Praise for *Your Evolving Soul*

"Finally! The revelatory, scientific, and evolutionary import of *The Urantia Book* has been situated within an integrative context for the 21st century and beyond. Byron Belitsos' wonderful book is a clarion call for all of us to (re)engage the Urantia cosmology and consider its provocative meta-view in a new and grounded way. The contribution Belitsos makes to our understanding of soul dynamics is essential reading in these turbulent times.

—**Sean Esbjörn-Hargens, PhD,** founder of MetaIntegral;
executive editor of the *Journal of Integral Theory and Practice*;
editor, *Metatheory for the Twenty-First Century*

"In this important book, Belitsos brings his great learning in the world's spiritual traditions to bear on the question of soul evolution. He illuminates the Urantia Revelation masterfully, placing this revelation within the larger context of the nature and function of our soul. In my view, this work truly makes a major contribution and deserves a wide readership."

—**Glen T. Martin, PhD,** professor of philosophy and
religious studies at Radford University;
author, *One World Renaissance* and *Millennium Dawn*

"Not that often do 'new revelations' have an exegetist and polyglot who links them immediately to a pluralistic or integral developmental framework and lens. More often, they linger for years with other adherents believing they have a 'one and only way.' Belitsos gives the Urantia message a fortuitous leap by linking it immediately to the modern oeuvre of interspiritual and integral worldviews."

—**Kurt Johnson, PhD**, coauthor, *The Coming Interspiritual Age*

"This extraordinary and brilliant book unveils the Urantia Revelation for those not yet ready to tackle such a lengthy tome. Byron not only makes a convincing case for its relevance today, but also manages to add a history of spiritual and philosophical thought that I found surprisingly interesting. Today's spiritual fashion seems to be pantheism, but Belitsos' lucid writing will awaken you to richer and far more inspiring ideas about the human soul and the nature of God."

—**Katie Darling,** spiritual teacher and founder of iWAVE Institute

"*Your Evolving Soul* is a magnificent and timeless work of genius that will inform, enlighten, and raise the consciousness of truth seekers for this and future generations."

—**Robert W. Hunt, PhD**, professor emeritus of mathematics, Humboldt State University

"*Your Evolving Soul* is intellectually brilliant and at the same time spiritually resonant. The author supports in a most eloquent way the immense value of the revelatory work, *The Urantia Book*. He has not only performed a great service on behalf of this revelatory text, but he makes it real and meaningful in the lives of readers."

—**The Honorable Martin Risacher** (Ret.)

""Byron has been a good friend of mine for over thirty years, and I very much appreciate his big heart and keen mind. His latest book is an impressive fruit of his long spiritual journey. Although I'm not a *Urantia Book* believer, this mysterious text is clearly full of inspiring spiritual teachings and deep theological insights, which Byron admirably brings to light. Moreover, *Your Evolving Soul* demonstrates the *Urantia Book's* strong affinities with integral philosophy."

—**Steve McIntosh**, author of *The Presence of the Infinite*, *Evolution's Purpose*, and *Integral Consciousness*

"*Your Evolving Soul* not only targets the *Urantia Book's* spirituality from the standpoint of the author's own insightful experience—placing it in a profoundly relevant historical context and destiny—but he also rips apart the very foundations of this normally elusive topic to reveal just how much spiritual consciousness one person can have. As I read *Your Evolving Soul* I most assuredly climbed the rungs of Jacob's ladder to soak in the living Paradise Father and his transforming love."

—**Rev. Dr. Rob Crickett**, global minister and teacher, and author of over twenty books on spirituality and Christianity

"Brilliant! Belitsos conveys a profound explanation of why we're here, where we're going, and our contribution to the evolving soul of creation. His seminal work gathers and integrates vast knowledge of our traditions and also explicates the epochal revelation of the age to come that is stunningly delivered by celestial authors. What a journey of mind-understanding and soul-awareness that enables the serious reader to connect with his own soul and cooperate in its growth."

—**Richard Rosen, PhD**, author of *Dear Abba* and *Life After Death*

Your Evolving Soul

Your Evolving Soul

The Cosmic Spirituality
of the Urantia Revelation

Byron Belitsos

Origin Press

Origin Press
PO Box 151117
San Rafael, CA 94915
www.OriginPress.org
www.Evolving-Souls.org

Front cover design by Mariah Parker (www.mettagraphics.com)
Interior design by Carla Green (claritydesignworks.com)

Library of Congress Cataloging-in-Publication Data

Belitsos, Byron, 1953- author.
    Your evolving soul : the cosmic spirituality of the
Urantia revelation / Byron Belitsos.
    pages cm
    Includes bibliographical references and index.
    LCCN 2017905453
    ISBN 978-1-57983-036-6 (paperback)
    ISBN 978-1-57983-054-0 (ebook)

    1. Urantia Book. 2. Soul.   I. Title.

BP605.U75B45 2017   299'.93
                                     QBI17-741

Printed in the United States of America

First printing: April 2017

**To the memory of my father,
Peter George Belitsos**

A heroic man of his time who supported me unconditionally
and who had a fervent faith in the value of progress

ΓΝΩΘΙ ΣΑΥΤΟΝ ("Know thyself")
The inscription found on the temple
at Delphi that my father often cited

Contents

Complete Contents

Contents

PART IV
FOUNDATIONS OF COSMIC SPIRITUALITY

SPECIAL SUPPLEMENT

APPENDICES

Note to the Reader

The manuscript of the *The Urantia Book* was completed in the 1940s, decades before gender-inclusive language entered into common usage. The Urantia text usually refers to Deity with male pronouns, although not in all cases. In my own discussion of theological topics, I take advantage of those few cases in which the *UB* does not use a male designation for a divine being. For example, the Supreme Being (evolutionary Deity) is referred to as both "he" or "she" in the Urantia text—but in my usage the Supreme is always designated as feminine. I use the same approach with the Third Person of the Eternal Trinity (technically known as the Infinite Spirit), who is sometime referred to as "she." But it should be well noted that Deity beyond the so-called local universe level is genderless, whereas the Creators of our local universe actually are male and female beings, known as Christ Michael (a male Deity who incarnated as Jesus Christ) and Mother Spirit.

Because various editions of *The Urantia Book* use different pagination systems, it has become the convention to designate quotes first by Paper number (the 196 chapters in the text are known as Papers), then section number, followed by the paragraph number within each section—for example, [101:4.2].

Some of the quotes from the Urantia text are lengthy, so I have taken the liberty of adding emphasis in bold to aid the reader by highlighting crucial points.

Introduction

In our technologically driven postmodern world, does it make sense anymore to speak of the human soul? Can a fresh new inquiry into this topic make a difference? I fervently believe so, given that so much is now at stake in our time of crisis, chaos, war—and widespread soullessness. I also sense an urgent need for such an investigation because of recent advances in neuroscience, consciousness studies, paranormal studies, and integral theory. The findings in these disciplines serve to make the issue of the nature of self and soul all the more relevant. *Your Evolving Soul* is one among many books that examine this topic. But it is unique as well, not only because it draws from all these disciplines but also in its reliance on an unusual esoteric source.

To get started with such an ambitious inquiry, we'll need to get inquisitive. We will want to ask questions such as: When we speak of the soul, what exactly are we referring to? Do we mean the subtle self or the *psyche*? Or, is the soul some aspect of the deep unconscious mind? Is the soul merely another name for our identity, or perhaps our true personality? These considerations also raise the crucial question of whether the soul is the same as—or distinct from—what some have called the inner spirit, the divine spark, the Buddha-nature, the *atman*, or the Self.

This possible distinction between soul and spirit, in turn, brings forward the issue of whether the soul is just one component of a larger self-system. If it is, how do we identify and define the other parts that may comprise that system? In other words, how would we describe our overall human design in relation to the human soul? And if a soul exists and is knowable apart from other aspects of selfhood, how should we understand it today—beyond the sometimes outworn definitions provided by the world's religions, and in the light of the current findings of scientific psychology?

Additional issues lurk around these questions. These include the classic problem of determining whether this entity we call the soul somehow survives death. And if we answer that question in the affirmative, we find ourselves compelled to consider whether the soul ascends to higher realms or perhaps returns to Earth in a new human body.

On the more practical side, does the soul evolve somehow in response to the kind of life we live? Answering that leads us to inquire about the technique of its evolution as well as the religious issue of the soul's destiny. And finally, if the soul is evolving toward an ultimate goal, might it be possible that the soul's movement in this direction contributes something important to the collective evolution of consciousness? If so, what practices can help us improve the personal soul and the collective soul during this life, and even in the afterlife?

Evolutionary religions and philosophies have developed doctrines in their well-meaning attempts to answer such questions. Some of these teachings about the soul are profound, and some are less so. But the research and analysis I will share make it clear that far too much of what is taught about the human soul in these traditional religious philosophies is vague and inconsistent. And the result in our time seems to me rather tragic. For centuries we have remained divided and confused on the central question of the nature, purpose, and destiny of the human soul—even while physics, for example, has achieved great success in sharpening its definitions and methods and has developed a worldwide consensus regarding its fundamental laws. *Your Evolving Soul* will present a unique model of the soul—and the larger self-system that contains it—in the hope that a new consensus may develop regarding the soul's fundamental definition and the best methods for enhancing its evolution.

And yet, the long legacy of the world's wisdom traditions is not to be scorned. Innumerable saints and sages of the past have been inspired and have built exemplary communities of faith. Many have displayed paranormal feats of body and mind and have performed miraculous healings. Along the way, they have offered teachings about self, spirit, soul, and human purposes that are so insightful and so helpful that their followers came to believe these teachers to be superhuman or their teachings and writings to be true revelations. And indeed, sparks of genuine divine revelation are contained in the evolving streams of wisdom known as Christianity, Judaism, Hinduism, Islam, Buddhism, and many esoteric and philosophical systems. In fact, I believe that each of these evolving religious communities provides a container for an ongoing stream of personal revelation that is gifted to their adepts, prophets, and mystics. In turn, these men and women find ways to distill their brilliant discoveries to meet the real needs of believers within their particular tradition.

According to the thesis of *Your Evolving Soul*, we are being graced once again by revelation suitable for our time, but in this case it's the gift of *epochal revelation* rather than merely personal revelation. This teaching provides what I believe is a revolutionary new picture of the human soul and self and also offers a profound new portrayal of the nature of the evolving cosmos, and of Deity itself. The Urantia Revelation has, in my view, set in motion a futuristic wisdom stream that is commensurate with the needs of the entire modern world, even though this mysterious text is chiefly seen as pertinent to Christianity. Establishing this bold claim is one part of the core argument of the present book. And because of this belief, *The Urantia Book*, a 2,097-page tome first published in 1955, will be a crucial reference to guide our discussion, but not the only one. (It will also be referred to in this book as the *UB*, the Urantia Revelation, the revelation, the Urantia Papers, and the Urantia text)

Part I of *Your Evolving Soul*, "Introducing an Epochal Revelation," unfolds the basic teachings and tenets of the Urantia Revelation, especially as it pertains to the soul, the self-system, and the cosmological basis of soul evolution. Several forms of evidence for the existence of our soul are examined in chapter 1, "Soul Glimpses: Poetic and Paranormal." In it I highlight intuited notions of the soul arrived at by poets, but I especially focus on the innumerable accounts of life reviews during near-death experiences (NDEs) that seem to validate aspects of the *UB* concept of an evolving soul. Chapter 2, "The Grand Cosmos: A Universal Theatre for

Soul Evolution," is devoted to a general overview of the Urantia text with special reference to its cosmology, theology, and psychospiritual teachings.

Among the many vital teachings presented in the Urantia Revelation, and the one that has stood out most prominently for me, is the description of the soul's nature, origin, evolution, and destiny. In particular, *The Urantia Book* states that a "sacred triad" (a simplifying phrase I have coined) comprises the human self. This threefold endowment, which I sometimes also call the inner trio or inner trinity, is the spiritual core of our God-given human design. It is composed of the *evolving soul* and the *Indwelling Spirit* (which is called by many names, including *God Fragment* and *Thought Adjuster*), and its third component is what I like to call the *unique personality* or *personhood*. In the *UB* each of these three elements is depicted as a distinct substance or ontological reality.

Nevertheless, this inner trio works together as one, not unlike the classic Christian conception of the divine Trinity—a threefold but indivisibly one God, wherein, paradoxically, each participant has unique and specific functions. In addition, our sacred triad has a mortal vehicle, the body-mind system, which, along with the trinitarian self-system, creates the conditions for soul evolution, personality unification, and the eventual eternal fusion of the sacred triad—a key topic of chapter 3, "The Synthesis Hypothesis."

From the strictly human point of view, our evolving soul is the heart of the inner triad, and its growth is largely under our control because of our precious endowment of free will, which is an integral feature of our God-bestowed personhood. According to the account offered in the Urantia Revelation, our soul is a nonphysical transcript of the valuable and salvageable elements of the experiences we choose to have. It is slowly cocreated on a daily basis by virtue of our spiritually significant thoughts, feelings, decisions, and subsequent actions, as these are recognized by the Indwelling Spirit and preserved, immortalized, *in and as our soul* by this divine action operating from within. These elements of real human experience get converted to personal soul memories and become a potentially eternal possession of the individual. In addition, our soul is able to survive death. In fact, it is the only purely personal asset that we possess going forward into the afterlife, if we later choose to ascend to higher realms.

These higher domains are described in the *UB* as a nested, sequential series of increasingly more advanced worlds upon which we sojourn in an afterlife of ever-more-rich education, socialization, and spiritualization. According to the Urantia account—easily the most detailed elucidation of the life after death in world literature—in this afterlife journey we eventually achieve *God Fusion* or *Father Fusion* (referenced earlier as eternal fusion), a status that assures eternal life and qualifies us for even more advanced challenges and cosmic experiences in our continuing ascent.

Meanwhile, here on Earth our chief evolutionary duty and, more important, our highest joy, is to engage in two core practices or activities that lead us to this goal. The first of these I like to call *soul-synthesis* or *soul-making*, and the second I call *circle-making* or *self-perfecting*—phrases I coined to stand for balanced personality integration, or what the *UB* sometimes calls *personality unification* or *cosmic individuation*. These topics are covered in chapter 4, "Cosmic Individuation: The Circles of Self-Perfecting." That chapter provides a wider psychospiritual framework for understanding personal evolution and our post-fusion ascension in the afterlife.

The activities of soul- and circle-making are, in my view, the core practices of the cosmic spirituality of the Urantia Revelation. Through such spiritual endeavors we each contribute toward what Teilhard de Chardin once called "the omega point"—the exhaustive realization of all possible experiential meanings and values through the actualization of all cosmic evolutionary potentials. In the *UB*, we are taught that humans truly are perfectible beings, both as individuals and as the collective of all conscious beings. But the journey to perfection described in *The Urantia Book* is far more complex, inclusive, engaging, and lengthy than anything conceived of in previous evolutionary cosmologies. This includes those of G. W. H. Hegel, Sri Aurobindo, Teilhard, or Alfred North Whitehead and his followers, all of which are evolutionary panentheistic systems comparable to the Urantia Revelation.

Our soul growth and self-perfecting continues into our eternal future. And this reality—this phenomenon of the collective evolution of trillions of evolving humans, from our world and from planets like ours—is the secret of what the *UB* calls the Supreme Being or the Finite God, the so-called evolving Deity of time and space. The Supreme is the God of cosmic evolution. "As we view the ceaseless struggles of the creature creation for perfection of status and divinity of being . . . these unending efforts bespeak the unceasing struggle of the Supreme for divine self-realization." [117:4.1]

The *UB* reveals that the grand evolution of the Supreme is (in part) constituted by—and is a cosmic summation of—the accumulated evolutionary growth of all beings on all worlds, including the angelic agencies and subinfinite Deities of the evolving realms that we briefly meet in chapters 2 and 3 and elsewhere in this book. This reality of experiential evolution, when combined with the physical evolution of the universe itself toward a state of conscious overcontrol, is the stupendous story of the Finite God who personalizes and future-eternalizes at the end of time, just as our soul personalizes and immortalizes within the very heart of this evolving Deity. And this face of the absolute—one of many facets of the divine—should be regarded as the space-time complement to the changeless, eternal, creator Deity that we worship as God, the Universal Father and Mother. God is infinitely more than a person, but cannot be anything less than a self-aware personality who is the Creator of a far-flung cosmic family of evolving personal beings destined for perfection in eternity.

Consider the fact that you and I are always in search of *more*—more truth, more beauty, more love and goodness. Informing and motivating this adventure is "the impulse of evolution," an apt phrase used often by evolutionary thinker Barbara Marx Hubbard, a friend who has been an inspiration for the writing of this book. As she might put it, our evolving soul is powered by this all-encompassing urge. She further points out that this same impulse animates the space-time universe as a whole. Likewise, the Urantia Revelation teaches that "*progress* is the watchword of the universe." [105:6.5]

But *Your Evolving Soul* is more than pantheistic—that being the typical metaphysical commitment of so many of today's evolutionary theorists. It is instead *panentheistic* in its theology. I conceive of the Divine Person as the utterly transcendent, all-loving Creator who at the same time is a full-time resident in his evolving universe by virtue of his choice to literally indwell each of us, both as a pure fragment of Godself—the nonpersonal Indwelling Spirit—and also as the *imago dei*, the distinct gift of personhood.

Underlying this theology is the claim that our self-system as a whole is a reflection, a true microcosm, of a much greater macrocosm. Our inner triad blends both evolutionary and eternal realities. It reflects the rough-and-tumble life of an evolving planet as well as attributes that stem from its origin in the central universe, a phrase soon to be defined. (You can also look up all such technical terms in the glossary). A key theme of the Urantia Revelation is the dialectical encounter of eternity and time—if you will, the *yin* of that which is originally perfect and the *yang* of that which is in the process of perfecting.

But big claims, especially about epochal celestial revelation, require big evidence. So, in this book I will treat my claims about the evolving soul as a hypothesis that I call the *soul-synthesis hypothesis*. We will test our hypothesis against common sense, logic, and what we know and believe to be the case as a result of the current findings of paranormal studies, the human sciences, the history of philosophy, and the finest ideas and ideals contained in previous spiritual teachings around the world. Toward that end, Part III, "A History of Self and Soul—East and West," provides several chapters that examine the intellectual history of the ideas of self, soul, and spirit, narrated with special reference to the unique definitions provided for these terms in Parts I and II of this book. Chapter 5 catalogues the dominant notions in the West, chiefly sourced from Plato, Aristotle, Apostle Paul, Augustine, and Aquinas. Chapter 6, "Gnosticism, Eastern Christianity, and *The Urantia Book*," covers crucial teachings about the self that were marginalized in traditional Western thought but have uncanny affinities with the Urantia Revelation.

My Part III survey of the best of evolutionary thought culminates in chapter 7, "Self and Soul in Modernity and Beyond," whose mission is to compare the highly original *UB* teachings about soul evolution and cosmic individuation with today's comprehensive theories of human development, especially as these are propounded by philosopher Ken Wilber and his associates.

Just as with chapter 6, chapter 7 points out a strong affinity between a particular feature of evolving thought (in this case, Wilber's theories of integral spirituality and integral psychology) and specific teachings of the Urantia Revelation. And the parallels in this case are significant. The *UB*'s psychospiritual teachings as well as Wilber's integral spirituality require our willingness to "wake up" to expanded states of awareness, "grow up" to higher levels of consciousness, and "show up" through incorporating the insights of science, culture, philosophy, and spirituality into our personal worldview—if I may borrow a few the terms used by today's integral theorists. In addition, I compare the *lines of development* in each system by tracking the role of our feeling, thinking, and willing faculties in our personal development. In particular, I take up the critical issue of which faculty or set of faculties of the self constitute the central line of human development. In this chapter I also invite the reader to entertain the possibility that the integral culture now flowering worldwide around the work of Wilber and his followers might be a suitable home for the Urantia teachings, given the similarities between the psychologies and philosophies of these two schools—with one system arising from evolving thought and the other from a revelatory text.

Part IV recapitulates the previous arguments of the book through the vehicle of a more advanced definition and detailed discussion of each element of the sacred triad. It begins with chapter 8, "The Nature of Personality Reality," a discussion that is necessary because of the intricacy and centrality of the *UB*'s teachings about the ontological nature of unique personhood, the theological import of the concept of personality, and the future destiny of human persons. Chapter 9, "The Gift of the Divine Indwelling," goes into greater depth on the crucial topic of the God Fragment, the divine spark plug in the engine of soul-making dynamics. This chapter also delves further into the core theme of the equal role that feeling, thinking, and willing play in symmetrical personal growth—with special emphasis on the faculty of feeling. Chapter 10, "Cultivating Contact with Spirit," continues on this general topic but with strong emphasis on those spiritual practices (including meditation and prayer) that enhance thinking and willing.

The concluding chapter, "Evolutionary Deity and Cosmic Spirituality," focuses especially on the self-perfecting mission of eternal life as this is uniquely revealed in the Urantia Revelation. It also explicates the doctrine of evolutionary Deity—the Supreme Being, in *UB* parlance. She is the emerging oversoul of all inhabited worlds and the nonlocal home of all evolving souls. Gaining an understanding of the Supreme provides the basis of a new cosmic spirituality based on the duty *and* the privilege of soul-making and self-perfecting in the light of truth, beauty, and goodness.

In essence, the Urantia Revelation explains the source, growth, and destiny of the soul in terms of our very personal relationship with the capacities of the sacred triad, as chosen in the mind and as worked out in our life experience. Our evolving soul is the ultimate repository of all of these experiences. The path of cosmic spirituality is the great quest to evolve an immortal soul that is rich in quality and broad in extent because of our life experiences. But the journey also contributes at each step to the evolution of all *other* selves and souls, here and throughout the universe, and into an endless future.

After the final chapter, *Your Evolving Soul* closes with what I call the Special Supplement, which contains five shaded sections. This background material is followed in turn by four appendices and a glossary.

The Supplement opens with an *apologia* that explores in more detail my views about the revelatory status of the *UB*. In this section I offer justification for my stance that the Urantia text was primarily authored by celestial beings. In addition, I take the position that these unseen writers performed an unprecedented feat: in association with human beings, they architected a revelatory scripture for the postmodern world that points the way to a unification of science, philosophy, history, and religion.

Because the *UB* is indeed a cocreative product, it makes sense to examine both its celestial authors (often referred to as the "revelators") and its so-called "human sources"—and I do just that in the following two sections. In my discussion of the complex issue of human sources, I offer an overview of the story about how several thousand exemplary ideas of human origin were selected by the revelators and then incorporated into the early drafts of the Urantia manuscript, providing a kind of skeleton of meaning around which the celestial writers wove the *UB*'s revelatory discourse. As I understand it, their method was to distill much of the best of the world's previous ideas in a wide variety of fields into a pool of acquired human knowledge, which they organized into a vast series of topics. These "gems of mentation" (as the *UB*'s authors call them) were then significantly augmented or very often superseded by superhuman input, thereby producing a blend of revelatory content with the finest "evolutionary" content available up until the time the manuscript was completed, which was no later than 1945.

As a result, many of the *UB*'s statements traceable to human sources—such as its coverage of sociology and anthropology—are now outdated or simply partial, if confronted with advances in the human sciences; and this is especially the case with regard to some of its physics and biology. On the other hand, a large body of avant-garde ideas that first appeared only in the Urantia Revelation when it was published in 1955 have now been validated. The revelators boldly assert that, although some of the *UB*'s scientific facts are only provisional and heuristic, its teachings about history, religion, theology, and spirituality will stand the test of time.

In Section 4 I provide a summary of the crucial and fascinating story of how the Urantia Revelation physically came into being as a manuscript in the hands of a half dozen devoted individuals based in Chicago in the mid-twentieth century who worked directly with the revelators and their angelic assistants over several decades. Following this, in Section 5, I broach the fascinating issue of the historicity of the *UB*. Any purported revelation will reflect, to some degree, the mentality and needs of its immediate audience. This is also the case with the *UB*, though I think far less so than any previous text of its kind. In many important respects, the Urantia

Revelation remains *ahead* of our time, even when we factor in its use of human sources.

While the Special Supplement, as well as many other parts of *Your Evolving Soul*, may read like an apologia, that doesn't mean we can't critically probe and skeptically test this material for veracity and usefulness. In particular, there is a great need to engage in comparative and critical analysis of the *UB*'s teachings in relation to current human advances in knowledge. That is one of my key aims in this work—and a task that has been admirably attempted by at least one other writer, my friend Sheila Keene-Lund, author of the monumental *Heaven Is Not the Last Stop* (2010). Because many key issues can't be resolved in a short book, I often suggest lines of inquiry for further research. It is my great hope that *Your Evolving Soul* will inspire others to follow in the footsteps of Sheila and me by delving more deeply into these topics, an activity that I believe is long overdue.

PART I

Introducing an Epochal Revelation

CHAPTER 1

Soul Glimpses: Poetic and Paranormal

Think of the Soul. I swear to you that body of yours
gives proportions to your Soul, somehow to live in
other spheres; I do not know how, but I know it is so.
—*Walt Whitman*

One hot and humid summer day in 1961 in suburban Cincinnati, I was engaged in aimless play at our neighborhood pool like any other nine-year-old boy. At one point, I jumped into the kids' end of the pool. Or so I thought. I was so startled by the unexpected depth of the water that I began to panic, for I had not yet learned to swim. Instead of gently hitting bottom four feet down, I was now lost in a full ten feet. I struggled and churned, frantic to get my bearings. In a flash, time slowed down as I entered a place of sheer terror. But before I could take a gulp of water, I was pulled free by a vigilant lifeguard.

In the few seconds before the rescue, I had what I would call a mini near-death experience (NDE). I saw my short life pass before me in a complete review: scenes of parents, siblings, school chums, teachers, our cat, my bedroom, me riding my bike—an explosion of distinct images of encounters with each important person or thing in my young world. And each scene that paraded through had an aura of truth and light around it. The feeling associated with this instantaneous experience was rapturous though my body was paralyzed with fear. I believe that this experience provided a rare glimpse of—as Walt Whitman might say—the proportions of my soul. Much later, I came across a poem by Emily Dickinson that seems to capture the essence of this modest childhood NDE:

> The Soul's distinct connection
> With immortality
> Is best disclosed by Danger
> Or quick Calamity—
> As Lightning on a Landscape
> Exhibits Sheets of Place—
> Not yet suspected—but for Flash—
> And Click—and Suddenness.

Looking back, I believe that the sudden "Danger" of drowning disclosed to me a "distinct connection," as Dickinson puts it. I caught a vivid peek of what I now believe was my youthful but immortal soul. I discovered ("as Lightning") that the deeper self on the inside (my "Landscape") is luminous. It's available all at once in a "Flash." And yet it was hidden away ("Not yet suspected"). An unfathomable self was hidden (as "Sheets of Place") under the surface person I thought I was.

Dickinson was prescient in declaring that the soul, the essential self, suddenly reveals itself in "quick Calamity." We'll shortly see that NDE life reviews offer paranormal proof of that poetic proposition.

John Keats and the "Vale of Soul-Making"

My own small life review led me to several provisional insights that I have carried with me ever since. We carry within us our life-story-as-a-whole; it contains our essential personal experiences that are somehow cumulatively stored up within us. This corpus of experiences can suddenly disclose itself when we face mortality; and the wondrous and numinous quality of these memories must be evidence of an immortal pedigree.

Further research inspired by the Urantia Revelation builds on these insights. According to my synthesis hypothesis, not only does the human soul consist of the sum total of the energetic record of all of our experiences, but these poignant moments of spiritual significance also have what the *UB* calls *survival value* beyond this life and may even contribute something unique to universal evolution.

As I see it, our evolving soul is a living, growing, shimmering entity of light, but its luminosity differs from the pure light of that "spark of God" that, according to poets and Gnostics, also indwells us. Instead, the evolving soul is a psychic product of an alchemical blend of widely divergent elements that, in certain moments of daily experience, get "mixed" behind the scenes in our deepest interior. The process of soul-synthesis occurs when worthy impulses, intentions, or states rise above the instinctive or reactive level of mind to what one could call the mid-mind. There they engage with the indwelling God-self that reaches down from the higher mind, which seeks an energetic resonance of recognition. These factors—a resonating mental content and its acknowledgment by the inner spirit—dissolve, so to speak, into one another, creating a blended substance of the subtle realm whose luster is unique.

In essence, the spirit-self selects and highlights those mind-moments it deems worthy of immortality, even if the immediate experience involved is painful or disturbing or seemingly ordinary. Our afflictions and predicaments and our sincere efforts to adjust to such difficulties—as well as our aspirations and our efforts to attain worthy goals—are especially soul-making. But a third factor is required, according to the *UB*: another part of us, which the text calls our unchanging and unique personhood, unifies and holds the space for these transactions to occur.

Even a child has such a psychic repository of life memories constitutive of a young soul, as I discovered. But to gain any direct awareness of the soul's subtle content is no small matter. The evolving soul seems to divulge its secrets only when we are in deep and sustained reflection and meditation—or else suddenly in dreams, epiphanies, or calamitous events.

The most potent soul-making situations, I believe, are those in which we wrestle with challenging dilemmas with an attitude of faith and hopefulness. We especially grow and stretch the soul when we are tested by demanding situations that summon creative choices among competing values. And if such choices and the resulting actions are infused with our highest consciousness of truth, beauty, and goodness, then our soul growth is all the more accelerated.

The brilliant John Keats intuited this process in a famous letter to his siblings, in which he opines that the world is "a vale of soul-making" ("vale" referring to "valley"). While making a point about Christianity's misguided theology of suffering, Keats takes a stand for courageous human development as the reason for our sojourn on Earth. To illustrate the idea, he contrasts his idea of soul-making with the traditional Christian idea that this world is a vale of tears. Note how his letter's description of the soul's purpose has an uncanny similarity to our synthesis hypothesis:

> The common cognomen of this world among the misguided and superstitious is "a vale of tears" from which we are to be redeemed by a certain arbitrary interposition of God and taken to heaven. What a little circumscribed straightened notion! Call the world if you please "the vale of soul-making." Then you will find out the use of the world. . . . There may be intelligences or sparks of the divinity . . . in short they are God. How then are souls to be made? How then are these sparks which are God to have identity given them, so as ever to possess a bliss peculiar to each one's individual existence? How, but by the medium of a world like this? . . . Do you not see how necessary a world of pains and troubles is to school an intelligence and make it a soul? A place where the heart must feel and suffer in a thousand diverse ways! . . . As various as the lives of men are, so various become their souls.[1]

This world of our travails is a "school for our souls," proclaims Keats, the author of "Ode to a Grecian Urn." And it's fascinating to note that *The Urantia Book* has a direct allusion to this very letter of Keats: "Jesus hardly regarded this world as a 'vale of tears.' He

---

[1] See the entire letter at: http://www.mrbauld.com/keatsva.html.

rather looked upon it as the birth sphere of the eternal and immortal spirits of Paradise ascension, the 'vale of soul making.'" [149:5.5]

In his letter, Keats prophetically distinguishes the evolving human soul from "the sparks which are God." The "sparks of divinity" have "identity given to them," as Keats puts it, and this evolving identity becomes increasingly able show to itself in our moments of crisis or penetrating thought—as Emily Dickinson points out.

Paranormal Revelations of the Soul

Can modern folks like us take inspiration from that which poets such as Walt Whitman, Emily Dickinson, and John Keats proclaimed about the soul in the nineteenth century? Can we find scientific support today for what the Urantia Revelation asserted about the evolving soul when it was published in the mid-twentieth century? We *can* find confirmation, I believe, when we examine the burgeoning scientific data about near-death experiences and related paranormal phenomena.

I first heard about NDEs from Dr. Raymond Moody's classic 1975 book, *Life after Life*. And I have long been aware that NDE research has generated other bestselling books and inspired feature films. But I was surprised when I later discovered that rigorous scientific research on NDEs has gone on for decades all over the world and is based on a vast archive of data. I've been even more amazed to discover that many of these same research scientists are stepping out as advocates for the existence of a soul or a nonmaterial self that survives into an afterlife. The NDE field has come a very long way from earlier days when experiencers who went public suffered ridicule, social ostracism, and even psychiatric and pastoral abuse and condemnation.

We now know that almost every account we have of the thousands of near-death experiencers (NDErs) includes a report of the joyful awareness of a discrete soul or nonphysical selfhood, along with the certain knowledge that it will survive death. These people are made aware of the same numinous qualities I felt in my mini-NDE, but with far more profundity. My terror of drowning induced a startling epiphany, but a "hard" NDEr actually does drown—as, for example, in the case of Dr. Mary Neal, the director of spine surgery at the University of Southern California, who perished in a whitewater kayaking accident but was revived after experiencing a spectacular NDE. "Before my near-death-experience," says Dr. Neal in an interview, "I believed in God and took my kids to Sunday school but was not particularly religious. . . . With my near-death-experience, the truth of God's promises and the reality of eternal life became a part of my every breath. I am in constant prayer and regardless of what I am doing, I try to reflect God's love and live for His glory."[2] A similar case is that of David Bennett, a commercial diver who drowned in a violent storm but returned to tell his own NDE story. Bennett, previously a brash and self-centered young man, is now a well-known inspirational speaker and spiritual teacher.[3]

Generally speaking, NDErs report the following experiences: a temporary (and verifiable) death; a sudden eruption into a supernatural domain of light usually populated by celestial beings and deceased relatives; the experience of being jettisoned back into their once-lifeless body to survive on Earth; and the report of a life-changing memory of these events. Among the most profoundly evidential aspects of their stories are the ensuing radical changes in these people's lives, as witnessed not only in the cases of Neal and Bennett but in hundreds of other instances as well.

NDE archives also include reports from deceased persons who channel from the other side, in what is technically known as After Death Communications (ADC).[4] Many such cases are known as "evidentiary mediumship," because their communications contain

---

[2] This interview is posted at the Amazon page for her book, *To Heaven and Back: A Doctor's Extraordinary Account of Her Death, Heaven, Angels, and Life Again; A True Story* (WaterBrook, 2012). Neal's book has more than 2,400 favorable Amazon reviews.

[3] Bennett had yet another NDE after a bout with stage IV cancer. See his story at http://ndestories.org/david-bennett/.

[4] Such reports may pose difficulty for *Urantia Book* students because the *UB* clearly states that contact with the dead is forbidden. Yet today's advocates for the phenomenon can point to a vast array of instances of evidentiary channeling, including cases documented in peer-reviewed scientific studies. I have personally come to the conclusion that the *UB*'s rule prohibiting ADC may have been suspended as an act of mercy during our time of planetary crisis.

verifiable facts and information that could not possibly have been known by the medium. Speaking from the unseen realms, these voices provide unprecedented information about the afterlife through reliable psychic mediums on Earth, some of whom have been studied in extremely rigorous, controlled scientific experiments going back more than a century.

One of the world leaders in the scientific validation of such phenomena is Dr. Gary Schwartz of the University of Arizona's Department of Psychology. He is the director of the Laboratory for Advances in Consciousness and Health, where he has conducted a myriad of double- and triple-blind studies. Schwartz, the author of *The Afterlife Experiments* and other important books in this field, has also published more than 450 scientific papers and has studied ADC and other paranormal phenomena for over three decades.

Perhaps the most reliable source of information and research on NDEs is IANDS, International Association for Near Death Studies. Other leading research centers of note in this field are the Institute for Noetic Sciences, led by its chief scientist, Dean Radin, PhD, and the Near Death Experience Research Foundation, led by former radiation oncologist Dr. Jeffrey Long. Both men are distinguished authors. Dr. Bruce Greyson, professor emeritus of psychiatry and neurobehavioral sciences at the University of Virginia, was a pioneer academic researcher and original editor of the *Journal of Near-Death Studies.*

In some spectacular, well-documented cases, the dead are known to speak to us directly through electronic media in a phenomenon known as instrumental trans-communication (ITC).[5] Such cases are included in NDE archives if they independently provide confirmable facts about an individual's life, and for other reasons. Schwartz insists that scholarly afterlife study should include the data that has been gathered regarding NDEs, ADC mediumship, and ITC.

Afterlife reports by NDErs do have wide variations in their particulars and the degree to which these paranormal experiences can be recalled. But the shared characteristics that have been noted

---

[5] The definitive documentary on the subject of ITC is *Calling Earth*, produced by Daniel Drasin. Drasin frames the controversy in ways that will quell the protests of all but the most hardened skeptic. See https://vimeo.com/101171248.

by peer-reviewed research scientists reveal uniform features across culture, religion, age, race, and gender. For example, according to premier early NDE researcher Kenneth Ring, author of the classic *Lessons from the Light*, "Religious orientation was not a factor affecting either the likelihood or the depth of the near-death experience. An atheist was as likely to have one as was a devoutly religious person."[6]

But what's most relevant for our inquiry is that innumerable NDE experiencers—including many children—report having had a life review. We now have at least five thousand documented NDE cases, and about a fifth of these include descriptions of some form of life review.

The cumulative weight of the vast body of life-review cases—along with the rigorous scrutiny of this data by scholars and scientists—points directly to my synthesis hypothesis: We carry within us an up-to-the-minute repository of the poignant experiences of our lifetime, and this record is radically distinct from the brain memories that get extinguished at death. Rather, a certain selection of our life history has been synthesized in and as an immortal soul that lives on *without* the physical body. This subtle entity survives into the afterlife and somehow displays itself in splendid detail in the NDE life review. It is possible, too, that elements of the life review are summoned from other extradimensional sources.

Such reports by NDE experiencers are all the more significant when we consider that, as author Roy L. Hill, puts it, "[NDErs] are not engaging in speculation. They are reporting consistent observations about the nature of the soul because they are reporting from direct experience. Put more simply, NDErs know the soul because they lived as the soul. Arriving back to their bodies, they were entrusted with more keys to their real essence."[7]

I see NDErs as modern-day Gnostics. NDEs in general, and life reviews in particular, infuse the experiencer with self-knowledge, offering a dramatic revelation of true gnosis—a word that we

---

[6] See a summary of Ring's seminal research at http://www.near-death.com/experiences/experts04.html.

[7] Roy L. Hill, PsyD, *Psychology and the Near-Death Experience: Searching for God* (White Crow Books, 2015), p 39.

examine in detail in chapter 6. "When you return to this life," writes experiencer Dr. Alan Ross Hugenot, "you are still a regular person; you haven't suddenly become a spiritual guru or a shaman, although you may become one later. On the other hand, everything in your paradigm has shifted and you possess a rare gnosis that life is eternally continuous. . . . I was *reborn to a new life* (reincarnated) in the same body."[8]

Very often, NDErs describing their life reviews report that they were surprised, deeply embarrassed, and even horrified by the disclosure of their soul's deepest secrets. They even beg to have the life review halted, but are always very lovingly reassured by any higher beings present that the outcome of the review will be beneficial.

According to analysts, the life review experience is obviously designed to educate the experiencer with a rich variety of unknown facts and new perspectives on their entire life story. These can include thoughts, actions, or motives withheld from self and others; vivid experiences of how their behavior impacted others—including strangers, animals, and even plants; deep insights into how and why the NDEr needs to change upon returning to Earth; and often a disclosure of their life mission.

NDEs and life reviews appear to offer unearned self-understanding, but I suggest that we think of these phenomena as a contemporary form of divine grace. Startling new experiential knowledge of the soul and the higher worlds is now being poured out as a revelatory gift to a skeptical postmodern world, perhaps also for the purpose of complementing and even validating verbal revelations such as the *UB* and other forms of channeled or transmitted wisdom. Further, the literature and lore of NDEs make clear that experiencers are being taught about soul development for the purpose of accelerating their growth when they return to their bodies, as well as to inspire others they meet to pursue a more spiritual life. Many experiencers go on to engage in various forms of missionary

---

[8] Dr. Alan Ross Hugenot, *The New Science of Consciousness Survival* (Dog Ear Publishing, 2016), p 72. In this book directed at fellow scientists, Hugenot, who has a doctorate in engineering, provides perhaps the most extensive scientific discussion of the paradigm-shattering implications of ADC and NDE research. See especially pp. 115–134. Hugenot is the current president of another important paranormal research organization called the Academy for Spiritual and Consciousness Studies.

or humanitarian outreach, personal healing ministries, or spiritual teaching not unlike that of a religious evangelist, but without the baggage of traditional religious doctrine.

NDE Life Reviews: Nonjudgmental and Multiperspectival

Life reviews are radical and startling. They are typically led by one or several angelic or celestial beings whose role is to help us distill our life lessons while communicating unconditional love for us. Contrary to the teachings of most religious traditions about the wrath of divine judgment in the afterlife, NDErs report without exception that these supervising beings are nonjudgmental, lavishly supportive, and deeply loving.[9] Here, for example, is a typical life review account provided by well-known author and speaker Dannion Brinkley:

> A powerful being enveloped me and I began to relive my entire life, one incident at a time. In what I call the panoramic life review I watched my life from a second person point of view. As I experienced this I was myself as well as every other person with whom I had ever interacted . . . When the panoramic life review ended, despite the many obvious mistakes I had made in my life, I experienced no retribution—no judgment and no punishment. I was the only judge presiding over my day in court! Given time to assimilate my life in retrospect, I was given the opportunity to know, first hand, both the happiness and the sorrow I had created through my actions.[10]

Much like Brinkley, many subjects report having a holographic experience overseen by benign beings, in which they engage in a vivid *reliving* of life episodes. Others compare a life review to watching a movie of one's entire life, or specific scenes and segments, viewed on screens of some sort. Directed at each step by loving

---

[9] See this helpful summary: http://www.near-death.com/science/research/life-review.html.

[10] http://www.dannion.com/dannion-brinkley-near-death-experience/

celestial beings of light, these experiencers will view their life in chronological sequence (or sometimes in reverse), or watch segments that can be fast-forwarded, slowed down, or paused to focus on a particular detail.

These descriptions strongly suggest, of course, some sort of heavenly storage medium that is being played back. Renowned medium Edgar Cayce, as well as theosophists and followers of Rudolf Steiner, claimed that our life chronology is embedded in the universal Akashic record, which contains the entire history of every soul that has ever lived.[11] I depict these events as being stored locally, in and as the personal soul, but there is reason to believe that duplicates of these life records are available elsewhere in the universe and can be accessed on demand by celestials beings or by humans with the requisite psychic skill and the proper permissions.

The NDEr receives specific coaching and guidance throughout the review. Deeds that are considered most valuable by the celestial guides are those that express pure and unconditional love or forgiveness—small and spontaneous acts of kindness. For example, in one endearing segment of a woman's life review, she was shown herself as a little girl spotting a tiny flower growing out of a crack in the sidewalk, then bending down and cupping the flower, giving it her full unconditional love and attention. In her life review, she discovered that this one incident was the most important event of her entire life.[12] Here's a similar case: "Reinee Pasarow described how the most positive thing she did . . . was to give special attention

---

[11] Cayce claimed the ability to access both the subconscious mind of the individual for whom he was giving a reading as well as their Akashic record, which he said was held in a great hall of records. "It is a hall without walls, without ceiling, but I am conscious of seeing an old man who hands me a large book, a record of the individual for whom I seek information. . . . Upon time and space is written the thoughts, the deeds, the activities of an entity. . . . Hence, as it has been oft called, the record is God's book of remembrance." (Excerpted from Edgar Cayce Reading 1650–1.) The *UB* broaches the idea that an additional record of our life is kept by our recording guardian seraphim, but little more is stated about that topic. In this connection, I discuss throughout this book the idea that our evolving souls—as they accrue wisdom and experience—contribute to the growth of the cosmic oversoul (also known in the *UB* as the Supreme Being). Further research should examine the possible connections between the seraphic records of one's life, the oversoul concept of the *UB*, the many traditions about an Akashic record, and perhaps the emerging philosophical idea of *nonlocality*.

[12] Quoted in: http://www.near-death.com/science/research/life-review.html

to a not-so-lovable boy at a summer camp so that he would know he was loved. During the review, she said this act of kindness was more important from her viewpoint of expanded awareness than if she had been president of the United States or the queen of England."[13]

Enjoy this excerpt from another classic account of a life review, this time from Betty Eadie in her 1992 bestseller, *Embraced by the Light*:

> My life appeared before me in the form of what we might consider extremely well defined holograms, but at tremendous speed. I was astonished that I could understand so much information at such a speed. My comprehension included much more than what I remember happening during each event of my life. **I not only re-experienced my own emotions at each moment, but also what others around me had felt. I experienced their thoughts and feelings about me.** . . . I saw how I had often wronged people and how they had often turned to others and committed a similar wrong. This chain continued from victim to victim, like a circle of dominoes, until it came back to the start—to me, the offender. The ripples went out, and they came back. **I had offended far more people than I knew, and my pain multiplied and became unbearable.** . . . **The Savior stepped toward me, full of concern and love.** His spirit gave me strength, and he said that I was judging myself too critically. "You're being too harsh on yourself," he said. Then he showed me the reversed side of the ripple effect. **I saw myself perform an act of kindness, just a simple act of unselfishness, and I saw the ripples go out again.** The friend I had been kind to was kind in turn to one of her friends, and the chain repeated itself. I saw love and happiness increase in others' lives because of that one simple act on my part. I saw their happiness grow and affect their lives in positive ways, some significantly. My pain was replaced with joy.[14]

---

[13] Ibid.

[14] Ibid.

Eadie's case helps illustrate that most life reviews are multiperspectival—that is, seen and felt as if from a God's-eye point of view that is inclusive of all who were involved with or even remotely connected to the experiencer.

Much of the life review account published by experiencer Rajiv Parti, MD, represented the actual experiences of his immediate family: "I was able to feel all points of view, my father's and grandfather's, and my mother's."[15] Parti's important book tells the story of how his NDE led to his transformation from an obsessive, materialistic anesthesiologist to a healer, speaker, and spiritual teacher. He had led a successful career as the chief of anesthesiology at the Bakersfield Heart Hospital in California, but Parti was not above physically abusing his own son and mistreating his wife. In his near-death experience, archangels and his deceased father led him on a journey in review of the violence that had plagued his family for generations. After his experience, Dr. Parti awoke as if "born again." He gave away his mansion, quit his career, opened a wellness clinic, and completely turned around his relationships with his family. To this day, he still teaches widely and converses with angels.

At the other end of the spectrum from Dr. Parti is Erik Medhus, an aimless young man who committed suicide at age twenty. Erik has become an evidentiary spokesperson for the spirit world, channeling through a respected medium—complete with the slang and expletives he once used as a teen hipster. The detailed story of his death and afterlife was edited by his mother, Elisa Medhus, MD. Here's a highlight from his life review that once again reveals the use of multiple perspectives as a radical teaching device:

> As my entire life unfolded before me, I was not only experiencing every single moment I ever lived but I was also observing and feeling what everybody else in my life went through in reaction to whatever I said or did to them. . . . Not only could I feel the emotions they had in response to my actions, but **I could**

---

[15] Rajiv Parti, MD, *Dying to Wake Up: A Doctor's Voyage into the Afterlife and the Wisdom He Brought Back* (Atria Books, 2016), p. 44.

actually see things from *their* perspective. It was like I *was* them."[16] [emphasis added]

Eadie reports, "I experienced their thoughts and feelings about me," but Erik's story—like numerous others in the literature—goes further by stating that he witnessed his behavior *as* the other person.

While some NDE accounts may seem to go far afield, scientists are discovering patterns that reassure us that something substantive is occurring. For example, a widely used scale to classify and measure NDEs for the sake of more precise academic study was developed by Professor Bruce Greyson. According to Greyson, the phenomenon of life review is unique to NDEs, and his data shows that they are reported by 22 percent of experiencers. Oddly, Greyson found that more atheists who reported NDEs (literally 100 percent) reported having a life review than any other category of experiencer.[17] One wonders: are their souls trying to tell them something?

I would suggest that our souls are *always* trying to tell us something. And it is for this reason that I can't agree with Greyson that life reviews are exclusive to NDEs. Bear in mind that our souls are constituted by our most intimate and heartfelt experiences. It stands to reason that this most precious of all of our life assets should become more accessible to us, especially as we mature, gain perspective, and grow in wisdom. Indeed, I am witness to the fact that in advanced psychospiritual settings, a partial review of a life event can tumble or even hurl itself into consciousness. You too have likely noted how certain special memories spontaneously arise during prayer, in deep reflection, or in therapy settings—especially those memories that need examination for drawing life lessons that may have been missed along the way. No longer can our psychological defenses hold back these crucial insights, some of which are embedded in traumas of the past. Certainly almost all of us need to be reminded of a key activity or a significant past relationship

---

[16] Erik Medhus and Elisa Medhus, MD, *My Life after Death: A Memoir From Heaven* (Atria Books/Beyond Words, 2015), p. 56

[17] http://www.near-death.com/experiences/atheists01.html

whose import has fallen into neglect, especially when a relevant lesson involved has ripened for integration. Might these be prompts provided because of our soul's superior intelligence?

I have watched in amazement as certain forgotten life experiences have arisen during long meditation retreats, dressed up in living color and almost demanding my scrutiny. These vivid, charged images appear almost as if on cue from some inner guide who seems to know my spiritual needs better than I do. And there are many other provocateurs of modified life reviews. The soul rises up in moments of danger, as Emily Dickinson teaches us. Falling in love can bring soul contents to our inner eyes—and I've even had such experiences while encountering powerful works of art such as operas, symphonies, and movies. Dreams can be symbolic media for life review, and no less than Carl Jung has made clear that a life review of sorts may take place if one connects the dots of a long series of dreams. But even given all these cases, it appears to me NDE life reviews unveil the soul like no other experience.

Shall we not at least follow the trails blazed by such poets as Dickinson and Keats, as well as NDE experiencers and scientists worldwide? They provide our point of departure in this book, but with the unprecedented detail in the Urantia Revelation, we can go further.

CHAPTER 2

The Grand Cosmos:
A Universal Theater
for Soul Evolution

To open the Eternal Worlds, to open the immortal Eyes
of Man inwards into the Worlds of Thought: into
Eternity Ever expanding in the Bosom of God,
the Human Imagination.
—*William Blake*

Consider the four-dimensional world we typically experience. From where you and I sit in 4D, it may seem that our inner life is a largely private affair. Our phones and computers may be under surveillance, but when it comes to our innermost thoughts and feelings, we assume that we live behind a veil of secrecy. We may believe that in our solitary, off-the-grid moments we can do or think whatever we like without notice or scrutiny. But in reality, at least especially according to NDE experiencers and the Urantia Revelation, we are always "on stage" for those beyond the veil. Beings in higher dimensions discreetly monitor our "live performance" through a cosmic one-way mirror and lovingly minister to us as needed. Plus, our spiritually significant thoughts and actions are in some measure recorded in our evolving souls, far beyond our awareness.

By all accounts, this illusory curtain of privacy disappears when we enter the afterlife. In a manner comparable to NDE stories, the Urantia Revelation explains that a celestial team in full possession of our soul transcript swings into action to enable the unforgettable moment of our reawakening after death and to welcome us. The *UB* gives a technically specific listing of what transpires next.[18] At death, we are told, we enter a resurrection chamber on high.[19] Our personality, soul, and Indwelling Spirit are placed in the custody of a celestial resurrection team. On cue, the team reassembles the constituent parts of our inner triad, minus the body-mind subsystem we knew on Earth. Our triad is coupled with a body similar to the previous human form (albeit of a slightly more rarefied substance), plus a supermaterial mind endowment—but unfortunately, no harps are handed out.[20] Presto! We emerge into the afterlife on a world at a slightly higher frequency than that of Earth,[21] where we continue to learn, love, rest, drink, and eat and enjoy a wider range of vision and sensory experience.

With the exception of those who passed on to the afterlife before adulthood, we begin our new heavenly career sporting a physiognomy and demeanor that approximates our adult self back on Earth. We will have been retrofitted with our old personality, so if you were Rodney Dangerfield back on Earth, you'll be instantly

---

[18] An important topic for further research will be a comparison of the best NDE accounts with *The Urantia Book*'s description of these resurrection events, which is narrated for us (purportedly) by celestial beings who have direct knowledge of how they are carried out.

[19] Some of us "graduate" immediately after death, whereas other, less advanced ascenders resurrect in very large groups at certain prescribed intervals, not unlike the traditional Christian idea of a universal resurrection at the Last Judgment. "There shall be a resurrection of the dead, both of the just and unjust" (Acts 24:15).

[20] Joking aside, ascenders do have personal communication devices, and we are told in the *UB* that these were referred to by the Apostle John as "harps of God" in the Book of Revelation. See 47:10.2.

[21] The first seven of the innumerable heavenly spheres upon which we sojourn in the afterlife are called mansion worlds. "The very center of all activities on the first mansion world is the resurrection hall, the enormous temple of personality assembly." [47:3.2] Life on these spherical worlds is explained in Paper 47, "The Seven Mansion Worlds." The revelators derived the word "mansion" from John 14:2: "In *my Father's* house are *many mansions*: if it were not so, I would *have* told you. I go to prepare a place for you."

recognizable on high by your former associates—except that perhaps now you'll "get some respect."

Aside from the thrill that accompanies our first moment of awareness in this new realm, our soul evolution does not skip a beat: "You will resume your intellectual training and spiritual development at the exact level whereon they were interrupted by death. . . . You begin over there right where you leave off down here." [47:3.7]

My sympathies to those of you who have hoped that your karma will be erased by the experience of surviving. Your strictly brain-based memories are gone forever—which is why the non-material record we call the soul is an essential ingredient. On the other hand, don't think of the higher worlds as being immaterial; they are physical spheres of another type known as architectural worlds, and are artificially constructed, not naturally evolved. "The material universe is always the arena wherein take place all spiritual activities; spirit beings and spirit ascenders live and work on physical spheres of material reality." [12:8.1]

In the immediate afterlife, we're not left alone and on our own like a solitary pioneer trekking into unknown parts. Those who were assigned a guardian seraphim on Earth will meet—and literally see—this loyal personal angel, who is one of the first to greet us. This being now becomes our daily companion.[22] Otherwise, we are assigned heavenly companions and teachers who are equally apprised of our developmental status. We're assigned a place to dwell and are given a ten-day "holiday" for looking up deceased friends and relatives. But for many of us, our advent on the first higher world of the afterlife is only brief cameo—we quickly move on.[23]

NDErs tell us that they are initially shocked at being greeted by deceased relatives who apparently had foreknowledge of our death.

---

[22] As explained in more detail in chapter 4, those who achieve the so-called third psychic circle on Earth are assigned a pair of seraphim to follow them throughout the mortal lifetime and on into the afterlife. We are told that one of the pair always functions as the "recorder of the undertaking," so the UB typically refers only to the one seraphim who is "on duty" as the ministering angel. [See 13:3.9 and the entirety of Paper 113.]

[23] Those who need the type of remediation and healing that take place on this first world of the afterlife remain for a longer period of time, but the rest of us continue on to the next mansion world in the sequence of heavenly spheres, known as mansonia number two. (For background see also note 27.)

They also report their surprise to discover that celestial beings have immediate access to their "soul reel" and are ready for immediate playback and scene-by-scene analysis in their life review. They soon realize that they've been like actors on a stage engaged in a performance that was monitored by a heavenly audience who never judged them harshly.

If you will permit me to continue with our movie metaphor, the Urantia Revelation adds much more detail to this picture, explaining that our immediate support crew is a tiny part of much bigger production. Apparently, a mighty celestial team is weaving everyone's performances into a vast story of cosmic evolution headed toward our collective denoument—the grandest musical of all, with an unheard-of richness of story and song and dance. But while existing NDE accounts of life reviews offer detailed close-ups, the Urantia Revelation offers a wider context—a long, wide shot, if you will—from which we can derive meaning from our contacts with spirit before and after death, and from here to eternity.

A Unified Stream of Guidance and Ministry

With the *UB*'s depiction in hand, we can now delight in these otherworldly descriptions with less embarrassment before the skeptical gaze of the modern world. I can say this because, at least in my view, the revelation provides for the first time a philosophically coherent and scientifically plausible framework for understanding the celestial realms. Because it frames the universe so widely, the Urantia text goes further than any other previous teaching in identifying the nature and purposes of our unseen friends on high. In its first two parts, comprising 56 Papers, we discover the vast family of affectionate personalities or entities who are sitting just off stage, mercifully ministering to each of us as individuals while nurturing the collective evolution of the whole.[24]

---

[24] One example from among the dozens of types revealed to us are the "social architect seraphim," one of my favorite angelic groups: **"These seraphim labor to enhance all sincere social contacts and to further the social evolution of universe creatures. . . . Social architects do everything within their province and power to bring together suitable individuals that they may constitute efficient and agreeable**

Not all our ready-at-hand spirit helpers are personal beings. The off-camera crew includes the impersonal divine reality of the God Fragment. Technically, this entity should be considered *prepersonal*, a term that will be explained later. The revelation of its nature is crucial to our study because, as noted, the Indwelling Spirit cocreates our souls in the highest reaches of our superconscious mind, working in liaison with our meaningful life decisions. It monitors our thoughts and feelings, and subtly adjusts our mental processes in a Godward direction without violating our free will. It patiently guides us, both during and after our life on Earth, to our ultimate destiny in perfection. The *UB* also calls the God Fragment by the odd names of *Thought Adjuster* and *Mystery Monitor*. I will say much more about this crucial divine gift in coming chapters.

When it comes to our personal spiritual practice, the Urantia Revelation invites us to consider that, moment-by-moment, our act is being witnessed, appreciated, and guided by loving beings and Deities. Each of us receives gentle stage direction sufficient for perfecting our role in each scene in our lives, so that we may deposit our best performance reel in the living cosmic archive of universal history.

Speaking in religious terms, our willingness to take direction is the equivalent of doing the will of God: "To do the will of God," states Jesus in the *UB*, "is the progressive experience of becoming more and more like God, and God is the source and destiny of all that is good and beautiful and true." [130:2.7] We know we are engaged with the divine will when we feel love and gratitude toward God, are increasingly inspired to love our fellows, feel an urge for unselfish social service, and when we are moved to choose the good, beautiful, or true option in each life decision.

---

working groups on earth; and sometimes such groups have found themselves reassociated on the mansion worlds for continued fruitful service. . . . Two beings are regarded as operating on the mating, complemental, or partnership basis, but when three or more are grouped for service, they constitute a social problem and therefore fall within the jurisdiction of the social architects." [39:3.4]

The Personal Heart of Cosmic Reality

This is my belief: *The Urantia Book* is a disclosure of ultimate cosmic realities and the divine personalities behind them. At the same time, I realize that a cursory look at the *UB*'s huge catalog of higher beings can be bewildering. I think it is fair to wonder why the text must go so far with its listings of odd-sounding beings such as Universe Circuit Supervisors, Perfectors of Wisdom, Tertiary Supernaphim, Ministering Spirits of the Central Universe, and Mighty Messengers. I am aware that many inquirers, upon viewing these unwieldy lists, conclude that the *UB* is another obscure channeled tome destined to be ignored on dusty bookshelves.

But be patient, dear reader—for it all depends on one's premise.

For some esotericists and New Agers, the supreme organizing principle of the cosmos is energy; for others, unity or nonduality. Mind or consciousness is the key for some, and for others, it's evolution. But for the Urantia Revelation, the supreme premise is *personhood*. The *centrality of personality* is the surprising core of this teaching, to which we now turn. Later chapters, especially chapter 8, offer a more advanced presentation of this issue, building upon the present discussion.

In any situation whatever, human or divine, we learn that the personalities involved are the most precious and crucial factor. "Everything nonspiritual in human experience, excepting personality, is a means to an end. Every true relationship of mortal man with other persons—human or divine—is an end in itself." [112:2.8] In other words, the reality of the personal—at any level and in any dimension—is the most vital element of the wide cosmos. The personal is the point.

"The universe is mind made and personality managed." [1:6.7] God in eternity plans and creates all things and beings. Deity personally sets in motion the impersonal laws of nature, and then oversees and manages the outworking of every facet of evolutionary reality through coordinate and subordinate Deity associates. For example, we read that single-celled life is formulated in their laboratories and then planted on newly habitable planets by specialized personal beings known as Life Carriers, who go on to carefully oversee and condition biological evolution over billions of years. (Paper 36 is entirely devoted to their story.) And the lawful physical evolution of stars and galaxies is planned and catalyzed by special supervising personalities—something like cosmic engineers. This über-science-fiction corps of beings are, like the Life Carriers, revealed for the first time in the Urantia Revelation. (See Paper 29, "The Universe Power Directors.")

Philosophically speaking, energy, mind, consciousness, evolution, and even spirit are subsidiary to that which is personal. They all function in service to the dignity of personality, which is superordinate in relation to all these factors. Thus it would be fair the call the Urantia Revelation a personalist teaching, in line with the contemporary philosophic movement known as personalism.[25] You'll recall that personality, or personhood, is also the central element of the inner triad of our self-system.

So, what is meant in the *UB* by having the status of personhood? The first point to bear in mind is that *Urantia Book*'s definition of personality diverges greatly from that of today's psychology, which regards personality as the pattern of our outward human behavior—the observable set of traits, attitudes, skills, or type of temperament we exhibit. But according to the Urantia text, each of us has a God-given personality that is *unchanging*. All other factors of self change or grow, but personality does not and cannot. "Throughout all stages of evolutionary growth, there is one part of you that remains absolutely unaltered, and that is personality—permanence in the presence of change." [112.1]

And yet, as we will see in much more detail later, personality is somehow able to host our living reality and unify the attributes of our subjectivity while also being the very source of will, creativity, and self-consciousness. Our unchanging personality is, paradoxically, the factual foundation of the objective reality of our ever-changing human subjectivity.

---

[25] According to the online Stanford Encyclopedia of Philosophy, "Personalism always underscores the centrality of the person as the primary locus of investigation for philosophical, theological, and humanistic studies. It is an approach or system of thought which regards or tends to regard the person as the ultimate explanatory, epistemological, ontological, and axiological principle of all reality."

To be a person is to enjoy an exclusive and singular perspective on reality that is unique in all universes. Personhood is that attribute of being that lets us exist as sovereigns in our own sphere of self-determination and creativity, allowing us to freely choose experiences, grow in knowledge and virtue, and evolve a personal soul.

Of course, at the same time, each unique human personality is only one of a near-infinite number of other unique persons. Angels and humans share this divine endowment of personality, not as something we attain, but as a sheer gift that remains with us and *as us* for an eternity. Further, being a person permits us to recognize and love other persons as equals—spontaneously so. Even after our radical transmutation in the resurrection halls of the afterlife, we can instantaneously recognize and be recognized by those we once knew on Earth. Because personality is supreme over all other factors of selfhood, an acquaintance we may run into at a high school reunion or even in the afterlife can intuitively seem like "that someone I knew before"—even if their physical appearance has changed drastically.

To be a person is to be adorable by nature, lovable almost by reason of divine fiat; behold any young child to confirm that truth. And that's why our Divine Parents cannot help but love each one of us, their children. Likewise, we can't help but fall in love with other persons once we get to know them over time. The glory of the idiosyncratic uniqueness of a free and living person is what arouses our love and affection for them.

If all this sounds too abstract, consider the lesson of Charles Dickens's *A Christmas Carol*. Recall the scene when the Ghost of Christmas Present shows Ebenezer Scrooge a God's-eye view of the personalities of Tiny Tim, Bob Cratchit, and the rest of Cratchit's humble family joyously celebrating Christmas Day with what little they have. Scrooge soon understands them in the way that those on the other side of the veil always do, sees the error of his ways, and falls in love with them. This story is in fact Dickens's own rendition of an NDE life review.

Personality is both that which knows and loves and that which can be loved and known. Theologically speaking, we can say that Deity personality is, by definition, absolute in its ability to know other persons and infinite in its capacity to love them. The Urantia Revelation (and most Christian theologians) teach that personhood is the central characteristic of God, who *is* absolute love personified. But the *UB* goes further in its celebration of the personal: "Personality is not simply an attribute of God. . . . Personality, in the supreme sense, is the revelation of God to the universe of universes." [1:5.13] As such, the personalness of Deity transcends God's other core characteristic—that of being pure spirit.

God as Father and Mother is the absolute person and the source and destiny of all personalities, and alone gifts us with personhood. We've noted as well that God confers on us a pure-spirit fragment as an additional and essential part of our self-system. But again, the personality portion of our selfhood is antecedent to and independent of our spirit endowment. In other words, for you and me, the component of personality in our self-system has logical (actually, theological) priority over the Indwelling Spirit feature in the inner trinity, especially since our personhood is the source of sovereign free will.

God as Infinite Love Personified and Self-Distributed

If God is infinite love personified, it follows that personality relationships of love and equality must be central to God's nature. God, the absolute Divine Person, is inherently relational, and yet is One God and One Universal Power. But how can God be unitary, self-determining, and self-subsisting, yet essentially loving and relational?

The *UB* asserts in its opening pages that all of reality emanates from three primal personalities, the Eternal Trinity—which are nonetheless perfectly one and seamlessly unified in the Father. Again, how can this be?

Divine personality is not self-centered; self-distribution and sharing of personality characterize divine freewill selfhood. Creatures crave association with other personal creatures; Creators are moved to share divinity with their universe children; the personality of the Infinite is disclosed as the Universal Father, who shares reality of being and equality of self with two co-ordinate personalities, the Eternal Son and the [Infinite Spirit]. [10:1.3]

In other words, it is God's ineluctible sharing of himself—his "fatherly" (or "motherly") bestowal of selfhood on others—that reveals the primal nature of personality for the ages. "There is inherent in the selfless, loving, and lovable nature of the Universal Father something which causes him to reserve to himself the exercise of only those powers and that authority which he apparently finds it impossible to delegate or to bestow." [10:1.1]

A community of absolute beings that we call the Eternal Trinity is the result of the Father's passion for the articulation and self-distribution of infinite love that occurred in the eternity of the past, establishing thereby the pattern for all subsequent communities and families in all domains.

According to the authors of the Urantia text, it was a virtual philosophic miracle that the theologians of the early Christian Church were able to establish—in broad outline—a generally correct doctrine of the Trinity, even in the face of a thousand years of Hebraic monotheism. This was possible because of their proximity to the powerful historic reality of the life of Jesus, whose claim to be the literal Son of God—one in essence with the Father yet distinct from him—was accepted by the early Church against other plausible interpretations of his miraculous career.[26]

---

[26] They achieved these theological heights because of the primary intuition of the Church Fathers who held that Jesus was *homoousios* (one in essence) with the Father and also fully human. Led in particular in the fourth century by St. Athanasius of Alexandria, the Council of Nicaea (325) repudiated Arianism (the belief that God the Son is fundamentally inferior to God the Father). Instead, they adopted the view that Jesus as Son was "light from light, true God of true God"—that is, ontologically equal to the Father. In addition, in Constantinople in 381, the Second Council spoke more clearly of the Holy Spirit as equal to the other two Persons, and proclaimed that he should be "worshiped together with the Father and the Son." (This essential teaching of the equality of the Third Person of the Trinity is affirmed and greatly expanded in *The Urantia Book*, as discussed shortly.) The *UB* singles out Athanasius in this passage: "It was a Greek, from Egypt, who so bravely stood up at Nicaea and so fearlessly challenged this assembly that it dared not so obscure the concept of the nature of Jesus that the real truth of his bestowal might have been in danger of being lost to the world. This Greek's name was Athanasius, and but for the eloquence and the logic of this believer, the persuasions of Arius would have triumphed." [130:0.18]

Neither Judaism nor Islam could accept the disruptive notion that the person of Jesus could be in any way the divine equivalent of the Creator Father and also human. Both religions held firm to the idea of God's indivisibility and oneness—that there can be no coequal Son of God. For example, perhaps Islam's most important belief about Allah (God) is summed up in the word *Tawhid*, the pristine notion of Allah's utter uniqueness. Tawhid signifies that God can have "no partners," no offspring that are equal in divinity. In Surah 112 of the Qur'an we read, "He is Allah, the One and Only; Allah, the Eternal, Absolute; None is born of Him, nor is He born; And there is none like Him."

No doubt about it, Muhammad's clear-cut monotheism offered a distinct advance over the polytheism of his contemporaries. To their credit, his followers have consistently taught and celebrated this great truth of the oneness and unity of a personal God of love and mercy, uplifting and blessing innumerable souls over the centuries.

Trinitarians hold high this same concept of the One God and consider it a great truth, but only one among other essential truths. Speaking to the nondualist mystic as well as to the monistic philosopher and the monotheist theologian, the *UB* asserts that the scope of the love and versatility of Deity can be even greater than to emanate from a single universal center. And the Urantia revelation stretches us with an equally important truth: the notion of God as parental at all levels. This reality exists even within the Father's exclusive sphere of eternity, where the phenomenon of fatherhood-and-sonship first appears in the cosmos—but of course, gender is not literal at this level.

Consider: what sort of God would populate a vast universe with human creatures raised by mothers and fathers? Doesn't it seem likely that such a God would co-parent us, along with other Deity partners? God as Father sets it all in motion, becoming the "first parent" in eternity by uniting with the Son to parent the third Person of the Trinity, the Infinite Spirit—and the three create and love all other living beings. No wonder Native Americans sometimes refer to the high God as "Grandfather."

In other words, a loving Father who is the ultimate parent of a universal family must have his own "family of equals" that allows a replete expression of God's regard for other beings—thereby providing the pattern of human parentage and human relationships of love, friendship, and mutual regard. And, more to the point of our inquiry: a loving and parental God would provide for our soul evolution by creating a rich array of divine agencies—some coordinate, and others subordinate—that nurture us from infancy to eventual perfection. The Urantia Revelation explains in detail how the two other coordinate divine personalities, the Eternal Son and the Infinite Spirit, provide additional reality domains that become discrete platforms for specific ministries to us as their beloved creatures. As we will discuss in the next section, the Son and the Spirit are genuinely coequal sources and centers of true realities that are essential factors in soul growth and self-perfection.

The Eternal Trinity and the Origin of Evolution

I imagine that you, dear reader, may be reaching for a stimulant. Instead, let's slow down and breathe deeply here, because I need to insert a preliminary philosophic step if we are to be intellectually rigorous. We cannot truly embrace a Trinitarian theology unless we first entertain the concept of infinity. So, with another big inhale, let's give this a try, as we join hands with Alice in Wonderland and leap down the rabbit hole of divinity reality. In this mysterious opening of infinity, we find that things can "eternalize" and "deitize"; that stuff can be both one and three at the same time; and that other paradoxes can abound "six ways before Sunday." So, to keep you by my side during this demanding section, a bit of humor will lighten up a dense discussion that provides essential background for understanding the method and scope of soul-making and self-perfecting.

God's first (theoretic) act of self-distribution led to a procession (outside of time) of two coequal divine personalities—as well as the promulgation of universal impersonal forces (as in, "the Force is with you") and the generation of time-space evolutionary reality (as in, you and me and Alice plus the White Rabbit).

But prior to that, God subsisted as the All—as a static infinite.

In a real sense, God's status of being nothing-but-infinite was limiting; and this is the great paradox. Consider: God is at first bound on all sides by an all-pervading infinity, subsumed in a "prison" of unqualified absoluteness with no formal distinctions between one thing and another.

Imagine: one could find no Alice, no White Rabbit, and not even the hole down to the center of the Earth, for they were all absorbed in unqualified infinity. To mix our metaphors recklessly, it was like a dark night in which all cows are black.

If there was to be any differentiation of things and beings, there had to be a liberation from what the *UB* calls the "fetters of infinitude," since God's infinity was "diffused" in an undifferentiated manner throughout the potentials of Total Deity. (About now, Alice is passing the marmalade jar.)

Thanks to God, the advent of the Trinity facilitates the Father's escape from this predicament.

> **The Paradise Trinity of eternal Deities facilitates the Father's escape from personality absolutism**. The Trinity perfectly associates the limitless expression of God's infinite personal will with the absoluteness of Deity. The Eternal Son and the various Sons of divine origin, together with the Conjoint Actor [i.e., the Third Person of the Trinity] and his universe children, effectively provide for the Father's liberation from the limitations otherwise inherent in primacy, perfection, changelessness, eternity, universality, absoluteness, and infinity. [1:0.1]

Imagine now that three great cosmic stages of unfolding are to be revealed as we sail farther down the rabbit role of eternity. In the Father's first stage of self-articulation, or what might be called his drama of trinitization, he takes a momentous leap so as to liberate himself from unqualified infinitude. He jumps back, so to speak, to unveil his own inherent attribute of absolute personhood. By this act, he eternalizes his Son, the Second Person of Deity.

We have hereupon cracked the undifferentiated cosmic egg and dropped it in the fryer, and a yoke appears in its center. Toast, tea, and marmalade are served.

The Father now fraternizes with his Son. He recognizes his divine equal in perfection of manifestation. God has discovered his attribute of fatherhood, and is now free to create additional sons and daughters. He can bestow personality on other intelligent beings who will dwell at successively lower levels of universe reality. And he can fraternize with them as well.

Prepare yourself now, you will be quizzed later on this further clarifying statement:

> **By the technique of trinitization the Father divests himself of that unqualified spirit personality which is the Son, but in so doing he constitutes himself the Father of this very Son** and thereby possesses himself of unlimited capacity to become the divine Father of all subsequently created, eventuated, or other personalized types of intelligent will creatures. As the *absolute and unqualified personality* the Father can function only as and with the Son, but as a *personal Father* he continues to bestow personality upon the diverse hosts of the differing levels of intelligent will creatures, and he forever maintains personal relations of loving association with this vast family of universe children. [10:2.1]

Well said! And now, the second crucial phase is made manifest as we fall deeper, down and down and down.

In constituting himself as the Father of an Eternal Son, the Father has eternalized a coordinate Deity who is the perfect revelation of the Father's personal nature. As such, the Son is the absolute paragon, the eternal pattern, of all personality reality. In addition, we are told that the Son—who shines in the heart of the heavens like a billion suns—pops up as the infinite source of spiritual energy to the universes. His drawing power as the Absolute Person is known as *spiritual gravity*.

But stop a moment. In this act of Deity-dualization, a new divinity tension is created. The Son should be described as the personality-absolute. But now an *impersonal* absolute known as Paradise must eternalize. We are told: "The Father, in eternalizing the Original Son, simultaneously revealed the infinity potential of his nonpersonal self as Paradise." [11:9.3]

It's as if the absolute of the personal must be balanced by the absolute of the impersonal. In fact, we are told, this *is* the case, since the infinite Father encompasses all possible realities, personal and impersonal and anything in between.

Therefore, because of the astounding transaction that led to the differentiation of the Eternal Son, an equally stupendous (but nonpersonal) center of energy, pattern, and power also comes into being in eternity. This center is the absolute source of all that is impersonal, and it steps up as the gravitational center of *material* reality.

We are falling ever deeper now, and a third great stage is deemed as inevitable: the procession to the Third Person, the Infinite Spirit. This august and magnificent being is sometimes called the Paradise Mother Spirit, so I will refer to her as "she." Also known as the Conjoint Actor, the Spirit is the personification of the conjoint partnership of the Father and Son. The Spirit is not just their rep—she *is* their union.

The Urantia Revelation teaches that an eternal central universe resides at the center of all things, with Paradise is its center. As the Third Person now manifests in eternity, we are told that space comes into being, and the central universe eternalizes.

The cycle of trinitization has concluded, and this primal association of the Father and Son, now manifest as the person of the Infinite Spirit, is pregnant with a great plan for even further self-distribution. This blueprint is the great project of the ages, the promulgation of experiential reality and all the things and beings that shall populate these evolving realms of space and time, including rabbits and their rabbit holes. (See "The Grand Project of the Ages" in chapter 11 for details.)

While the Father is *love absolute*, the Son is *unqualified mercy*. The Eternal Son is the first being in the universe to experience sonship, which affords him a special feeling of solidarity for all of us, who are also children of parents. And while the Father is perfect love and the Son is divine mercy, the Paradise Mother Spirit is *applied love*. She now becomes the chief divine administrator, and her portfolio embraces the mission of extending her "love app" to the vast multiplicity of creatures on the habitable worlds of space.

All these children want to come forth, but someone has to be their Mother! So the Infinite Mother Spirit steps up. And with this, the Eternal Trinity launches creature life in space and time. As the *Tao Te Ching* put it, "the One became the three, which became the ten thousand."

The secret is out: an evolutionary universe of trillions of children was all along *in potentia* (as Thomas Aquinas might have said) in the Father's unfathomable infinitude.

Let us get some ice cream and recap: Once the Father had demonstrated the absolute pattern for personality, which was eternally personified as the Eternal Son, then the absolute of nonpersonal reality appeared, and in fact had to materialize for the sake of balance and symmetry. Again, in this eternity-moment, we witness the appearance of the absolute of matter, Paradise. Because Paradise is the singularity at the center of all universes, this principle establishes the fact that matter exists in all dimensions of reality. This means that all worlds, including the most rarefied spheres and even Paradise itself, operate on a physical foundation.[27]

Recapping further, we've seen that the two primal Deities, the Father and Son, have agreed to a conjoint program of universal creation upon this foundation. They decide to create evolving and experiential children in the universes of space and time as a counterpoise to the eternal, nonevolving residents of the central universe (that *de facto* already exist). Their agreement *personalizes* as a Deity, often known as the Conjoint Actor, who thereby completes the trinitization party. She is also called the God of Action, the Infinite Spirit, and the Divine Mother. She is the detail-oriented minister for the astonishing plan of self-distribution into the evolutionary realms of creature life and creature ascension to Paradise.

---

[27] With regard to these higher worlds, the "denser" portion of their constituent physical elements maps to our atomic chart. But the remainder of their elements consist of materials (which, by the way, are not "pearly") beyond our range of vision. In these higher-dimensional spheres, the "atomic chart" is inclusive of the one we use on Earth but has double or triple the number of elements. The atomic chart of Paradise has 300 elements, and that of intermediate worlds has 200. "All of these [intermediate] worlds are architectural spheres, and **they have just double the number of elements of the evolved planets.** Such made-to-order worlds not only abound in the heavy metals and crystals, having one hundred physical elements, but likewise have exactly one hundred forms of a unique energy organization called *morontia material*." [48:1.3]

Following the momentum of creation already set in motion by her two Deity partners, the Infinite Mother Spirit carries forward the seven possible permutations (or expressions) of the original Deity threesome. Alice, who loved numbers, would likely have been thrilled because each of these permutations receives it own personalization as a Deity. Collectively they are known as the *Seven Master Spirits*. These beings are previously unrevealed on our world, but the sacred significance of the number seven has certainly been intuited over the centuries by prophets and numerologists.

This diversification of God into seven Master Deities is why—as exclusively revealed in the Urantia Revelation—seven great inhabitable superuniverses evolve into being in space in an orderly and majestic rendition of the Big Bang. If you are interested in the astrophysics of the seven superuniverses, you may enjoy Appendix A, "Urantia Cosmology and Current Astrophysics," which details the fact that said superuniverses are actually immense galaxy superclusters, many of which have been identified by our scientists. Our Milky Way is a member of one these great agglomerations, known as the Virgo Supercluster. Further, we are told that these great formations rotate (counterclockwise) around a universal center or Great Attractor (that is, Paradise)—which, as you will recall, is the source of material gravity.

In general, then, by working with her Deity compatriots in the Trinity, the Infinite Spirit now places derivative Deities in charge of seven domains of space-time. Their cosmic charter includes the evolution of humanoid creatures like us. Curioser and curioser, is it not, dear Alice?

A Brief Anatomy of the Universe of Universes

Calling the grand cosmos a "universe of universes" provides an apt description, for the cosmic realities depicted in *The Urantia Book* are bigger and far older than that described in today's astrophysics.

Space-time is unbelievably far flung, we learn, but the evolutionary domains are not diffuse and unstructured, despite appearances. The organization of galaxies is not random and inchoate, since they are planned and created by infinite personalities. And, as we have seen, at the center of this cosmic holarchy is the central universe, with Paradise as its heart. This center is stationary; the evolving physical universes comprise its periphery and are always in motion. They rotate in the shape of a stupendous cosmic disk around the central universe in a configuration of five vast rings, each one composed of innumerable galaxy clusters, galaxy super-clusters, and even bigger agglomerations that today's astrophysicists call galaxy filaments. This great disk strikes an image not unlike the Medicine Wheel of Native American cosmology.[28]

The innermost ring of the five is the only currently inhabited zone of the evolving cosmos; stop to ponder that the four other rings of galaxies are not inhabited at this time. The inhabited inner ring is known as the *grand universe*. It consists of the seven great galaxy superclusters that we have introduced as superuniverses, each of which consists of one-hundred thousand local universes. Whereas a superuniverse contains up to a trillion inhabited planets, each local universe can evolve up to ten million of them.

And finally, the entirety of cosmic reality, inclusive of the grand universe and the central universe, is referred to as the *master universe*. The master universe has a center, as we have noted, but if a spaceship were to approach the horizon of this cosmic gravitational center, it would seem to disappear at any one point.[29] The eternally existent central universe, we are told, is inhabited by perfect beings and the absolute Creator Deities, who provide the unique patterns for personalities such as us in the perfecting universes. These

---

[28] We are told in the *UB* that in addition to the rotation of this great disk, all domains of space are also expanding outward at unbelievable speeds—just as today's astrophysics describes—but the revelators teach that this vast expanse of the space of the cosmos behaves in an accordion-like manner. It inflates and then contracts in a two-billion year cycle, in a process called space respiration. See 11:2.2.

[29] And that's because, at least according to my own interpretation, the governing geometry of the master universe is toroidal, like so many other systems in nature. Consider the possibility that the universe is one immense torus that contains an endless array of lesser toroidal structures all the way down to the human level. A key characteristic of a torus is that it has a dynamic center. At its core, the entire physical system comes to a point of ultimate balance and stillness—also known as the singularity of the torus. The singularity at the greatest scale, I believe, is Paradise. I further speculate that this unifying force of the transcendent oneness of the universal torus of the cosmos is the cause of the phenomenon of indissoluble wholeness now under discussion in the new theories of evolutionary holism.

exalted beings lack one precious thing: the challenge and the thrill of soul-making and self-perfecting described in this book.

The Trinity in Time and Space

Eternity *loves* the creatures of time; and in a real sense, the eternals need us as we need them. Therefore, eternity makes provision for the sustainable administration of the time domains.

The evolving universes are managed by divine personalities who are designed for the outworking of eternal love in these imperfect realms. In fact, our personal growth is meaningful only if understood in the context of the divine activities of these loving beings, both Deities and angelic beings. (Section 2 in the Special Supplement offers a listing of only a few of these affectionate beings who serve at different levels of the evolving universes, and who also had a hand in authoring Papers in the *UB*.)

The galaxy superclusters—the great superuniverses—constitute the largest unit of cosmic administration. Managing a universe of thousands of inhabited galaxies requires inconceivably efficient organization, and the *UB* offers an exclusive glimpse of this apparatus.

But let's take a few steps down to the local universe level of administration. At this level, we discover the very important beings known as our immediate Creator Parents, who, we are told, are of direct origin from the members of the Trinity.[30] The identities of our own two local universe Deities may come as a surprise. They are Christ himself—he who incarnated here as Jesus—and his divine feminine consort, who is known as the local universe Mother Spirit. Christ is often known as Christ Michael, or simply Michael. These two, Michael and Mother, are complemental Creators, roughly akin to the gendered divine couples we find in world mythology such as Isis and Osiris or Shiva and Shakti.

Together as our Creator Parents, Michael and Mother originated our "local" family, which currently includes nearly four

---

[30] Deities at this level are differentiated as literally male and female; they are gendered personalities who are coequal as divine partners and cocreators.

million inhabited planets. One of these worlds is Earth—which is known on high by the name "Urantia." It was the Deity prerogative of Michael and Mother to set in motion the evolution of life on each of these worlds through their various agencies of life origination and evolutionary overcontrol (detailed at length in Part II of the Urantia text, "The Local Universe").

Christ and Mother create the material infrastructure of the local universe. They also create the angelic host and the planetary celestial government that carefully watch over us, including the seraphim (the direct offspring of the Mother) who are personally assigned to guide us in coordination with our Indwelling Spirit—all in order to grow our souls toward fusion. Germane as well to our evolving soul is the fact that Christ and Mother Spirit maintain personal relationships with every one of their human creatures through their Spirit of Truth (the spirit of Christ) and Holy Spirit (the spirit of the Mother), influences that also guide our decisions and actions. Learn more about them in Appendix B, "The Local Universe Creators: Mother Spirit and Christ Michael."

The Goal of Perfection in the Afterlife

We begin our ascent from our local universe, with Paradise as the ultimate goal. But all along the way inward and upward to the central universe, we make stops at intermediate destinations. You and I will inhabit many heavenly places in our long career of ascension after death. These worlds constitute an educational regime that is far, far beyond the conception of anything envisioned in any scripture. After a long journey, we will meet and fraternize with perfect beings in the central universe who will teach us the ways of perfection, and we will share with them our discoveries on the enthralling path of experiential achievement—the work of soul evolution.

Simplistic ideas about the soul's destiny are provided in the Gospel of John, where Jesus teaches that believers will be rewarded with an eternal life in heaven. In fact, those who are "born again" actually gain an eternal life *now*: "I give them eternal life, and they shall never perish" (John 10:28). This offer of an eternal existence now and in an endless afterlife strikes some of us as a great truism.

But at the time of Jesus or in the ensuing centuries, almost nothing specific was known about what goes on in the heavenly estate. Before the rise of the NDE phenomenon, modern Western ideas about the afterlife mainly derived from the stark and eccentric images of St. John's Book of Revelation, a few passages in the Old and New Testaments, and especially from Dante Alighieri's *Divine Comedy*. As a result, a certain archaic and quaint lore has come down to the modern world.

For example, imagine the typical Christian living in Chicago in the 1930s, such as those who read the original Papers of the Urantia Revelation. (See their story in the Special Supplement.) If they thought of it at all, they might have imagined heaven as a place populated by robed saints and Rubenesque angels—a one-stop haven of happiness where disembodied humans dwelled in adoration of Christ and Mary.

Educated Catholics among them might have drawn from Dante's vision of heaven in *The Divine Comedy*. And it is interesting to note that some of Dante's images poetically foreshadow the Urantia Revelation. Throughout his journey in the *Paradiso*, Dante has been led upward through the spheres, first by the Roman poet Virgil, then by Beatrice. Upon attaining the Seventh Sphere, Dante views and then climbs the ladder of Jacob (a famous biblical image that appears in Jacob's dream at Genesis 28:12), which signifies the ascent of the soul to God.

Finally, having ascended to the "sphere of the fixed stars," Dante is met by St. Bernard, who escorts him to the empyrean, the dimensionless highest heaven, the moral center of the cosmos that both contains and exceeds all time and space. Dante now stands before circular rows of seats reserved for all the souls of the saved. With much help, especially from Mary, the Queen of Heaven, he finally sees the blazing "Point of Light and Love," which is God. The Source of all things is surrounded by the angelic hierarchies, which appear as nine orders of angels who take the form of nine concentric circles that spin around the brilliant point of God's light at the very center of the empyrean. An immense circular light emanates from God, and "living light pours round and through" the poet.

Like Paul on the road to Damascus, Dante is overwhelmed by this great light from heaven; also like Paul, he is blinded. But he then is given new sight that bestows the beatific vision. Standing alone before the divine luminosity and gazing at its holy center, he observes that God's light becomes three concentric circles shining, like a halo, around His countenance.

> Within its depthless clarity of substance
> I saw the Great Light shine into three circles
> In three clear colors bound in one same space.[31]

It is a pleasure to contemplate this rich imagery. But in a monumental leap beyond such mythic and poetic notions, the *UB* unveils its stupendous ascension scheme, featuring reams of almost technical detail about the regime of afterlife education, socialization, and consciousness growth. This vast plan of mortal ascension, we are told, is one of three key components of the Father's Plan of Perfection Attainment [7:4.3].

This plan has built-in equipment. The potential for survival is inherent in God's bestowal of the Indwelling Spirit and a unique personality. And we've already noted how these two elements of the inner triad provide the conditions for the evolution of a personal soul, in concert with our intrinsic body-mind endowment.[32]

The other two components of the Perfection Plan are the personnel support features: the Plan of Bestowal and the Plan of Mercy Ministry. To recap: In addition to the endowments from the Father, our efforts are also supported by the grace of the downreach of Deity in the form of periodic avatar incarnations and daily angelic ministry. These habiliments of progress explain why willing humans always graduate upward. If and when we do, we sojourn in the afterlife on increasingly higher worlds in the company of our

---

[31] Dante Alighieri, *The Divine Comedy: Volume III: Paradise*, trans. Mark Mussa (Penguin Classics, 1986), 33-115-17.

[32] This divine scheme "is the Universal Father's plan of evolutionary ascension, a program unreservedly accepted by the Eternal Son when he concurred in the Father's proposal 'Let us make mortal creatures in our own image.' This provision for upstepping the creatures of time involves the Father's bestowal of the Thought Adjusters and the endowing of material creatures with the prerogatives of personality." [7:7.4]

compatriots, who are also self-perfecting mortals from innumerable inhabited planets like ours, real extraterrestrials.

Like Dante, ascenders are led forth by heavenly personal guides (our guardian seraphim and many others) on the slow journey inward to the extradimensional heart of the cosmos, eventually to be taught the truths of eternity on the spheres of the central universe, which is named *Havona*. Here we meet those superb inhabitants of eternity, beings who dwell in a zone of unimaginable grandeur but who drink in our narratives of the rugged experiential life that we led as we climbed "Jacob's ladder."

Our goal is Paradise, the culmination of our heavenly ascension. We complete the journey there, having become perfected beings known as *finaliters*—exalted and deified persons. Finaliters have by definition finalized their evolution in the afterlife. They have exhausted all cosmic potentials for personal advancement in every dimension of selfhood. They are perfected souls of light, complete in their development of God-consciousness and replete in their range of universe experience and cosmic socialization.

I know that at first glance, this description of the Paradise ascent may sound a little daunting, like the misplaced dream of an uptight perfectionist. But after years of contemplating the details of this path, I feel increasingly relaxed about the journey. For I know that the ladder of divinization was conceived by infinitely loving beings who understand us better than we understand ourselves. They provide more than enough support and structure, and the Deities give us millions of years to relish the experiential riches of our voyage. The ascent is intensively educational, but it is almost leisurely in its pace. It is almost as if God is saying to each of us, "Each moment is sufficient unto itself, for the joys of Paradise are even now within your grasp."

PART II

Self and Soul in the Urantia Revelation

The Synthesis Hypothesis

Every moment and every event of every
man's life plants something in his soul.
—*Thomas Merton*

The soul's center is God.
—*St. John of the Cross*

T he long road to Paradise begins with our soul-making decisions
on the humble soil of Earth. As we have seen, we make decisions of
spiritual import along the way, literally synthesizing a new reality
in the universe—an immortal substance called the soul, a peculiar
material that was perhaps alluded to in a well-known biblical statement by Paul the Apostle: "Ye have in heaven a better and an enduring substance" (Hebrews 10:34).

The Urantia Revelation makes clear that, to the extent that
we exercise a form of self-reflective and truth-discerning awareness called faith, our daily choices lend themselves to the further
accumulation of this mysterious soul-substance—and eventually to
God-realization. That is the synthesis hypothesis I offer for your
consideration in this chapter.

Growing a soul is a highly personal enterprise with profound
consequences. This slowly evolving entity becomes the living
embryo of our emerging identity, now and into eternity. It represents

our truest self as seen from the standpoint of the Indwelling Spirit, the cocreator of the soul along with the human mind.

At first, our soul's immortality is provisional. In a sense, the soul is "on loan" to us. And the great question we all must one day face is: will we *eternalize* our soul to make it our permanent possession? In other words, will we irreversibly opt in to the Paradise ascent after death? We are taught in the *UB* that in the early phases of the afterlife, we are confronted with the greatest decision one can ever make: do we wish to continue on into an eternal life of service? Even now we can affirm this choice. But in the exalted moment when we make this choice *irrevocably*, our soul fuses with our Indwelling Spirit. True immortality factualizes because the seat of our identity becomes the inner spirit itself. This level of attainment is so profound that, if achieved while on Earth, the physical body is consumed in that moment and the person translates directly to the afterlife.[33]

On the other hand, if we opt out of ascension, the soul's substance continues on, but not as a part of our personal identity. The *UB* explains that while the soul is a very distinct substance, it is always technically in the custody of the Indwelling Spirit, its coauthor. If we decide against serving and loving God in eternity, the soul "divorces" itself from our personhood, and now becomes the exclusive possession of the Thought Adjuster. Thereupon, the soul's previous achievements contribute to the Indwelling Spirit's future career as the indweller of another person, if such an assignment is made.[34]

---

[33] I return to the theme of God Fusion in detail in the last section of this chapter. Bear in mind that getting to this point of attainment requires a profound enlightenment beyond anything we have witnessed on Earth in recorded history, with the few exceptions that we will examine in that section. In later chapters I explain the conditions required for fusion in terms of human development theory.

[34] But this event is not the same thing as reincarnation in the conventional sense—as explained in more detail at the close of chapter 10. If we opt out of survival, our inner triad gets broken up: our personhood (our unique self with its power of will and self-consciousness) gets absorbed into the cosmic oversoul, and our soul becomes the ward of the Thought Adjuster: "If mortal man fails to survive natural death, the real spiritual values of his human experience survive as a part of the continuing experience of the Thought Adjuster. The personality values of such a nonsurvivor persist as a factor in the personality of the actualizing Supreme Being. Such persisting qualities of personality are deprived of identity but not of experiential values accumulated during the mortal

While on Earth, the average person's soul evolves largely outside of their awareness. And this better self within us has its own growth trajectory. As it matures, it slowly diverges from that scrappy character that constitutes our limited self-sense—our so-called ego. This differentiation of soul and ego happens because most of us are taught to identify with our strictly material self—our body, appearance, family, nationality, race, education, occupation, and so on.

But such is not the case so when we become citizens of the Kingdom of God, if I may use the old biblical metaphor. Now we become aware—dimly at first and "through a glass, darkly"—that a more exalted selfhood is surfacing. We are now citizens of another and higher world, and this newly chosen identity eventually supersedes all lesser identifications.[35] This new status was explained by Jesus in his ordination sermon to the Apostles, as restated in the Urantia Revelation.

> "Now that you are ambassadors of my Father's kingdom, you have thereby become a class of men separate and distinct from all other men on earth. **You are not now as men among men but as the enlightened citizens of another and heavenly country** among the ignorant creatures of this dark world. It is not enough that you live as you were before this hour, but henceforth must you live as those who have tasted the glories of a better life and have been sent back to earth as ambassadors of the Sovereign of that new and better world." [140:3.1]

The Human Soul: An Alchemical Synthesis

When we become citizens of this "heavenly country" that Jesus spoke of, we increasingly allow the Indwelling Spirit to stamp its

---

life in the flesh. The survival of identity is dependent on the survival of the immortal soul of morontia status and increasingly divine value. Personality identity survives in and by the survival of the soul." [16:9.3]

[35] It may be more precise to say that the soul transcends and includes the results of these lesser activities. Our compromised efforts to adapt to our life conditions can grow the soul *quantitatively*, but may fall short in achieving the refined qualities of a noble soul whose chief pursuit was faith and truth-discernment. This issue is a chief concern of chapter 4.

vibrational signature on our life experiences. Here's how the Urantia text summarizes this special transaction: "[Your] memory of human experience on the material worlds of origin survives death in the flesh because **the [Indwelling Spirit] has acquired a spirit counterpart, or transcript,** of those events of human life which were of spiritual significance." [40:9.4–5]

Each day, our Thought Adjuster creates a new set of transcripts of our worthy life experiences. Allow me to emphasize again that each soul memory is an imperishable record—and it is literally deposited within us after each soul-making choice.

The inner spirit also values our clear thinking, making energetic copies of our concepts: "Adjusters work in the spheres of the higher levels of the human mind, unceasingly seeking to produce . . . duplicates of every concept of the mortal intellect." [110:2.4]

With each such instance of "spiritual counterparting," a novel substance is created within us that remains eternally in the safekeeping of the Indwelling Spirit. And this growing entity is energetically distinct from either the human mind or the inner spirit, who are the parents of this new reality. The *UB* compares the soul to a loom: the warp of the loom is spiritual energy, while the woof is derived from the material energies of the mind. In each moment of soul-making, the loom generates a unique and original bit of fabric. It is spun and threaded like metaphysical silk in the subtle domains that abide within the human heart.

Allow me to offer another metaphor. The evolving structure we call the soul can be compared to an alchemical synthesis, a concoction of "chemical" constituents contributed by the choosing mortal mind and the approving inner spirit. With each event of counterparting that occurs, the "solution" in which these constituent elements are dissolved precipitates out a new transcript, which then gets deposited as a tiny crystal of soul memory. Such memories are of a different species from the short-term or long-term material memories lodged in the hippocampus, all of which vanish at death.

[After death] those mental associations that were purely animalistic and wholly material naturally perished with the physical brain, but everything in your mental life

which was worthwhile, and which had survival value, was counterparted by the Adjuster and is retained as a part of personal memory all the way through the ascendant career. You will be conscious of all your worthwhile experiences as you advance from one section of the universe to another—even to Paradise. [47:4.5]

Bear in mind that the third member of the sacred triad, our unique personality, is also active in soul-making. It provides the precious faculty of volition to this complex process. The human will can only manifest—at first—through the vehicle of the material mind, bound up as the mind is with the brain. As I will discuss in detail in chapters 8 and 9, the locus of this crucial faculty will one day transfer its seat to the soul—exactly to the extent of our consecrated identification with the things of the spirit. Obviously, this step precedes the much more advanced transfer of personal identity from the soul to the Indwelling Spirit.

The cocreated energetic substance that comprises the soul is so unusual that a special word had to be coined to describe it, so the revelators invented an odd new term—*morontia*.[36] "As a mortal creature chooses to 'do the will of the Father in heaven,' so the Indwelling Spirit becomes the father of a *new reality* in human experience. The mortal and material mind is the mother of this same emerging reality. The substance of this new reality is neither material nor spiritual—it is *morontial*. This is the emerging and immortal soul which is destined to survive mortal death and begin the Paradise ascension." [0:5.10]

---

[36] The term "morontia" has more meanings beyond the scope of the present discussion. It can also designate the subtle realm between the material and the spiritual. "*Morontia* is a term designating a vast level intervening between the material and the spiritual. It may designate personal or impersonal realities, living or nonliving energies. The warp of morontia is spiritual; its woof is physical." [0:5.12] Further, "morontia" also is used to refer to those higher worlds that bridge the gulf between mortal origin and the more advanced spiritual status: "Much of the reality of the spiritual worlds is of the morontia order, a phase of universe reality wholly unknown on Urantia. The goal of personality existence is spiritual, but the morontia creations always intervene, bridging the gulf between the material realms of mortal origin and the superuniverse spheres of advancing spiritual status." [16:4.6]

Soul Evolution as a Faith Adventure

Paper 111, entitled "The Adjuster and the Soul," provides the *UB's* core discussion of the morontia soul. In one of the text's inimitable breathless sentences, the revelators summarize the chief function of the soul in the following way: "The soul partakes of the qualities of both the human mind and the divine spirit but persistently evolves toward **augmentation of spirit control through the fostering of a mind function whose meanings seek to coordinate with true spirit value.**"

The "mind function" fostered by the soul, as technical as that phrase may sound, is the beautiful phenomenon of human *faith*. Our soul-making depends in large part on the proper function of faith, an oft-misused word that gets redefined and rehabilitated in the Urantia Revelation.

Think of faith as truth-seeking and truth-finding awareness. Faith pursues its purposes in deep reflection. It searches out the imponderables of experience through mindfulness, prayer, and insight. The explorations sponsored by faith lead to firmly held convictions that are known through what might be called sublime thinking—true soul consciousness. Such persuasions reach the status of genuine faith when they become so compelling that they inform all of our decisions and actions.

But faith is much more than belief; mere belief is secondary and can even be beside the point. "Belief is binding, but faith liberates," teaches the Urantia Revelation in an especially profound discourse.[37] Faith liberates spiritual energy so that we can carry out the great work. Mere belief in a series of intellectual propositions about

---

[37] "Belief has attained the level of faith when it motivates life and shapes the mode of living. The acceptance of a teaching as true is not faith; that is mere belief. Neither is certainty nor conviction faith. A state of mind attains to faith levels only when it actually dominates the mode of living. Faith is a living attribute of genuine personal religious experience. One believes truth, admires beauty, and reverences goodness, but does not worship them; such an attitude of saving faith is centered on God alone, who is all of these personified and infinitely more. Belief is always limiting and binding; faith is expanding and releasing. Belief fixates, faith liberates. But living religious faith is more than the association of noble beliefs; it is more than an exalted system of philosophy; it is a living experience concerned with spiritual meanings, divine ideals, and supreme values." [101:8.2]

God or the soul will not suffice to energetically transform the self. Only a robust faith—a profound and unshakeable consecration of the whole self to a great ideal born of deep reflection—can mobilize the entire personality in service to higher values.

Of course, the passionately held conclusions of faithful awareness may ultimately be wrong. But its certainties are heuristic—that is, they give us an essential framework for growth and learning. It is better that a child has sincere faith in some childish idea of God learned in Sunday school than have no faith at all; it is beneficial when warring tribes drop their weapons and unite around a common faith in a mythic religion, as did the ancient Hebrews. Primitive faith is better than having no beliefs because it provides a baseline for the further evolution of individual souls as well as whole societies.[38]

Sincere faith inspires and refreshes awareness. A person with strong faith exercises a "mind function" that sweeps aside frivolity, worry, and fixations, allowing them to be more receptive to the higher impulses of the Indwelling Spirit. "Faith acts to release the superhuman activities of the divine spark, the immortal germ, that lives within the mind." [132:3.6] This sort of faith guided Joan of Arc, a teenager of peasant origin, to become the unlikely leader of the French nation; it led Martin Luther King to transform race relations in America and go on to powerfully condemn the immorality of the Vietnam War. Both became martyrs because of their convictions. Faith may not always be prudent or wise, but it always acts, and these actions are soul-making events that can sometimes transform nations.

While faith consorts with certainties felt in the soul, human reason works with probabilities calculated in the mind. "Science appeals to the understanding of the mind; religion appeals to the loyalty and devotion of the body, mind, and spirit, even to the whole personality." [102:1.4]

---

[38] Albeit there may be exceptions when toxic doctrines are forced on youthful souls, which can lead to the arrest of any further development of faith. The point here is not so much the intellectual content of the belief system but rather the psychological experience of a consecrated personal commitment to a perceived truth. I have in mind here especially the *UB* section entitled "The Supremacy of Purposive Potential" at 102:5.

Rational thought uses the human senses and logic to build new knowledge from verifiable material facts. Intellectual doubt must always remain if science is to evolve. By contrast, the approach of religious faith is to expand consciousness through prayer, wonder, and imagination—or any helpful technique of deep personal immersion in meanings and values. Based on repeated instances of such communion, faithful persons develop a confidence that dominates their mode of living. But not unlike science, enlightened faith allows its assurances to evolve and become more refined through never-ending spiritual exploration. And a healthy faith has an enthusiastic respect for the results of scientific method.

The great revelations to humankind are designed to enhance our faithfulness to higher values. They assure us that we live in a friendly universe that supports our ongoing search for truth, beauty, and goodness. They depict the Creator as a divine parent who cares for the daily needs of his children, who forgives them and calls them home when they go astray. When we perceive the signs of such divine solicitude, we are inspired to care for our fellow siblings in this universal family of God. We are stirred to a lifetime of loving action based on faith.

> Religious experience is the realization of the consciousness of having found God. And when a human being does find God, there is experienced within the soul of that being such an indescribable restlessness of triumph in discovery that he is impelled to seek loving service-contact with his less illuminated fellows, not to disclose that he has found God, but rather to allow the overflow of the welling-up of eternal goodness within his own soul to refresh and ennoble his fellows. Real religion leads to increased social service. [102:3.4]

Pope Francis referred to this kind of faith in a homily he gave after celebrating Mass in early 2017 at the Vatican. The pope described Christianity as a religion of loving service, not a "religion of talk." He complained about "fake" Christians who treat the faith as though it were window dressing rather than as a call to service, especially to the needy. "To be a Christian means to *do*—to do the will of God," said Francis. "And on the Last Day—because all of us will have one—what shall the Lord ask us? Will He say: 'What have you said about me?' No. He shall ask us about the things we did."[39]

The Urantia Revelation also insists on the centrality of "doing unto others" in religious life. But according to the *UB*, the Lord not only asks "on the Last Day" what we have done; the divine spark asks us *every day*, "What actions of yours are worth immortalizing in and as your soul?" Our answer each day of our lives is the sum and substance of our soul evolution.

In practical terms, the cosmic spirituality of the *UB* is about doing the right thing according to the law of reciprocity of the Golden Rule. Faith assures us that such a life of giving and receiving is realistic and sustainable. Faith says: the resources required to love both self and others are abundantly available. But with greater faith, we can go even further. We can love others as we imagine God would love them. In a response to a question by Nathaniel—whom the *UB* calls the "philosophic apostle"—we are told that Jesus astonished his apostles by distinguishing six levels of the Golden Rule, describing the sixth as "the divine command to treat all men as we conceive God would treat them. That is the universe ideal of human relationships." [147:4.9]

This philosophic teaching about ethics, which occurred on the occasion of a visit to the home of Lazarus in Bethany, illustrates that doing the right thing is also matter of deep thinking. Clarity of thought, supported by wholehearted faith, attunes us to cosmic reality. "Truth, beauty, and goodness [are] man's intellectual approach to the universe of matter, mind, and spirit." [56:10.11] Living courageously according to such core values is the thinking

---

[39] "Pope Francis: God is real, too many Christians are fake," Vatican Radio, February 23, 2016. *Urantia Book* students have observed that numerous statements by the pope seem to harmonize with the *UB*. It is also known that a circle of Catholic priests in Argentina had been studying *El Libro de Urantia*, and it is possible that that their superior at the time, Archbishop Jorge Mario Bergoglio—now Pope Francis—might have known about their interest in the revelation. The Spanish-speaking world in general may be more aware of the existence of the Urantia Revelation than even the U.S. population, because of a novelization of Part IV of the *UB* entitled *Caballo de Troya*, by bestselling Spanish author J. J. Benitez, has sold more than three million copies in twenty-eight editions. The series of eight books that followed has sold another two million. The Spanish translation of *The Urantia Book* has sold over 250,000 copies, in part because of the influence of Benitez.

person's gateway to cosmic spirituality. "Spirituality enhances the ability to discover beauty in things, recognize truth in meanings, and discover goodness in values." [100:2.4]

In order to exercise my own personal faith while in prayer or meditation, I relax my body, still my mind, and focus my awareness within. I ask for what is true, beautiful, or good in the matters at hand. I wait and listen. Then I direct my attention to the images, ideas, and impulses that emanate from the Indwelling Spirit. Experience has taught me that what I can receive in these moments depends on my level of faith. "Truth can never become man's possession without the exercise of faith. This is true because man's thoughts, wisdom, ethics, and ideals will never rise higher than his faith, his sublime hope." [132:3.5]

Faith Marries Potentials to Actuals

When it comes to faith, our predicament can be summed up, metaphorically, with one question: Is the sun rising or is it setting? Pure faith answers: the sun is *always* rising, regardless of the time of day.

Faith wakes us up to the bright light of cosmic reality. Living faith, born of trust in a friendly universe, opens the aperture of the mind to the light of a deeper awakening.

From one point of view, the exercise of faith involves mindfulness—an improved attention to one's experience. Faith in this sense is the act of mobilizing a single-pointed focus on the needs of the moment. "Man's sole contribution to growth is the mobilization of the total powers of his personality—living faith." [103.7] But faith has other tenses. Faithfulness refers to the future as well: we are evolving beings, but we have the potential to perfect ourselves. Genuine faith believes in the sacred promise of such God-given potential.

In the *UB* we are told that the design of cosmic reality in the evolving realms involves the translation of potentials into actuals. "In the time universes, potential is always supreme over the actual. In the evolving cosmos the potential is what is to be, and what is to be is the unfolding of the purposive mandates of Deity." The Urantia Revelation calls this *the supremacy of purposive potential.* (See

102:5.1.) There is no limit to the cosmic potential for our growth in the eternity of the future, because the prospect of our unending progress is God's purpose and God's delight.

We can sense how this cosmic design applies to our children. Many parents are struck with an almost overwhelming awareness of their child's unrealized potential, especially when contrasted with the apparent insignificance of their progeny's current preoccupations. The best parents inspire their child's growth in the light of their unlimited potential but never exert undue pressure for performance or unwisely manipulate the youth's available choices. And the Deities treat the growth of us adults with the same consideration. The best forms of personal growth are joyous, creative, and spontaneous.

A robust faith harnesses "the power of now" while maintaining an abiding awareness of the unfolding potentials of the future. We are progressing beings; therefore, faith must translate the prospect of better things into present awareness. Stated otherwise, hope reflects the hoped-for future into the present, allowing us to freely translate these potentials into personal growth. But our bouts of anxiety short-circuit the faithfulness that supports the patient and orderly unfolding of our potentials.

During the period of Jesus's so-called lost years, we are told in the *UB* that in his late twenties he traveled around the Roman world as an assistant to a wealthy Indian merchant, which included tutoring the merchant's teenage son. After months of observing how adept Jesus was as a teacher, one day the boy asked Jesus why he did not begin immediately begin his public ministry. This was the reply of Jesus:

My son, everything must await the coming of its time. You are born into the world, but no amount of anxiety and no manifestation of impatience will help you to grow up. You must, in all such matters, wait upon time. Time alone will ripen the green fruit upon the tree. Season follows season and sundown follows sunrise only with the passing of time. I am now on the way to Rome with you and your father, and that is sufficient for today. My tomorrow is wholly in the hands of my Father in heaven. [130:5.3]

Even Jesus was infused with wise and hopeful patience in the face of his unrealized divine potentials. His faith made him effective at transferring potentials into actuals sufficient for the day—every day.

The theological basis of this translation from potentials to actuals grows out of the nature of the Third Person of the Trinity. As noted in chapter 2, she carries out the integration of the far-flung bifurcation of energy and spirit through the agency of mind—her Absolute Mind. She is the source of all minds, and it is the purpose of mind to correlate the divergence of energy and spirit. This labor of consciousness is the secret of evolution in time and space, and the theological foundation of soul synthesis. And this characteristic action of mind is the divine source of that mind function we call faith.[40]

Exploring the God of Experience

To further understand soul-synthesis, we must remember to separate God's existence in the perfect (eternal) universe from God's *experience of our experiences* in the perfecting universes. The synthesis hypothesis is built in part on a great reformation of theology that allows a perfect God to cocreate a perfected universe in partnership with his imperfect creatures. But this sort of cosmic transaction was inconceivable in traditional theology.

Classical theology in the Abrahamic tradition (inclusive of Judaism, Christianity, and Islam) suffers from an authoritarian premise that does not countenance a cooperative relationship between God and his creatures. The Creator-creature relationship goes only one way. The traditional God is absolute, complete,

---

[40] As I will explore later in the book, the chief faculties of the human mind are willing, thinking, and feeling. And it is with mind alone that we carry out our soul-making decisions, ideally by harmonizing the use of all three of these constitutive faculties. And if these choices are deemed by our Indwelling Spirit to be soul-worthy, they dynamically link our material life with the high values of the realm of spirit. But always remember that personality is ontologically prior—ancestral—even to all of these factors. The personal is *causal* in relation to the spiritual and the mindal. Our personality is the source of our free-will capacity that operates through our mind endowment to bring us home to Paradise. If faith is "the supreme assertion of human thought" [3:5.4], this faith is ultimately a free expression of unique personality.

perfect, eternal, and self-sufficient, needing nothing from his creation. God's creativity lets him populate his universe with evolving life, but his creatures lack a corresponding creative power of their own. Humans may grow up to be wise and loving, and even build great civilizations, but in so doing they contribute nothing of cosmic significance to their Creator.

In the traditional conception of Deity, God as King receives our love and is aware of our needs, and can send us divine grace and gifts in many forms. We can offer faith and homage, but it is not within our ability to make a difference to God. Being "saved" qualifies us for membership in God's Kingdom, but not for participation in God's divine enterprise as an essential partner in the cosmic evolution that God originally set in motion. This idea of a far-distant and transcendent Creator God is especially stark in Islam, but it predominates in all forms of Western theology and much of Hindu thought as well, even when they speak of a loving Deity—such as Jesus or Krishna—who incarnates to fraternize with and teach his creatures. Among Hindu thinkers, only Sri Aurobindo made a distinct breakthrough to a cocreative form of evolutionary panentheism.

The singular achievement of the *UB*'s version of evolutionary theology is that it rejoins the majesty of the concept of an utterly transcendent personal God with an original concept of a finite God of evolution who *depends* on human decisions. In this equation, the God of Experience is constituted by human activity, while the Eternal God is an inexhaustible singularity of endless love and infinite energy who wishes to explore his own divinity through sharing it with finite beings upon whom he confers free will and spiritual potential. Such an overarching panentheistic structure is at the heart of our synthesis hypothesis. And there are even phases of the universal unfolding of God's purposes that can be called postevolutional.[41]

---

[41] We are told in the *UB* to view the eternal God as the *First Personality*, the First Source of all things; and we can best think of the God of Experience as the *Last Personality*, the unifier on Deity levels of the meanings and values of all soul-making and self-perfecting experience. The final chapter of this book explains how the personhood of God as *Supreme* emerges as this Last Person at the culmination of space-time evolution. (Beyond the scope of this book is the *UB*'s revelation that new personalizations of Deity

We are fortunate that a major new philosophic movement has arrived just in time to help us better understand this idea of a dynamic God of evolution within the context of belief in a transcendent Deity. Early in the twentieth century, the philosopher Alfred North Whitehead, followed by theologians such as Charles Hartshorne, John Cobb, and David Ray Griffin, offered a way to undo the disempowering features of classical theism. Their work allows us to better conceive of a cocreative process of soul-synthesis while building on the findings of evolutionary holism. It's known as *process theology*, and it amounts to what might be called an exalted theory of God in time. Building upon the ideas of earlier evolutionary philosophers such as G. W. F. Hegel and Henri Bergson, Whitehead argued that God and humanity are always intrinsically related in and through the process of cosmic evolution. In fact, the two behave like one coevolving being. With God in the lead as primordial, God and humans are involved in cocreative acts that generate an evolving universe.

Only God sees the big picture of evolution, so God becomes the prime mover of the universal process. God's role is to *initiate* the action. But because man's free will is sacrosanct, the God of process theology has no other option but to lead by means of love, persuasion, and inspirational appeals.

God especially works through the medium of primary values. He ensures, for example, that beauty is clearly visible in our immediate environment. Because of the unmistakable presence of that which is attractive, God's human partners are aroused and awakened. For example, the aura of a lovely woman motivates ordinary men to unselfish and courageous behavior far beyond expectations; likewise, the presence of an appealing man inspires a woman to amazing feats of love and devotion. The same can be said for the presence of the innocence of a child, the wonder of gazing at a starry sky, or the awe of viewing a living cell under a high-powered microscope. And these vivid experiences may lead us to seek out other and less obvious values.

---

will occur in the far distant future when the billions of galaxies in deep space become inhabited and then completed in their development, thereby bringing into being *God the Ultimate* and *God the Absolute*.)

Whitehead's God leads us forward with compassionate patience by offering us the lure of such inspiring values. Philosophers all seem to agree that these can be summarized as truth, beauty, and goodness. Humans are indispensable partners with God in this creative process, since only we can choose to activate those values that serve to move things forward. If we miss the mark, God gently and faithfully returns with yet another attempt to entice us to higher ground. Our spiritual practice is to cultivate an ever-deeper receptivity to the presence of these clues in our daily lives.

In process philosophy, the divine may initiate the action, but thereafter God and humankind are engaged in a mutually reinforced progressive pursuit of the values of truth, beauty, and goodness. We've noted that humans are acting at their cognitive limit when they recognize these primary values. Truth, beauty, and goodness, according to the *UB*, are the "comprehensible elements of Deity,"[42] and to act upon them is to do the will of God.

As cocreators with God, we are always able to reinvent ourselves, our families, and our societies as we follow the cues of this Great Attractor who is always just out ahead of us; both the process thinkers and the *Urantia Book*-informed philosophers will agree on this proposition as far as it goes. But the process God, while retaining some of the attributes of traditional Godhood, is not an infinite being endowed with personal qualities of love and self-awareness who can endow us with transcendent factors such as a God Fragment and a unique personality.

All that said, much more research is needed in comparing these two postmodern theological systems.

---

[42] In reference to higher stages of evolution on advanced planets, the Urantia text states, "Throughout this glorious age the chief pursuit of the ever-advancing mortals is the quest for a better understanding and a fuller realization of the comprehensible elements of Deity—truth, beauty, and goodness. This represents man's effort to discern God in mind, matter, and spirit. And as the mortal pursues this quest, he finds himself increasingly absorbed in the experiential study of philosophy, cosmology, and divinity. . . .The worlds settled in light and life are so fully concerned with the comprehension of truth, beauty, and goodness because these quality values embrace the revelation of Deity to the realms of time and space." [See 56:10.]

The Drama of the Evolving Soul

According to the Urantia Revelation, the Divine Heart is unfathomable in its willingness to share life, love, and light. The Father consents to indwell our mortal minds, patiently residing in the deepest recesses of our psyches. The Thought Adjuster acts as our pilot without violating our will, faithfully creating an immortal counterpart of our personal decisions. Process theologians evoke the beauty of the cocreative qualities of this relationship, but revelation is needed to teach us that something eternal is in the making through this unlikely partnership.

This, then, is the drama of soul-making: the all-loving, all-knowing, all-pervading Creator fractalizes as each of us. A spark of the absolute gets placed, unnoticed, within us. The God Fragment is devoted entirely to our watchcare, however lost or lowly we may be, and subjects itself to our decisions. It patiently waits for us to *wake up* and *grow up*. It remains loyal through our failures, always exuding forgiveness and guidance. What a tragic waste that so many folks squander this opportunity to interact with a gentle and pure spirit while residing in a dense physical body. The God of universes who bears the highest possible signature of energy and spirit is utterly at our service, even if we sit in relative oblivion on the other end of the energetic spectrum, foolish, confused, and self-centered.

But the indwelt child starts out as an innocent. Even a kid who goes astray and becomes a soldier for the Islamic State begins life as a noncombatant. The child has been thrown into life by some inscrutable force, according to the vivid description of the German existentialist philosopher Martin Heidegger. The "throwness" refers to the arbitrary and apparently random influences it must bear: the infant gets a certain set of parents with all their faults and strengths, inheriting a randomized mix of their DNA. And even if the child's soul somehow chose these parents before its conception in order to learn life lessons, the infant has no idea of that, and the adult most likely will never know of a possible previous life. So the upstart babe has no choice but to improvise from day one. The growing child must respond somehow to quirky parents and sibling rivalries. Without knowing why, it must take up strange duties such as learning to walk on the hard ground, speak the local tongue, and do mindless chores like cutting the grass on a hot day in August.

But even if the growing boy or girl rebels against these impositions, the rudiments of soul-making begin to accrue as soon as the Thought Adjuster arrives. The God Fragment, hailing from the center of infinity, has the power and the prerogative to make the most of each life, even a life that is incoherent and misguided. This even holds true in the case of Erik Medhus, the hapless boy we met in chapter 1 who committed suicide at a young age. If you can buy it, his account assures us that some spiritual agency made a proper record of his life and painstakingly preserved it for playback after his death. Even in the case of Erik's harebrained antics, those decisions that displayed the rudiments of soul-making were held sacrosanct.

Each of us is a budding hero in God's eyes, and every moment of our life is lovingly attended and recorded. The divine indweller remains unconditionally steadfast. Imperfect decisions are not spurned, as they represent the precious reality of the child's singular gropings in a vast universe. Just as a human father or mother loves their child despite its gross errors or mediocre choices, our Divine Parents cherish and even memorialize these all-too-human choices in the photo album of our soul. Each significant life event is worthy of review later on.

But to what end can all this be?

We are told that the Infinite Oneness of the I Am is existentially self-sufficient in its exclusive sphere of eternity. But now it initiates an adventure of self-discovery in time by creating a universe of experiential children. Because God's myriads of finite children are free to make their own lives, they release God from infinitude, providing a vehicle for their Divine Parent to gain self-knowledge as their choices unfold. God wants to know all possible points of view, so God's Mystery Monitor provides a window on the concrete particulars of life experience as seen through the eyes of the trillions of creatures of time. God weaves these perspectives into one unified field of cosmic experience known as the Supreme. The Father overcomes existential Oneness by bringing into being a new modality of *experiential Oneness*, a unity-in-diversity achieved through the eventual attainment of completion and perfection by all of his creatures over eons of time.

Indeed, we are not only one pair of eyes through which the Creator learns of his creation, but are also his ears, hands, and feet. We are the intrepid explorers and the experiencers who traverse the vast and unknown expanses of space to become an integral part of the whole equation of universe reality. We become one of trillions of unique answers that complete the Creator's initial question: "Who Am I in time and space?"

And thus began God's great poetry-factory of soul-making and self-perfecting. Humans engage in adventures and write their story, and the Thought Adjuster takes on our life story, especially the story of our personal relationships—in particular, those connections that were powerful and reciprocal. As noted earlier, the *UB* reveals that our soul contains the totality of our significant experiences, but it makes clear that only divinity itself is competent to know the criteria for such significance.

Strictly speaking, you and I are not the authors of our stories. The soul portrays our lives as *God* perceives them. God immortalizes the divine perspective on how we live by selecting worthy events from the raw material of our experiences. This means that soul-making can occur even, for example, in times when we harbor painful illusions that we conveniently omit or suppress from memory. Let's say that as a college sophomore you became a Marxist organizer. This experience was vividly real when it occurred. But now you run a hedge fund in Manhattan, and you'd rather delete that whole year from memory. The God Fragment retains the poignance of this audacious college adventure in your soul. It honors those times when you fought for what you thought was right and true in your heart, regardless of the futile, or even delusionary, nature of your effort.

When all is said and done, the finished film of our soul's evolution is a masterful edit of the uncut footage that we provided through our decisions and actions, now set aside for download and viewing. It's God's own visual anthropology, cocreated with the assent of the natives on the ground, who lack critical insight into the meanings of their tribal activities.

To pursue the metaphor a bit further: the intellectual property rights to our story don't belong to us at first. We are technically the coauthor of our soul, but the story is held in trust by the Father Fragment until we fully claim it. If we reject survival after death, our personal presence in the universe comes to an end, but as we noted, the soul transcripts held by the Thought Adjuster remain with it eternally. We may give up on eternal life in total defeat, but our story of failure has a valued place in the library of universal evolution.

And this may be one reason why NDE life reviews are multiperspectival. Our life story is more than a first-person narration. Many others are also protagonists whose lives intersect with ours in strategic ways. How did our love, or our lack of love, affect their soul's trajectory, and vice versa? We can't know the full story locked inside the heart of those persons who were closest to us. But their experiences are crucial in the bigger scheme of things. So, God's heavenly recording service captures their hidden thoughts and feelings, like an omniscient narrator of a nineteenth-century Russian novel. God divinely witnesses the vicissitudes of our noblest successes and our most foolish shenanigans, seeing our choices in terms of their ripple effect on his children throughout his domains. God knows our whole lives in totality, and from his absolute position of love and wisdom, determines what crosses the threshold of spiritual significance to become immortal in our souls and in the universe.

God Fusion: The Ultimate Destiny of the Soul

Finally, let us turn to the "augmentation of spirit control" alluded to in a previous quote. We've noted that the Indwelling Spirit is classified as prepersonal—technically devoid of personhood—yet we are told that it carries within itself a transcendent agenda.

While not a true personality, the God Fragment is an active agent of change: it radiates a superb affection for us, adjusts our thinking in a Godward direction, catalyzes our soul-making choices, and even operates during our dream life. The indwelling God is, after all, the "spirit nucleus" of the human soul and the very secret of our soul evolution. Its manifold activities are a tip-off that it possesses volition of some sort, or what the revelators call *prewill*. Yet we are told that its choices are always subservient to our will, as hard as that may be to fathom. We are in the presence of a great and universal mystery—the inscrutable fact that God's love for his creatures leads him to make a pure part of himself subject to our imperfect and sometimes catastrophic decisions.[43]

In other words, personality is always superordinate in relation to all other elements of universal reality, as we've already noted. Hopefully, our decisions will become increasingly conformed to the Thought Adjuster's spiritual agenda, but our personality will always call the final shots.

> You as a personal creature have mind and will. The Adjuster as a prepersonal creature has premind and prewill. **If you so fully conform to the Adjuster's mind that you see eye to eye, then your minds become one**, and you receive the reinforcement of the Adjuster's mind. Subsequently, if your will orders and enforces the execution of the decisions of this new or combined mind, the Adjuster's prepersonal will attains to personality expression through your decision, and as far as that particular project is concerned, you and the Adjuster are one. **Your mind has attained to divinity attunement, and the Adjuster's will has achieved personality expression**. [110:2.5]

Our spirit-self is a driver; it has a grand goal. This intrepid God-entity has romance and marriage in mind. It stands at the door and patiently knocks, holding a fresh bouquet of divine roses and the very finest chocolate.[44] It aims to achieve the one thing it lacks: personalness. And this is only possible through an eternal union with the host of its indwelling, consummated in a dramatic wedding

---

[43] "Human will functions on the personality level of universe reality, and throughout the cosmos the impersonal—the nonpersonal, the subpersonal, and the prepersonal—is ever responsive to the will and acts of existent personality." [107:7:14]

[44] In ancient mythology, the phrase *hieros gamos* refers to the ritual marriage of a god and a goddess; in a real sense, the great fusion we are speaking of is comparable to a hieros gamos where one of the parties is prepersonal but achieves personhood because of the union.

of energies, values, and meanings. Our spirit-suitor has been guiding its human subject all along through our circles of growth with this very purpose in mind. The technical designation of this event is *Thought Adjuster fusion*, and we are taught in the *UB* that such a union is an irrevocable marriage of the God Fragment with the personality and its associated human soul, wherein they become one—forever, into all future eternity.

We know that God's other high gift to human selves, according to Urantia cosmology, is *unique personality*. We also have noted that intrinsic to unique personhood are the prerogatives of free-will choice—the ability to enact decisions through the vehicle of a human intellect housed (for now) in an animal-origin physical body. Attaining personhood is the goal of the Father Fragment because personality houses the precious attribute of sovereign free will and the capacity for reflection and self-awareness.

This marriage of the indwelling God and an evolving human is a two-way street. The Indwelling Spirit ennobles its human partner by providing us with a direct window onto pure divinity; but it also affords God with a first-person perspective on the drama of a human ascender. The sacred reciprocity of this relationship is encapsulated in this eloquent statement: "Morontia evolution is inherent in the two universal urges of mind, the impulse of the finite mind of the creature to know God and attain the divinity of the Creator, and the impulse of the infinite mind of the Creator to know man and attain the experience of the creature." [111:2.2]

We are synthesizing an immortal soul destined to unite with the indwelling God, after which the fused partners enter into an even greater adventure: the effort to find perfection in an eternal afterlife. This effort to achieve fusion is, then, the *telos* or destiny of our personal human evolution. Soul-making and self-perfecting dynamics lead inexorably to the soul's own completion and fulfillment—not in the blissful passivity of nondual realization but ultimately as a union of our evolving soul with the Indwelling Spirit entity that reorganizes the personality for an eternal life of service.

The Urantia Book depicts such fusion events as routine during the soul's ascent in the afterlife in the higher worlds. Such a fusion can occur during bodily existence on the more advanced material planets. But it is extremely rare on our planet. It may possibly be evidenced by the so-called rainbow body phenomenon of Tibetan masters. It is also alluded to in the biblical records of the sudden ascent of Elijah (2 Kings 2:11) and of Enoch (Genesis 5:19); and it is perhaps symbolized in the Catholic dogma of the bodily assumption of the Virgin Mary to heaven. The *UB* affirms that Elijah and Enoch of old are the only cases of fusion while in the flesh on our world.[45]

Our model of the soul relies especially on the crucial distinction between the soul as an evolutionary, experiential reality and the Indwelling Spirit as a self-acting, existential reality impinging on and guiding human consciousness. Equally crucial is that all of this transformative activity occurs in an environment of existential and unchanging personhood endowed with relative free will. Our "sacred trinity" houses human endowments that have substantive reality and exist in separate but intimately related domains that each contribute to the ultimate fusion event. In the next chapter we explore in more detail how we can proceed on our personal spiritual path to this marvelous goal. For now I leave you with this profound summary:

> Fusion with a fragment of the Universal Father is equivalent to a divine validation of eventual Paradise attainment, and such Adjuster-fused mortals are the only class of human beings who all traverse the Havona circuits and find God on Paradise. To the Adjuster-fused mortal the career of universal service is wide open. What dignity of destiny and glory of attainment await every one of you! Do you fully appreciate what has been done for you? Do you comprehend the grandeur of the heights of eternal achievement which are spread out before you?—even you who now trudge on in the lowly path of life through your so-called "vale of tears"? [40:7.5]

---

[45] In this connection, the Reverend Dr. Rob Crickett, a veteran *Urantia Book* student, has just announced the formation of the St. Enoch and St. Elijah Society for the Father Fusion of Jesus Monastery. See: http://www.rcim.org/sffj.org/Welcome.html. Rob is also the autahor of a series of books on Father Fusion.

Cosmic Individuation: The Circles of Self-Perfecting

Be perfect, therefore, as your heavenly Father is perfect.
—*Matthew 5:48*

From the Universal Father who inhabits eternity there
has gone forth the supreme mandate, "Be you perfect,
even as I am perfect."
—*The Urantia Book* 1:0.3

The eons-long process of self-perfecting, which begins with the soul's first emergence, entails what the *UB* calls *cosmic circles attainment*—the subject of this chapter. The revelators designate this progression with various other coined phrases, including "psychic circles of cosmic growth," "levels of cosmic evolution," "personality unification," or "circles of human achievement." I especially favor their phrase "cosmic individuation," and I will sometimes designate the idea as circle-making, a phrase I have coined. Some of this language may sound like jargon, but these new terms permit us to make important distinctions about the attainment of spiritual perfection.

The Urantia Revelation states that there are seven levels of cosmic circles attainment. Moving through these circles entails balanced progress toward God Fusion, and it is accomplished through the same process of soul-making and personality unification that Jesus mastered while on Earth, as depicted in Part IV of *The Urantia Book*. The *UB*'s greatly expanded narrative shows how Jesus engaged in circle-making throughout his life, including the so-called missing years. Later in this chapter I focus on two crucial dimensions of personal growth toward perfection, the qualitative and the quantitative aspects, and conclude with a look at how this distinction might be applied to the life of Jesus in the *UB*'s revelatory account, providing us with a pattern that we can emulate throughout our own lives.

The circles are all-encompassing levels that we traverse via the practice of cosmic spirituality. They are more inclusive than the faith of a Catholic saint or the higher levels of consciousness of a Hindu yogi. The revelators give the name "circles" to these stages of progress because they encircle all the elements of human selfhood: physical health, cognitive development, emotional intelligence, interpersonal facility, psychosexual maturity, cultural sophistication, and spiritual faith—or what development theorists call states of consciousness and the levels and lines of human development. In the course of circles attainment, we use the leverage of faith to experience ever-higher stages of consciousness, leading up through subtle-realm awareness (that is, the direct perception of the morontial soul), and finally toward nondual union with the Indwelling Spirit.

Two examples of contemporary personal growth disciplines that approach the depth and breadth of circle-making as it is described in the *UB* include Integral Transformative Practice and Integral Life Practice.[46] We may also say, along with depth psychologist Carl Jung, that the circles refer to levels of individuation—the balanced and harmonious growth of all the powers of the self. The theory

---

[46] Integral Transformative Practice (ITP), developed by human potential pioneers George Leonard and Michael Murphy, offers what it calls "cross-training for the body, mind, heart, and soul." Integral Life Practice, developed by Ken Wilber and his associates, builds on ITP and other integrated practice systems. Both approaches hearken back to the practice of integral yoga advocated by Indian master Sri Aurobindo.

and practice of circle-making are broached in this chapter, then picked up again in chapter 7 in greater detail.

Circle-making is not only about our life here; it also refers to the quest to become a high-functioning and deeply self-realizing cosmic citizen in the afterlife. For circle-makers, achieving higher states of being and doing great works in this world and on higher worlds are equally essential. These people increasingly wake up to embody the key virtues of mindfulness, sincerity, faith, hope, charity, and love; and they also grow up by getting into action to improve life conditions in society through their chosen work in the world.[47]

Cosmic citizens, while on Earth, contribute with increasing effectiveness to social and cultural evolution as mature and responsible adults who build sustainable and thriving families, communities, schools, businesses, industries, charitable organizations, governmental institutions, and entire civilizations. Abraham Lincoln, Mahatma Gandhi, and Martin Luther King are outstanding exemplars of circle achievers because they were individuals of strong faith, extraordinary courage, and high ethical awareness who also helped advance the collective evolution of humanity in practical ways, and in the face of great opposition. But we can also find women and men in the most ordinary of occupations quietly, and even profoundly, achieving their circles through balanced personal growth and consecrated devotion to their life purpose.

And all this progress in cosmic individuation occurs because the universe itself is in the process of completion through universal evolution. To become good universe citizens, we must allow this grand process, the great Tao if you will, to carry us forward on the inexorable current of progress toward perfection in the space-time cosmos.

---

[47] The terminology of "waking up" and "growing up" is borrowed from Ken Wilber's *Integral Spirituality* (2006), an important inspiration for this chapter, which we examine more closely in chapter 7. Other important elements of Wilber's personal growth system include "cleaning up" (or shadow work) and "showing up."

Ideal Conditions for Cosmic Individuation

Our God Fragment is the lead partner in the endeavor of circle attainment: "The indwelling Thought Adjuster unfailingly arouses in man's soul a true and searching hunger for perfection together with a far-reaching curiosity which can be adequately satisfied only by communion with God, the divine source of that Adjuster." [102:1.6] The Indwelling Spirit always points home—to God, to the promise of perfection, to the source of those potentials that are turned into actuals through steadfast faith.

Technically speaking, our inner spirit points to itself, a pure fragment of divinity, which represents, or rather *is*, the will of God revealing itself to our consciousness in any given moment—always gently and in deference to our free will.

The will of God will always be our most creative choice in any moment. But to perceive God's will, we need to drop our compulsive habits and liberate our minds from "the slavery of antecedent causation," as the *UB* calls it. In fact, true moral freedom and the capacity for spontaneous creativity are inherent in the divine gift of personhood, that most mysterious member of our inner trio.[48]

To clear the way for the freedom to choose what is most real, it is essential to arrest the gross material currents of the discursive mind that so often carry us downstream in the wrong direction toward distractions, negative fantasies, or anxieties. We must somehow purify the mind and remove clutter, thereby opening a space in awareness so that the more subtle frequencies of the Indwelling Spirit can interpose themselves and communicate the tone and flavor of the better way forward. For most of us, achieving this state of consciousness requires the regular practice of deep relaxation or stillness combined with focused meditation, prayer, and communion. Higher-quality discriminations and a greater quantity of useful decisions result when we respond in faith to the sublime overtures

---

[48] "The bestowal of creature personality confers relative liberation from slavish response to antecedent causation, and the personalities of all such moral beings, evolutionary or otherwise, are centered in the personality of the Universal Father. They are ever drawn towards his Paradise presence by that kinship of being which constitutes the vast and universal family circle and fraternal circuit of the eternal God. There is a kinship of divine spontaneity in all personality." [5:6.9]

of the inner spirit, whose impulses are coordinated with—and are in fact largely indistinguishable from—other influences such as angelic ministry and the presence of the Holy Spirit and the Spirit of Truth. But we must prepare a royal road in our mortal minds to receive this higher input.

To further accelerate our cosmic individuation, we can consciously align our will throughout the day with the divine will that is already self-manifesting within us. A firm intention clears the way—provided that our field of view is not warped by unhealed psychological wounds or obstructed by negative emotions such as envy, intolerance, slothfulness, or anxiety, or simple lack of discipline.

Our God Fragment is, by definition, our inerrant source of truth. And if the "truth is the whole," as Hegel once famously said, then our spirit always offers to our human will those choices that point us toward balanced development, physical wellness, and psychological wholeness. The spirit-self intrinsically aims us toward a wholeness that arises from the proportionate and symmetrical growth of the physical and nonphysical factors of self. Such is the nature of genuine circle-making. But as Carl Jung made clear in his writings, this inner drive toward wholeness and integration naturally shows up in our psychic life unless it is obstructed by our willful ignorance, selfish motives, or by complexes that develop as a result of childhood or adult trauma.

Understood in this way, our circle-making entails balanced personal growth, and circle-makers are men and women who by definition become poised, elegant, and unified personalities:

> [Circle attainment] has to do with personality status, mind attainment, soul growth, and Adjuster attunement. The successful traversal of these levels demands the harmonious functioning of the *entire personality*, not merely of some one phase thereof. The growth of the parts does not equal the true maturation of the whole; the parts really grow in proportion to the expansion of the entire self—the whole self— material, intellectual, and spiritual. [110:6.1]

The more sane and balanced we are as persons, the more we can reliably and safely receive the influence of the divine spirit, expand our selfhood, and achieve our circles.

Circle-Making and the Quest for Selfhood Reality

In the last chapter I noted that the God Fragment brings with it something specific and highly personal: a blueprint of our model career and ideal life. (See 110:2.1.) We can best realize this divinely appointed destiny through many-sided self-development: "Circle by circle your intellectual decisions, moral choosings, and spiritual development add to the ability of the Adjuster to . . . register his picturizations of destiny with augmenting vividness and conviction." [110:6.2]

Practically speaking, this quote tells us that if a young person's growth is balanced intellectually, morally, and spiritually, then his or her ideal lifework will naturally emerge into view. If the child's family or social environment is not oppressive or especially deprived, the impulses of the inner spirit will gently point the youth toward God-given aptitudes. Stated another way, a reasonable self-appraisal spontaneously arises within the average person unless specifically thwarted. And much of this unconscious growth is the unacknowledged influence of the God Fragment, which is slowly building an enduring identity in and as the evolving soul.

Discovering our unique mission and actualizing this model career is the essence of cosmic individuation. Every significant choice we make hinders or facilitates our progress in circle-realization in the light of our true purpose, we are told in the *UB*.

But always bear in mind our original unity-in-diversity premise from chapter 2: divinity is not monochromatic, nor is the self or its model career. Our selfhood comprises an inner triad that is rich and multifaceted, just as Deity self-manifests as a unified Trinity of divine personalities.

The following passage (quoted from 110:6.11) defines circle achievement from the standpoint of each member of our sacred inner trio:

1. *Adjuster attunement.* The spiritizing mind nears the Adjuster presence proportional to circle attainment.

2. *Soul evolution.* The emergence of the morontia soul indicates the extent and depth of circle mastery.

3. *Personality reality.* The degree of selfhood reality is directly determined by circle conquest. Persons become more real as they ascend from the seventh to the first level of mortal existence.

As we spiritize our minds and evolve our souls on this Earth and in the afterlife, we achieve selfhood reality—true personality realization. Circle-makers base their lives upon that which is cosmically real as they pursue their quest for self-perfection. And, if "the good is the real,"[49] then those who perpetrate sin or iniquity become, so to speak, cosmic deviants. (Note in the quotation below the *UB*'s unique distinctions between evil, sin, and iniquity.) They stray from cosmic reality as well as from their own personality reality. In the single-minded pursuit of selfish ends at all costs, they stifle their own soul growth, immobilize their circle-making, and slow down the pace evolution for the rest of us.

There are many ways of looking at sin, but from the universe philosophic viewpoint **sin is the attitude of a personality who is knowingly resisting cosmic reality**. Error might be regarded as a misconception or distortion of reality. Evil is a partial realization of, or maladjustment to, universe realities. But sin is a purposeful resistance to divine reality—a conscious choosing to oppose spiritual progress—**while iniquity consists in an open and persistent defiance of recognized reality** and signifies such a degree of personality disintegration as to border on cosmic insanity. (Emphasis added.) [67:1.4]

By contrast, circle makers are reality-centric. They identify with the substance of cosmic reality, which we are told presents itself to

---

[49] "The *eternal real* is the good of the universe and not the time illusions of space evil. In the spiritual experience of all personalities, always is it true that the real is the good and the good is the real." [102:3.15]

us as three primary reality domains: the physical world of matter-energy, the intermediate realm of mind or soul, and the higher realm of spirit. Each of these is of origin from the Eternal Trinity, as we saw in chapter 2 (and all three are "hosted" and unified by personality). We gain mastery of these realms through the human endeavors we call science, moral philosophy, and the faith of religious experience. Circle mastery correlates with and eventually harmonizes our manifold life experiences in and through these three domains of action.

Because our minds are crafted by divine beings, we inherently possess the intellectual tools required to recognize, interact with, and identify with these three manifestations of the real. As broached earlier, the Infinite Spirit *is* Universal Mind, and human mind as it functions in the evolving universes is sourced from the seven Deity manifestations of the Trinity, which are a subabsolute derivative of Universal Mind, according to an important section in Paper 16.[50] In these revelatory passages, the *UB* makes it clear that, by Creator design, the human mind is inherently endowed with three *cosmic intuitions* that make it possible for sincere persons to penetrate the many-sided realities of the evolving universes in the form of energy, mind, or spirit. Reality recognition is only possible because these three "scientific, moral, and spiritual insights, these cosmic responses . . . are innate." [16:6.9]

These specialized responses, we are told in this passage, are the fundamental cosmic discriminations that underlie circles attainment. They are the very architecture of reality-based thinking, allowing us to (1) differentiate the factual from the nonfactual through the discernment of causation using the physical senses; (2) recognize relative right and wrong by the perception of our moral duty; and (3) recognize spirit values through faith and reflective meditation, which the text calls "the reverential and worshipful form of the cosmic discrimination." Practicing and coordinating all three modes

---

[50] This intricate structure is beyond the scope of this introductory book, but suffice it to say that the mind of the Infinite Spirit unfolds as the seven possible permutations of the Eternal Trinity, generating the so-called *cosmic mind*, which is "the intellectual potential of the grand universe." [16:6.1] See also the discussion of the Seven Master Spirits in the Special Supplement, Section B.

of awareness offers the best route to balanced living, integral con-sciousness, and eventual God Fusion.

We exercise these three cosmic insights by acquiring a liberal education in the broadest sense, inclusive of the passionate pursuit of the facts of science, the reason of philosophic inquiry, and the spiritual values of faith. These foundational insights comprise what the *UB* calls reality responsiveness, and they naturally emerge and function in the reflective thinking of any self-realizing person.[51]

Traversing the Seven Circles

While today's developmental psychologists have attempted to define in detail the consecutive stages of human maturation, the revelators decline to be so specific, citing the wide variations in personality endowment. Yet the *UB*'s authors do point to crucial signposts, to which we now turn.

The text identifies three key stages of circle realization: the seventh, the third, and the first (in ascending order), while skip-ping a full discussion of the other four. These three are singled out because of the key spiritual influences that are brought to bear at each level. These transitions of the self can be thought of as super-natural initiations.

The *seventh circle* is described as the first step in cosmic individ-uation. According to the Urantia Revelation—and contrary to many contemporary teachings and beliefs—a *personal soul is not present at birth*. The soul's birth occurs in early childhood, we learn, coming into being on the occasion of the child's first autonomous moral decision. This highly significant event signals the activation of moral intuition, one of the three innate reality responses noted above.

---

[51] "There exists in all personality associations of the cosmic mind a quality which might be denominated the 'reality response.' It is this universal cosmic endowment of will creatures which saves them from becoming helpless victims of the implied a priori as-sumptions of science, philosophy, and religion. This reality sensitivity of the cosmic mind responds to certain phases of reality just as energy-material responds to gravity. It would be still more correct to say that these supermaterial realities so respond to the mind of the cosmos. The cosmic mind unfailingly responds (recognizes response) on three levels of universe reality. These responses are self-evident to clear-reasoning and deep-thinking minds." [16:6.4-5]

This is the great moment when the infinite enters into the finite mind, there to begin an eternal partnership of soul-making and self-perfecting. Apparently, the first function of genuine moral sensitivity in the child's mind sends out a vital signal that is noted on high. In response, we're told, the child receives a God Fragment that is directly bestowed from the eternal central-universe headquarters of these exalted entities. No wonder the Urantia Revelation calls us cosmic citizens as well as sons and daughters of God!

The literal birth of the soul (technically speaking) is the next transaction that occurs.[52] At the first sign of moral awareness, a pure spirit-spark emanates "downward" from the newly arrived God Fragment in recognition of the activation. In this meeting, *spark meets thought*, and a fiery new immortal entity is born. A luminous bit of soul-substance results from this sacred rendezvous.

For better illustration, allow me to offer a contrasting metaphor.

A sudden sprouting of eternalized thought appears in the Petri dish of the child's embryonic soul. A "culture" of immortal self-hood now begins to grow in this medium. In balanced psychological development, the God Fragment deposits "spores" into the child's Petri dish each time a soul-making event occurs. If the child is healthy, these deposits are evenly distributed in the dish—they cover all the psychological bases, so to speak. But if the child's early development is asymmetrical, patchy holes and gaps begin to show up in the soul's culture. The Petri dish, we might say, displays a disordered array of sprouts. Some areas are filled in, but other equally important portions are blank or may look diseased.

For example, imagine a young boy who suffers from an overdeveloped altruistic drive because of the influence of a psychologically unbalanced parent. His one-sided choices will favor the demands of others over his own legitimate needs. The boy's "unselfish" choices are valued, and technically they are soul-making, but when the soul's disposition is dominated by any one virtue, an otherwise noble impulse can actually become a liability. The net result may

---

[52] We are not told the exact sequence of events—or even whether this process follows a strict linear progression; so I offer here a step-by-step model for the sake of simplicity.

be distorted soul growth, or what secular psychology would call a budding personal neurosis.

If left unchecked, our overly altruistic boy may grow up to identify so earnestly with his pet virtue that he develops a psychological complex. His basic life orientation lacks the essential balancing quality of self-care.[53] Such a condition may cause no end to problems in adult life. And this is why Plato and so many other philosophers have called for the balanced and unified development of the moral virtues. A therapist could correct this tendency by encouraging the child to make wholesome choices based on the rights of the self as conceived in proper proportion to the rights of others. We call this sensitivity to interpersonal reciprocity the Golden Rule, as noted earlier.

We might wisely conclude from this that all of us need to develop a broad set of virtues in order to be cosmically individuated, starting from the earliest arrival of the Mystery Monitor in our mind in early childhood. And young people need role models who exhibit psychological balance—or what the *UB* calls personality unification—if they hope to advance in circle-making.

In his masterwork on the philosophy of living, *Living in Truth, Beauty, and Goodness*, philosopher Jeff Wattles explains that the classic moral philosophers of the West highlighted a core set of virtues that they deemed sufficient to develop a noble and balanced character, but often elevated one or another virtue to the head of the group. Plato regarded "self-mastery regarding pleasure, courage, justice, and wisdom" as sufficient. Aristotle supplied a list of moral virtues but argued that these were unified by the crowning virtue of practical wisdom. Thomas Aquinas added faith, hope, and love to Aristotle's list, declaring love to be the greatest of virtues.

Wattles believes that any cultivation of the virtues is helpful, but argues that the better path to a unified and strong character is through "wholehearted commitment to the will and way of God," and declares that "a total engagement of the divine way is the *core* of greatness of character." In other words, through a consecrated

---

[53] Carl Jung showed that such complexes generate archetypal images that represent these distortions in our dreams and fantasies, thereby pointing toward the need for balance and compensation.

attitude of receptivity to the divine presence through faith, prayer, and worship, the Indwelling Spirit communicates the core virtues directly to the soul in a way that unifies and balances selfhood. As a result, "other qualities continue to develop naturally around that ever-growing core."[54] Thus we can see the crucial importance of early religious training (in the context of broad education and healthy socialization) to the development of a noble character in a growing child.

The revelators largely skip through the sixth, fifth, and fourth levels to describe the *third circle* of attainment. We are told that when we achieve this cosmic level—normally far into adulthood, if at all in our lifetime on Earth—we are assigned a personal angel, or what is technically called a *seraphim guardian of destiny*.[55] Thereupon, this loving celestial being extends toward us "continuous ministry and unceasing watchcare." [113:1.5]

Having a personal angelic attendant markedly accelerates our growth. Indeed, these ministers are charged with becoming powerful agents of soul evolution.

Seraphim are mind stimulators; they continually seek to promote circle-making decisions in human mind. **They do this, not as does the Adjuster, operating from within and through the soul, but rather from the outside inward, working through the social, ethical, and moral environment of human beings**. . . . Seraphim function as teachers of men by guiding the footsteps of the human personality into paths of new and progressive experiences. To

---

[54] See Jeff Wattles, *Living in Truth, Beauty, and Goodness: Values and Virtues* (Wipf and Stock, 2016), pp. 197–202.

[55] "Human beings in the initial or seventh circle have one guardian angel . . . assigned to the watchcare and custody of one thousand mortals. In the **sixth circle**, a seraphic pair . . . is assigned to guide these ascending mortals in groups of five hundred. When the **fifth circle** is attained, human beings are grouped in companies of approximately one hundred . . . Upon attainment of the **fourth circle**, mortal beings are assembled in groups of ten." [113:1.7]

accept the guidance of a seraphim rarely means attaining a life of ease. In following this leading you are sure to encounter, and if you have the courage, to traverse, the rugged hills of moral choosing and spiritual progress. [113:4.1]

In other words, seraphim (and other orders of angels) stimulate our circle growth by bringing about relationships that stretch us as we are confronted with challenging new opportunities for moral decisions.

In chapter 2 we discussed in this connection the Plan of Mercy Ministry. This vast project of angelic ministry to mortals is an exclusive function of the divine personalities of origin in the Third Person of the Trinity—that is, the Infinite Mother Spirit and her derivative daughters, the Mother Spirits of the local universes.[56] Recall also that the Second Person of the Trinity (the Eternal Son) directs the Plan of Bestowal, the splendid project of the successive divine incarnations on evolving planets, such as that of Jesus. Both of these divine ministries to the inhabited worlds operate from the outside in, via the social and interpersonal environment of evolving human civilization, and as such are designed to supplement the influence of the Father Fragment, which operates only from the inside out—once again illustrating the wisdom of trinitization. This arrangement creates diverse avenues through which Deity fosters progressive evolution.[57]

All of these influences serve to move us toward the final goal of terrestrial evolution: achieving the first circle of cosmic individuation. But here's a key point: because these Deity initiatives shape us

---

[56] Their divine consorts, the local universe Creators known as Michael Sons—in our case, Christ Michael, who incarnated as Jesus—create other orders of celestial beings that do not function as direct angelic ministers to mortals.

[57] We've noted that all three operations are called the Father's Plan of Perfection Attainment. Seen from the widest perspective, these differential influences emanate from the existential Trinity, which acts as one power, and then diverges into particular ministries as they are applied to meet specific human needs in the space-time universes. But in the far-distant future they will be *experientially unified* as the self-perfecting activities of the evolving worlds find their completion. I should point out also that these angelic and incarnation ministries of the Eternal Son and the Infinite Mother Spirit are illustrative of the principle of personhood in the universes. For those religions that lack a personal God of love, no such personal influences can be theologically possible.

both from the outside in *and* the inside out, they are more likely to induce the symmetrical growth of the self. And the result of such balanced personal development is that first circlers actually attain *direct* God-contact :

> The Adjuster cannot, ordinarily, speak directly and immediately with you until you attain the first and final circle of progressive mortal achievement. This level represents the highest possible realization of mind-Adjuster relationship in the human experience prior to the liberation of the evolving morontia soul from the habiliments of the material body. [110:6.15]

First circlers have not only become profoundly God-conscious individuals, they've also reached the highest levels of maturity in their emotional, intellectual, and social lives. They show up as creative world citizens whose work makes a difference on the planet. Their noble characters display a variety of virtues organized around a singular devotion to love and service. And now the God Fragment can "speak" to them or even through them directly. What's more, their inner spirit can contact them reliably and *safely*.

Does this actually mean that premature contact with one's Indwelling Spirit can be dangerous? It certainly does, and life experience bears this out for most of us. The revelators sternly warn that things can go awry if a God-conscious person's maturation is not replete.

> [When Adjusters] find it possible to flash a gleam of new truth to the evolving mortal soul, this spiritual revelation often so blinds the creature as to precipitate a convulsion of fanaticism or to initiate some other intellectual upheaval which results disastrously. Many a new religion and strange "ism" has arisen from the aborted, imperfect, misunderstood, and garbled communications of the Thought Adjusters. [110:4.5]

I translate this important statement to mean that first circlers will never show up as power-hungry cult leaders or stubborn fanatics who create schismatic religious sects. Instead, those abiding at the first circle can be trusted to handle direct flashes of divine truth.

By definition, these individuals will have attained profound psychological integration. They are sane and stable enough to accurately perceive the voice of the spirit within—as described in this passage:

> [Thought Adjusters are] the founts of everlasting progression. And how they do enjoy communicating with their subjects in more or less direct channels! How they rejoice when they can dispense with symbols and other methods of indirection and flash their messages straight to the intellects of their human partners! [108:6.7]

The founders of the world's enduring religions of peace and enlightenment, such as Gautama Buddha, must have enjoyed this sort of contact. And Jesus, especially as he is depicted in the *UB*, is the paragon of such wholesome integration at the first circle of cosmic individuation.

Jesus and the Two Axes of Self-Perfecting

We are just getting started in this discussion. Circle-making is a vast subject that will require much more research in the interdisciplinary interpretation of the *UB*, along with immersion in today's sophisticated theories of human developmental and transpersonal psychology. In this section we turn to another aspect of circle-making that may bring more clarity, one that has echoes in contemporary theories of psychospiritual development that we further discuss in chapter 7.

To help us better understand the seven levels of cosmic circle attainment, the *UB* suggests what appear to be two key axes of integrated growth. These are alluded to in the text as the *qualitative* and the *quantitative* aspects of soul evolution:

> The mastery of the cosmic circles is related to the quantitative growth of the soul, the comprehension of supreme meanings. But the qualitative status of this immortal soul is *wholly* dependent on the grasp of living faith. [110:6.1]

I have found it helpful to chart these facets of adult maturity on a Cartesian grid of sorts, illustrating the fact that the two axes of growth have a reciprocal relationship. In general, the vertical axis represents growth in the quality of consciousness as it ascends the "stages of faith."[58] The horizontal axis corresponds to quantitative expansion through the realization of new depths of meaning as a result of wide-ranging life experiences—especially situations that require one to apply all three of the innate cosmic intuitions to solving the practical problems of living (the factual, moral, and reverential insights discussed earlier).

For example, seventh circlers can, at least in theory, attain the highest states of spiritual achievement and energetic awareness; they can truly feel what has value. So, their faith-realization can match the *quality* of consciousness achieved by a first circler who directly receives the guidance of their God Fragment. But these people are one-dimensional. They may turn out to be otherworldly mystics or "fools for God"—but they may also become self-deceived cult leaders.

First circlers have acquired more depth and dimensionality of character; they have actualized the entire grid in its vertical and horizontal dimensions. They are inclusive in their outlook and behavior. In addition to having a high-pitched awareness of the value of love, they have also learned to love others skillfully and wisely. Simply put, these two reciprocal factors of personal growth involve:

1. **Growth in value consciousness**—the increasing grasp of living faith achieved in contemplative states of feeling the presence of the energies of God, the source of all value; a growing awakening to the centrality of love—that is, the qualitative depths of feeling the truth of the infinite value

---

[58] I have in mind here James Fowler's classic book, *Stages of Faith: The Psychology of Human Development and the Quest for Meaning* (1981), and in particular his last two stages: "conjunctive" faith, which acknowledges paradox and the multidimensionality of truth, and "universalizing" faith, which leads one to treat all others as members of a global or cosmic community, in accord with universal principles of love and justice.

of personality. The *UB* puts this feeling capacity succinctly: "Quality—values—is *felt.*" [111:3.6]

2. **Comprehension of meanings**—the growth of wisdom through the achievement of discriminating awareness of facts, moral clarity in personal and professional life, advanced skills in social intercourse, and "well-traveled" cultural sophistication—through the frequent exercise of the three cosmic intuitions.

Awareness of value is a matter of feeling and faith, but meanings are understood in the mind and realized in action. A life of increasing meaning is a life of wisdom that is achieved only through practical life experience and engagement in diverse personal and professional relationships that ultimately contribute to evolutionary Deity.

> A seventh or sixth circler can be almost as truly God-knowing—sonship conscious—as a second or first circler, but such lower circle beings are far less conscious of experiential relation to the Supreme Being, universe citizenship. . . . The motivation of faith makes experiential the full realization of man's sonship with God, but *action*, completion of decisions, is essential to the evolutionary attainment of consciousness of progressive kinship with the *cosmic actuality* of the Supreme Being. Faith transmutes potentials to actuals in the spiritual world, but potentials become actuals in the finite realms of the Supreme only by and through the realization of choice-experience. [110:6.16-17]

Perhaps the most fruitful direction for research into these distinctions is to study the life of Jesus, who is depicted in the *UB* as the ideal of self-perfecting. In this summary passage in particular, Jesus is described as adept at balancing the values of extraordinary faith with the meanings of seasoned wisdom—in other words, he was able to coordinate the qualitative and quantitative dimensions of his soul growth in order to avoid a fanatical overreaction to his gift of religious genius.

In a religious genius, strong spiritual faith so many times leads directly to disastrous fanaticism, to exaggeration of the religious ego, but it was not so with Jesus. **He was not unfavorably affected in his practical life by his extraordinary faith and spirit attainment**. . . . The all-consuming and indomitable spiritual faith of Jesus never became fanatical, for it never attempted to run away with his well-balanced intellectual judgments concerning the proportional values of practical and commonplace social, economic, and moral life situations. The Son of Man was a splendidly unified human personality. . . . **Always did the Master co-ordinate the faith of the soul with the wisdom-appraisals of seasoned experience**. [196:0.6]

With this depiction of the character of Jesus in mind, let's delve a bit deeper into the two axes of cosmic individuation.

The Vertical Growth of Value-Consciousness

The vertical axis relates to achieving ever-deeper states of awareness of the presence of God. Such refined states are energetic and metacognitive. They go far beyond pious belief in a religious doctrine. Vertical growth of value-consciousness refers to the existential stance of the whole person in relation to their actual experience in the present moment—in a word, their *faith*.

Faith in this sense is a question of *feeling*. As they go about their day, true mystics feel the reality of values—such as beauty or truth or love—as these present themselves in ordinary life situations, even to the point of bursting into momentary experiences of bliss and rapture. Think of the little girl back in chapter 1 who spotted a small flower growing out of a crack in the sidewalk and gave it her fullest attention. In her life review, she discovered that this event was memorialized in her soul as one of the most important experiences of her life.

I also believe that an additional human faculty always comes into play in the exercise of faith: *the power of imagination*. Our faith cannot rise much higher than our level of willingness to imagine how much we are divinely loved; and we can derive inspiration from such visualizations of how God's grace is or may be showing up in our lives. *"Faith is the inspiration of the spiritized imagination."* [132:3.6]

For example, genuine faith inspires a young man and woman to agree to marry. It helps them envisage the value of the superb experiences they will enjoy together. They are on fire with the imagination of their future state of bliss. So the couple resolves to actualize their value-consciousness in relation to marriage, including the value of having children. Their faith tells them that living according to the particular set of family values that they share is more important than the immediate pleasures of a sexual life and the comforts of couplehood without a life commitment.

We saw earlier that the highest possible cognition that humans can have is the conceptual grasp of truth, beauty, and goodness as supreme values. But faith aims even higher. Here again I refer to an existential state of transconceptual awareness during which the whole person approaches the divine source of higher values. This source is God, who also appears as a *whole person*—as God as our Father or Mother, even God who incarnates for us. Our worshipful communion with this God is the ultimate religious experience, and the sublime feelings of trust and reassurance made possible in such an experience are what makes possible courageous living—a life infused with hope, inspiration, and love. Practically speaking, this experience leads one to choose to be *like* the Divine Person—to fully identify with God's qualities as we understand them. And this would naturally lead us to strive *to do what God would do* in every life situation, as did Jesus.

> The human Jesus saw God as being holy, just, and great, as well as being true, beautiful, and good. All these attributes of divinity he focused in his mind as the "will of the Father in heaven." . . . Jesus' great contribution to the values of human experience was not that he revealed so many new ideas about the Father in heaven, but rather that he so magnificently and humanly demonstrated a new and higher type of *living faith in God*. Never on all the worlds of this universe, in the life of any one mortal, did God ever become such a *living reality* as in the human experience of Jesus of Nazareth. [196:02.3]

Quantitative Soul Growth through
Seasoned Experience

We noted earlier that Jesus attained the highest circle because he was able to coordinate his sublime faith with worldly wisdom. And we are told that Jesus lived a perfect life on earth because he mastered the art of the symmetrical development of the fullness of his human capacities, both qualitative and quantitative.

For those who accept the Urantia Revelation, Jesus is our model of proportional growth in the two dimensions of soul evolution and self-perfecting. We already know—even from the New Testament account—how Jesus became a master in the qualitative domains of faith and spiritual experience. So instead let's focus our concluding discussion in this chapter on his quantitative achievement of seasoned wisdom, which is far less understood because most of this singular accomplishment is revealed only in the Urantia Revelation.

Quantitative soul growth requires wide exposure to and intimate contact with all kinds of people, the mastery of many useful skills, the development of self-confidence in the face of numerous harsh challenges, and the experience of problem solving in the face of every sort of predicament.[59] This list of experiences fits well the description of Jesus provided in Part IV of the *UB*, where we learn that he was so well grounded and so highly effective in his public teaching career because of his formidable experiences in his earlier private life.

> Jesus did not want simply to produce a *religious man*, a mortal wholly occupied with religious feelings and actuated only by spiritual impulses. **Could you have had but one look at him, you would have known that Jesus was a real man of great**

---

[59] It is interesting to note that male heroes in film and literature are often depicted as displaying such worldly wisdom and cleverness—abilities that, in the light of the argument I provide here, are necessary but not sufficient for human fulfillment. Heroines, by contrast, display a higher quality of moral and spiritual consciousness but will be dependent on the man to rescue them from worldly dilemmas. But we are speaking here of a blending of these capabilities in one person. I recently published a book that explores this distinction in terms of brain hemispheres, entitled *How Whole Brain Thinking Can Save the Future* (Origin Press, 2017) by James Olson.

experience in the things of this world. The teachings of Jesus in this respect have been grossly perverted and much misrepresented all down through the centuries of the Christian era; you have also held perverted ideas about the Master's meekness and humility. What he aimed at in his life appears to have been a *superb self-respect*. [140:8.20]

Please bear this statement in mind as I briefly tell the story of Jesus's heretofore unknown life on Earth, narrated for you with special reference to this quantitative aspect of his development.

Jesus was a normal and healthy Jewish child of his time, but was known to be highly inquisitive. He very early learned numerous practical skills from his mother, including care for animals and horticulture. From his father he learned to read and write in two languages (Aramaic and Greek) before entering the synagogue school, where he was taught Hebrew. He later traveled throughout the Roman world as a master linguist and translator.

Joseph taught Jesus carpentry, and the boy became a master carpenter at an early age. He later became adept at leatherwork and the skills of a smith, and his two uncles taught the young lad how to farm and fish. The location of the family's carpentry shop just outside of Nazareth—at a stop on a major route of commerce in those days—provided innumerable opportunities for Jesus to meet people traveling by caravan from all over the Mediterranean world and the lands of the Near East. Jesus learned the news of the larger world while making repairs for the travelers. Joseph also took Jesus with him on business trips, providing more occasions for learning about the world beyond Nazareth;

At this point, we depart entirely from the biblical account of Jesus's life as we read the revelators' account of the "lost years." The first great event of this period is the death of Joseph in a construction accident when Jesus was barely fourteen years old. As the eldest son of the family, Jesus suddenly became the head of a large household of eight siblings, with another child on the way. He now assumed responsibility for his pregnant mother and his brothers and sisters, ages one through ten. Jesus became a "father-brother" to his siblings, dedicating himself to their care and upbringing. He saw to their education, and even home schooled his four sisters at a time when females were not permitted an education. But the family slowly slipped into poverty after Joseph's land holdings were sold off to meet the family's basic needs. In this difficult situation, young Jesus was the sole provider for the destitute family until he could train his eldest brother James to assist in the shop.

While certain channeled accounts of the lost years depict Jesus as a wandering mystic who attended mystery schools and traveled to monasteries in Tibet, the Urantia account depicts a man who is developing "seasoned experience" in all aspects of living an ordinary life on Earth, facing many more practical problems and adversities than the average person of his era or any other. Throughout a dozen years of labor as the head of his family, he not only supported their immediate needs and educated the children, but also was able to buy the full ownership rights to the family's shop, and even set aside enough money to later fund the purchase of a second home. As the chief breadwinner for a large family from the time he was an early teen, he was afforded a full opportunity to experience the difficulties faced by even the most challenged earthly parent of his time or anytime since.

As a divine incarnation, Jesus was not in a position to marry, but he attracted the attention of all the eligible women in his town, befriended many, and even turned down one proposal of marriage. He was considered the natural leader of the more advanced youth of Nazareth, but turned away offers of a political position as he awaited the call to his spiritual mission.

Finally, at age twenty-six, when the youngest child in the family was twelve and the older siblings were able to take over the household thanks to the training Jesus had provided, he left home for good. After departing Nazareth, Jesus worked at building boats beside the Sea of Galilee, even creating a novel method of boat construction. From there, Jesus embarked on a two-year trip to Rome as an interpreter for a wealthy businessman from India and a tutor for his seventeen-year-old son. This trip began a long period of personal ministry work, during which he gained an intimate understanding of all races and classes of people in the Roman world, once even meeting Emperor Tiberius while acting—at the royal court—as a lay advocate for a friend. While sojourning in Rome with his Indian client, Jesus had occasion to meet and teach every leading religious teacher based in the imperial city.

Upon his return from Rome, another opportunity for travel presented itself when Jesus became the conductor of a large caravan, traveling as far as present-day Iran and back again to Palestine. The *UB* account clarifies the fact that Jesus never visited the Far East, but he no doubt met people from these lands and from Africa in the family's carpentry shop and on his lengthy travels. Soon after this period, Jesus began his public ministry, about which there is more information in the biblical account, as well as in the *UB*.

This summary illustrates that Jesus truly achieved personal growth in the worldly wisdom dimension, without which he could never have achieved the kind of balanced and majestic personality that was able to change our world forever. Jesus was not a gentle and kindly mystic, or a "man of sorrows," as sometimes depicted in traditional accounts. He was a highly dynamic and perfectly self-actualized man among men whose enemies both feared and respected him.

The *UB* explains that he traversed his circles and would have achieved God Fusion at the age of thirty-two—which would have resulted in his immediate ascension without physical death. But he elected to remain on Earth to inaugurate a new era as a fully self-realized divine incarnation, teaching with full authority the truths of soul evolution and cosmic individuation. In the final four years of his life, Jesus, both God and man in one person, inspired humanity with the revelation that our soul's destiny is an eternal life during which we *will* become perfect, "even as our Father in heaven is perfect."

A History of Self and Soul—East and West

CHAPTER 5

Early Beliefs about Self and Soul

In the three chapters of Part III, I draw from my training in the history of ideas to provide you with greater perspective on our core themes. My hope is that other *Urantia Book* students can pick up where I leave off with more in-depth comparative studies of these significant periods in the unfolding of religious consciousness. I end this section with a look at the writings of Ken Wilber, whose work in certain ways culminates the global history of ideas and, in my view, points toward the historic significance of the Urantia Revelation. I am delighted to have been associated in small ways with Ken's efforts over the years.

The Urantia Revelation offers sophisticated conceptions of Deity, evolution, personhood, soul, spirit, and the afterlife, which I summarized in Parts I and II. But how original are these purportedly revealed concepts? Are the *UB*'s teachings about such things a radical departure from the pool of human knowledge, East and West, or were some of these notions foreshadowed in traditional beliefs and scriptures? At a minimum, did the wisdom traditions at least break out some of the *UB*'s key distinctions, such as that between soul and spirit and personhood, or did they confuse or conflate these ideas? In addition, does *The Urantia Book* make a contribution by clarifying other vital issues in regard to self and soul that have remained mysterious, such as the nature of personhood or the destiny of the soul after death?

Part III offers a brief history of the wisdom traditions in which I attempt to tease out answers to these questions. Chapters 5 and 6 survey premodern beliefs, practices, and philosophies from around the world, but I especially concentrate on those traditional teachings (mainly in the West) that are most frequently referenced in the *UB*—especially those found in the Bible or in other Christian sources.

Chapter 7 changes gears a bit and focuses mainly on the work of contemporary philosopher Ken Wilber, founder of the integral movement. Wilber and his colleagues have created an impressive integrative philosophic system that highlights essential truths of the world's wisdom traditions. Integral theory reframes these noble ideas of the past in terms of current scholarship—especially contemporary philosophy, modern evolutionary theory, scientific psychology, and human development theory. Because the integral vision is so inclusive and spiritually rich, it has important affinities with the Urantia text. The modest goal of chapter 7 is to compare and contrast the two with respect to a few key questions in psychology and spirituality, especially with an eye to how each system may enhance the other.

The Invention of the Soul in Primitive Religion

Let's turn for a moment to the prehistory of humankind, when primitive tribes roamed the Earth in search of the means of survival and clues as to the mysteries of life.

We can only imagine how pummeled these earliest peoples must have felt by the unpredictable phenomena of nature. How would they cope with these overwhelming forces? Anthropologists tell us that indigenous peoples were constantly rocked by fright as well as awe in the face of the inexplicable. The water, the land, the night sky, the parade of wild animals and quirky natural events—all seemed to be animated from within by invisible forces or beings. Without exception, our forbears concluded that there must be a realm of unseen spirits that governed these wonders. But what if these powerful beings were venerated and given sacrifices? What if seers or medicine men could contact and then coax the spirit world to help the tribe in its daily struggles?

It turned out that some medicine men had their own magical powers. They stumbled upon practices or substances that induced altered states, allowing what seemed to be direct communication with the forces and spirits. While in heightened states of awareness, the shamans and seers could also sense a luminous presence *within each person*. This energy was akin to the magic and power of the spirit world. Did this inner entity or force, they wondered, have its source in the realms that were inhabited by the spirits?

The shamans gave way to priests—designated managers of the innate worship impulse. These individuals supplied the community with stories, symbols, and rituals, and later with scriptures that described the higher forces or principles operating within the spirit world as well as in the human realm.

Death was the greatest mystery to be managed, then as it is now. But the ancient scriptures were often indefinite on this subject. After death, would the aliveness of each person ascend to the upper world where they would meet the spirits? Would it instead descend to the lower world? Or would it return to Earth in a new body?

It had long been observed that when members of the group died, or when animals had been hunted down and killed, their breath disappeared. Was the faculty of breathing, then, the secret of life? And how did the power of breath enter into a newborn in the first place? Where did it go at death? If not breath, what *was* this animating force in each person, plant, and animal as well as in the weather, the sun, and the stars?

Later, teachers and philosophers arose to systematize the slowly evolving beliefs of their forbears. Their doctrines described a sacred entity within, or a soul of ultimate value, which was perhaps gifted upon humankind by a creator God or Goddess high above. This soul was life itself, the very power of breath. It looked out on the world through the eyes, and it had the ability to think and feel. It could survive death and live on in another realm if certain rules and rites were followed. And it might intercede for us with the higher spirits, if we requested an intervention, especially if the request were directed to deceased ancestors or holy men.

In almost every human tradition around the world, this animating soul was held to be both immaterial and potentially immortal, and the very source of life. But it was rarely described as a repository of one's daily life experience, with the notable exception of Egyptian religion, the Hindu belief in karma, and some versions of esoteric Christian thought. Nor was it clearly distinguished from other attributes of selfhood, such as an indwelling spark of God or an autonomous selfhood and personality that could reflect and choose. Ancient thinkers, even Plato, most often conflated all these attributes as the self or soul. But at a minimum, some notion of a soul apart from the body was handed down in virtually every indigenous and premodern setting.

Self and Soul in the Ancient Near East

In traditional Western thought deriving from either the religion of Abraham, ancient Egyptian beliefs, or Greek philosophy, the soul was indeed described as an immortal essence that could survive the death of the body. It might live on in a higher world after being vested with a heavenly body, or be deposited in a new body through reincarnation. In the Mediterranean world during the Greco-Roman era, such dualist conceptions were most often rooted in or influenced by Platonism. Plato taught that the soul was the seat of personhood and the source of life. He believed that this nonphysical entity was the totality of a person's true identity, and that the body was merely incidental as a vehicle for the soul; but this soul did not evolve.

Before Hellenism came to dominate the Eastern Mediterranean world, the Jews taught contradictory doctrines on the question of a soul and an afterlife. For example, in the times of Jesus, the Pharisees believed in a resurrection of the soul after death and held that God punished the wicked and rewarded the righteous in the afterlife; but the more literal-minded Sadducee sect repudiated the idea because there was no mention of life after death in the Torah. Still, a few hints of the promise of an eternal life to come are sprinkled in the Old Testament; for example, "Your dead shall live. . . . Awake and sing you dwellers in the dust" (Isaiah 25:8). The Jesus of the New Testament built upon these rudimentary ideas to proclaim the teaching of life eternal, attainable through belief in him and his gospel. And he dramatically and publicly demonstrated the existence of the soul and the afterlife in the most magnificent way possible in his resurrection and ascension.

But as to what and who this personal self was that survived death, and what really happened in the afterlife, little is said in either the Old or the New Testament. In the West, esotericists, mystery schools, and Gnostics influenced by Plato and Jesus attempted in later centuries to fill in the gaps.

It should be well noted, however, that Hebrew tradition does refer to the divinity of the human self. The book of Genesis inscribed upon the Western psyche the notion of the *imago dei*, the "image of God." A divine "imprimatur" is stamped by the deities upon each human creature. This scriptural passage (see Genesis 1:27) clearly states that before the fall into sin, the high Gods (the *Elohim*) determined that they would create man to be "like themselves." But soon after we were placed on Earth, our intrinsic divine nature was deeply stained by the sin of the rebellion of Adam and Eve.

Jesus later taught that "the Kingdom of God is within you." Judaism and Islam also embraced the vague notion of the *imago dei*. But for each of these Abrahamic traditions, Adam's fall had marred this divine inheritance. Could the original state be recovered? A special deliverance was needed if the self was to be salvaged so that it might survive death. Christian dogma stated that survival of the soul depended on participation in the sacraments of the church and, especially, on a personal belief in Christ, whose blood sacrifice on the cross had "ransomed" humanity from suffering the wages of Original Sin.

Soul and Spirit in the Classic Western Religions

In the religiophilosophic cauldron of Roman times, Greek ideas mixed with Hebrew, Christian, Egyptian, Roman, and many other influences. The linguistic possibility of a distinction between between soul and spirit emerged. The Greek word *pneuma*, the Arabic word *ruh*, and the Hebrew *ruakh* all referred originally to "vital breath," later translatable as "spirit." The Greek word for soul, *psyche*, also had equivalents in the other languages. In Sufism, a distinction was later made between *qalb* (heart or soul) and *ruh* (spirit).

In some unusual cases the idea of an inner spirit became more sharply defined as an otherworldly entity or preexistent divine spark that abides within as a gift from a higher being. In particular, the ancient Gnostic sects (which we will explore in chapter 6), most notably Valentinianism, posited an indwelling *pneuma* that was trapped in the physical world. But perhaps the purest version of this notion emerges much later in liberal Quakerism; its teaching of the "inward light" is strongly reminiscent of the God Fragment of the Urantia Revelation. But these vivid ideas of an Indwelling Spirit sometimes eclipsed the notion of an evolving personal soul in traditional thought; the two concepts rarely coexisted.

By some interpretations, it may also be said that traditional Chinese religion distinguished soul from spirit, as *yang* and *yin*. The Egyptians at times distinguished two entities known as the *ka* and the *ba*; the soul (*ba*) contained spiritual characteristics unique to each individual, and the *ka* was a preexistent life force. Various versions of the Egyptian *Book of the Dead* describe a judgment after death, called the Weighing of the Heart ritual, in which the *ba* (which faithfully recorded a person's good and bad deeds during life) was weighed on a scale against "truth and justice." If the person was judged sufficiently moral, then an ascent of the *ba* or personal soul into the next world could occur. This Egyptian concept of the *ba* and its afterlife journey provides perhaps the first ancient version of an ascending personal soul of the sort described in the Urantia Revelation; it was also seen as distinct from a divinely gifted spirit-self. At first, states the Urantia Revelation, "only kings and the rich were promised a resurrection [of an immortal soul]; therefore did they so carefully embalm and preserve their bodies in tombs against the day of judgment. But the democracy of salvation and resurrection as taught by Ikhnaton eventually prevailed, even to the extent that the Egyptians later believed in the survival of dumb animals." [95:5.13]

Much later, the influence of the great Christian mystics and possibly the influence of Asian ideas led some Christians beyond the classical dualism of body and soul-spirit toward an awareness of a spectrum of levels of being, ranging from body to mind, soul (*psyche*), and spirit (*pneuma*). But Christians and Jews have long been handicapped by the fact that the terms "soul" and "spirit" are used interchangeably in many biblical passages, as some scholars point out, and also by the dualism of body and soul inherited from Platonism. Apostle Paul and other New Testament writers held to Plato's dichotomy or fundamental duality of body and soul: each of us is composed of flesh and "soul-spirit," and the two poles oppose each other in a war of sorts, which can be resolved in favor of salvation and survival after death only by faith in the grace of Jesus Christ. Nevertheless, the possibility of a clear distinction between soul and spirit remained latent even in Hebrew scripture. The Hebrew word *nefesh* (the instinctive part of the self) was translated as *psyche* in the original Greek of the New Testament. We've noted that the Hebrew word *ruakh*, "vital breath," was translated as the Greek word *pneuma* (spirit), which later becomes *pneumatic hagio* (the Holy Spirit). The term takes on a special meaning after Pentecost, which poured out on all flesh the spirit of the "Comforter."

The Special Role of Greek Philosophy

Plato is, of course, the original source in the West of what has come to be known as *substance dualism*. His dialogues depict the human body as a lesser reality that is distinct from the immortal soul, and describe the soul as the source of life itself and the principle of life. The soul preexisted the body and would survive the death of the body. In Plato's *Phaedo*, Socrates teaches his students that after his death, his soul would for a time exist on its own in another world where he will be "in a state of heavenly happiness." While there, his soul would be able to think and feel and know itself *as* himself, as Socrates, and would eventually be reborn in subsequent bodies on Earth.

In general, Plato thought the soul was uniform and unitary; it did not have substantive parts, only properties. From the *UB* point of view, he conflated mind, soul, spirit, and personhood.[60] First of all, for him the soul was naturally and *unconditionally* immortal or eternal—not experiential or evolving. The body and all material things, according to Plato, are subject to change and dissolution, but the soul is an otherworldly entity that repeatedly incarnates in new bodies. The soul remains the same in essence throughout its incarnations. It was not influenced by the impulses of an additional entity or external power—that is, the inner spirit as conceived by later esotericists and the *UB*—but it was guided by its own native capacity to reason. To Plato, the soul's only aspiration was to return to its eternal nature in a discarnate state, which had been forgotten at birth.

This, of course, is the famed theory of *anamnesis*, the idea that all true knowledge actually abides in the soul from eternity, and if it is to be retrieved, it must be *recollected* through conscious effort. "Seeking and learning are in fact nothing but recollection," says Socrates in *Meno*. We can recover knowledge by rational philosophic discourse or by directly contemplating it through a kind of noetic cognition, which will reveal the divine patterns and ideal Forms of each idea or thing that the soul *had already understood* previous to the current incarnation. These "innate ideas" were self-evident notions intrinsic to the soul's nature.

For example, at the most basic level, we're born with souls that automatically understand simple ideas such as 2 + 2 = 4 or the shape of a triangle. Plato illustrates this famously in *Meno*, where Socrates leads an uneducated slave to solve a complex geometrical puzzle. At a more advanced level, we can discover the apparent existence

---

[60] But Plato was sometimes inconsistent on this point. In *The Republic* he speaks of the soul as having higher and lower parts: the appetitive (the lowest), the vital, and the rational. He left this discrepancy unresolved, but he made clear that only the rational part had volition and that it governed the lower parts. It could rally its vital center to provide emotional support for its rational purposes.

in our minds of ideals or ideal concepts that cannot have been derived from any worldly experience. For example, consider the *idea* of perfect equality. We can never have an actual experience of this ideal, so how does it arise in the mind? The same goes for ideas of truth, beauty, goodness, and other abstract concepts—whence do such ideals originate if they are not observable in this world? Plato wondered. In fact, every philosophically significant word we use in everyday speech, such as "justice" or "infinity," is a particular instance of a corresponding abstract Idea, or ideal Form. Plato posits these ideas as being eternal and incorruptible. Just as physical things are detectible to our bodily senses, these eternal ideas are only intelligible to our intellect. Ergo, the reasoning soul is itself eternal!

In essence, then, copies of ideal Forms actually abide *in and as* the soul, according to Plato, but they are obscured from view by the trauma of rebirth, and by bodily existence itself, which he compared to a prison. The purpose of education in this life is the *recovery* of the inborn ideas that one lost awareness of upon entering a new human body.

In this light, consider a unique but rather esoteric comparison: the Urantia Revelation, which is friendly to other cardinal points in Greek philosophy, suggests that the exalted residents of the central universe—who dwell in that highest domain in the cosmos known as Havona—actually instantiate, in their very existence as persons, divine ideals or eternal patterns. And they do so *in perfection*. In other words, these glorious persons are like walking and talking Platonic ideal Forms. They are nonexperiential beings who have existed from eternity.[61] And all this makes one think that Plato was on to something rather profound with his theory of eternal Forms and the soul's aspiration to abide in eternity.

Again, Plato never envisioned that the human soul evolves or can itself be modified by experience. Nor could he have ever imagined that the experiential soul—through its quest for perfection through evolution—has a vital contribution to make to these perfect beings

---

[61] Imagine the thrill of meeting the person who is the perfect archetype of some long-held ideal of yours when you sojourn someday on one of the worlds of Havona. Can you picture what sort of ecstatic conversation you might have?

residing in the domains of eternity. Yet, as I have noted (and which will be covered in more detail in the final chapter), making such a contribution is one of the primary reasons for our journey through the central universe in the afterlife, according to the *UB*.[62]

Another proof of the soul on differing grounds is presented in *Phaedrus* and elsewhere by Plato, which depicts the soul as something that is uniquely able to "move itself"—as the "self-mover." At one point he defines the soul as "the motion which can set itself moving" and which alone is able to move the body. Plato's speculations along these lines led to Aristotle's formulation that God must be the "Unmoved Mover," later adopted into Catholic theology. From the point of view of the *UB*, the ultimate mover must be some other part of the inner triad—that is, the divine spark or the autonomous personality,[63] with its God-given attribute of free will. Again, Plato conflated these ideas and attributes into one entity, the soul. But he still managed to provide a rich concept of the ontological soul.

Aristotle's Monistic Concept of the Soul

Whereas Plato was a substance dualist, Aristotle was a monist in regard to the human person and our attributes and capacities. Aristotle represents a significant minority position in Western tradition that holds that no transcendent soul or spirit of any sort exists on its own and, further, that although what we call the soul may be the seat of reason and insight—and as such may even be incorporeal—it is *not* immortal; in other words, there can be no instance of a soul without the presence of a material body. Conversely, there could never be a human body without what we call a soul. Soul and body are seen as one in Aristotle's monist conception, but the word "soul" is used to refer to an intrinsic capacity of a person to feel,

---

[62] "Through their contacts with ascending pilgrims [humans in the afterlife], the Havoners [individuals residing in the central universe] gain an experience [that] overcomes the experiential handicap of having always lived a life of divine perfection." [UB: 19:6.2]

[63] But the soul is able to self-initiate action at some point in its maturity, the *UB* says.

think, perceive, or make decisions. It's not a separate substance that acts on its own.

In *De Anima* and elsewhere, Aristotle roundly criticized Plato's arguments for the soul's separate existence. For Aristotle, the soul is simply the "form" or "principle" of the body. A famous sculptor, for example, is commissioned to represent the emperor Augustus in stone, and the result is a life-sized statue. It may seem as if the artist has enabled the "spirit of Augustus" to enter into and animate his raw materials—but that's only an illusion created by the artist. In the same way, the soul is merely the form of the body that allows the body to activate itself—or, as Aristotle would say, "strive for its full actualization."[64]

It is remarkable to what extent Western thought inherited an antinomy, a stark opposition, between its Platonic and Aristotelian lineages. On one hand, the soul is seen an independent, immortal entity divinely endowed with reason and innate ideas according to the Platonic tradition. But in the Aristotelian view, our "soul" is by nature *one* with us, embedded in our physical form and function and indistinguishable as a separate substance.

Earlier Christian thought, especially in the Hellenistic East, tended toward Plato's substance dualism; this was especially so with Gnostic esotericism. But the medieval scholastics in Western Europe constructed a workable alternative view based on Aristotle. St. Thomas Aquinas gently overhauled Aristotle's antidualism, constructing an Aristotelian edifice around the Christian dogma of the immortality and resurrection of the soul. But the result was awkward. Yes, the body and soul were a unity, as Aristotle had insisted, but it was a *complex* unity. Given that the soul is the abstract "form" of the body, it could for a time lead a separate existence after death

---

[64] Plato believed that the eye, for example, was just a "pass-through" receptacle; the act of seeing was actually carried out by the soul. But for Aristotle, the actual form of the eye is what imparts to it the capacity to see. Its morphology "actualizes" the eye by allowing it to fulfill its practical function. In that sense, our capacity for vision can't be understood as a separate substance that is somehow a thing apart from the physical eye. By the same token, our ability to engage in abstract thought, said Aristotle, may seem to be a grand thing—possibly something divine—but it is merely another (albeit higher) form or capacity intrinsic to the body, which is itself contingent and mortal.

before the general resurrection to come. We'll return to Aquinas in a moment.

The Question of the Indestructibility of the Soul

It is important to remember that in all schools of mainstream Christian thought, salvation means the eventual reconstitution of the *whole person* in the afterlife, both soul and body.[65] (The Apostle's Creed states in part, "I believe in . . . the resurrection of the body, and the life everlasting.") This afterlife unity of body and soul must be so, they believed, because Jesus had himself experienced bodily resurrection while on Earth.

Jesus's immediate followers and the later Church Fathers concluded that Christ's resurrection made all believers capable of having their own personal resurrection, first of the soul immediately upon death, and then of our literal terrestrial body as it rejoins the soul after the End of Days. As the idea matured into later Catholic doctrine, the general sequence became as follows: After death, the individual soul is judged. It is either sent to Purgatory for purification and rehabilitation, to heaven for an existence of eternal bliss, or is relegated to hell for an eternity of punishment and pain. But regardless of the soul's afterlife status, it will unite again with the body on the Last Day. In other words, after the final resurrection of the dead, the bodies of all of the dead—sinners and saints—will reunite with the detached soul that has gone before it either into heaven or into hell; *all* souls will live on eternally.

Recent scholarship has made clear that this Christian notion of an indestructible soul—which achieves eternal life in heaven or else an eternal damnation in hell, was a vestige of Platonism that somehow survived in Christian doctrine. It was Plato's old idea of inherent immortality in a new form! This idea of unconditional immortality first originated from the prominent early Church

---

[65] These notions go back to the Old Testament, as one can see, for example, in this passage from Ezekiel 37: "This is what the Sovereign Lord says: My people, I am going to open your graves and bring you up from them. . . . you, my people, will know that I am the Lord, when I open your graves and bring you up from them. I will put my Spirit in you and you will live."

thinkers known as the Alexandrians—Origen and Clement—and then was especially elaborated and propagated by Augustine, from there passing into traditional Church teaching.

But it is well worth noting that today a minority view is gaining prominence, at least among Protestant scholars. It is known as *conditional immortality* or *annihilationism*. This new development is of special interest to us because conditional immortality of the soul is the position that the *UB* takes in its complex teaching about the afterlife.

According to this trend in academic Protestant theology, no specific scripture clearly points to unconditional immortality. Biblical passages that describe the fate of unrepentant sinners, they say, strongly imply that the impenitent person *ceases to exist*. (For example, in Matthew 13:40–42 Jesus speaks of divine judgment by comparing it to weeds being thrown into a furnace; in Romans 6:23, Paul writes that the "wages of sin is death"; and Revelations vaguely refers to a "second death.") The loss of immortality by those who utterly reject God is consistent with a loving and merciful God who would never condemn his children to an eternity of conscious pain and suffering.

But isn't a God who annihilates his errant children also less than loving? Not at all, according to this view. God simply *complies* with the person's decision to no longer live on in God's universe. The annihilation is a mutual decision, not a unilateral ruling of an authoritarian and punishing God. "One of God's essential considerations on our behalf is to respect our freedom," according to Robert Wild, one of the rare Catholic scholars to adopt the conditionalist view. "This withdrawl [*sic*] of existence is not unjust since existence was a perfectly free gift in the first place. God does not owe us continued existence if we refuse to accept the purpose of existence."

The *UB* makes clear that *all* of us will survive into the afterlife; the decision as to whether to engage in the long ascension to Paradise or to else to reject the afterlife career can only be made *after* our resurrection on high.[66] Only then are we provided with

---

[66] According to the *UB*, this resurrection occurs very shortly after death for those who had achieved the third circle. For all others it happens much later at one of the periodic group resurrections that occur at the end of a dispensation. See 189:3 for a fascinating

sufficient knowledge of the ascension plan to make an informed decision. Says the Urantia text: "All will creatures are to experience one true opportunity to make one undoubted, self-conscious, and final choice. The sovereign Judges of the universes will not deprive any being of personality status who has not finally and fully made the eternal choice; the soul of man must and will be given full and ample opportunity to reveal its true intent and real purpose." [112.5.9] The very high beings called the Ancients of Days (who were introduced earlier as the rulers of our superuniverse) have the exclusive power to annihilate a person that has decided against eternal life, if this person freely chooses this fate. But if we soldier on in our soul growth until God Fusion occurs, an eternal life is assured.

Aquinas on the Aristotelian Self

The Urantia Book may at first glance seem to be Neo-Platonic. But it turns out that the *UB*'s concept of the soul also shares an important feature with the Aristotelian view, especially in the interpretation of Aristotle's monism that comes down to us in the work of Aquinas, perhaps the greatest of all medieval philosophers in the West.

We saw that Aristotle described the soul as *that which configures* the structure and organization of the totality of the self, enabling it to live and breathe and operate in the world. In other words, the soul infuses form and function into the body; plus it actually animates the body with life itself.

A human being is, in other words, a fusion of soul and body. This fusion of elements is comparable to water: oxygen and hydrogen combine to create something new, a distinct substance existing at a higher level. Water has a unique and unitary substance in the same way that a person is a unified self with singular qualities. The "waterness" of water is present because of a chemical affinity (of two parts hydrogen and one part oxygen) that resulted in the formation of a water molecule with its exclusive structure.

---

account of the great dispensational resurrection that took place concurrently with Jesus's own resurrection on Easter Sunday. Also in this connection, we've noted earlier the very exceptional cases of those who translate directly from Earth to the afterlife because they achieved God Fusion while in the flesh.

Aquinas accepts all of these Aristotelian notions about the unitary self, and simply adds that the Christian God makes it all happen. The soul is directly created by God, who pours it into matter, giving the disembodied soul a locus in which it may actualize itself.

But if the soul and body are unitary, how can there be life after death once the bodily form has dropped away? If the soul is not a separate and distinct substance, as is claimed by Plato and the dualists, how can the person have a heavenly existence in the afterlife? Aquinas answers that the soul can *subsist* (that is, maintain itself at a rudimentary level) on its own in its temporary heavenly estate. It is an incomplete self that lacks the form of personhood, but it possesses the intrinsic spark of life and can maintain itself and even have a functional existence, surviving on high until it is reunited with the body in the great resurrection at the end of the age.

To illustrate this, Aquinas makes clear that when Catholics are praying to the saints in heaven, they are not praying to the *actual person* of, say, Peter or Paul, but only to their souls, which are not the entirety of the personhood of these men. But when Peter and Paul one day become reconstituted after the final resurrection of the dead—that is, when their resurrected bodies unite with their souls on high—they once again become bona fide persons.

Along the same line, we've seen how the Urantia Revelation sharply distinguishes personhood from the evolving soul, not unlike Aquinas. Its teaching on the repersonalization of the self after death is based on the idea that personality, the locus of will and self-awareness, is the superordinate power in the self-system, as we've earlier noted. The soul and spirit do have a universe reality apart from their unification in personality, but they cannot constitute a living being with a true identity unless personhood is also present as the organizing principle. *Personality alone* confers unity and being on the other constituent parts of the system—the surviving soul and the Indwelling Spirit. And when personality is present once again (in the reconstitution of the self after death), we witness a recapitulation of our inner triad, but this time in the raiment of a heavenly body (technically, a morontia form) whose identity is now manifest in and as the surviving soul.

Neither Aristotle nor Aquinas was able to grasp the presence of the Indwelling Spirit as the cocreator of the evolving immortal soul, but they did understand that selfhood must be an unified system that displays identity, will, and self-consciousness through the fusion of form and function. We revisit these ideas in chapter 8.

Saint Augustine and the Human Soul

Of all ancient Western thinkers, St. Augustine offered perhaps the richest set of ideas about the soul in his *Confessions* and the other monumental works he wrote in the fourth and early fifth centuries, yet he never conceived that souls evolve or that a distinct spark of God exists within. The idea that the virtuous efforts of an experiencing self could generate a surviving soul in cooperation with God simply did not have a place in the early Western Christian theological equation.

Augustine struggled throughout his philosophic career with questions about self and soul. For example, is the soul bestowed by God? Does it pass to a new child through sexual procreation? He also puzzled over the question of exactly how Adam's sin enters into each new soul. But he was firm in the belief that each soul automatically inherits the stain of ancestral sin as well as the guilt of Adam—a doctrine he adopted wholesale from St. Paul, who himself originated the idea of original sin despite the fact that it had virtually no scriptural precedent.

Because of the Fall, it was said, humans are depraved in nature. We lack the freedom to do good, and cannot perform the will of God without unearned grace. This doctrine of inherited moral depravity greatly influenced the medieval Church's view of the soul, and was later revivified by Martin Luther and John Calvin, becoming a bedrock belief that has existed within Protestantism ever since.[67]

Like Plato, St. Augustine conceived of the human soul as immaterial. The soul was unitary, but it was a complex unity, endowed with reason and many other faculties. Reason enabled the soul to control

---

[67] This discussion is in part guided by Goetz and Taliaferro, *A Brief History of the Soul* (Wiley-Blackwell, 2011).

the body, Augustine thought, but reason and human will alone could never save the soul. For unless the soul was first redeemed by belief in Christ and by sacramental grace, its pedigree of original sin made its survival in heaven an impossibility. Augustine even believed that unbaptized childen who had died must suffer in hell, an idea that is fortunately no longer subscribed to by the Catholic Church.

Augustine followed Platonists in the belief that the soul is naturally immortal, always destined either for heaven or hell in eternity. But he departed from Plato in his description of the soul as "embodied"; it infused the entire body and could be simultaneously aware of pleasure or pains and other feelings occurring in the parts of the body. Indeed, Augustine came close to the belief that the soul is equivalent to what we today know of as awareness or consciousness. Thus he can be seen to have conflated the soul with what the *UB* would call the *material intellect.* But he added the idea that all souls, including consciousness itself, are tainted by the rebellion of Adam and Eve.

The soul not only is the seat of consciousness, but it is also intrinsically self-aware or capable of self-reflection, according to Augustine. In contrast, the *UB* states that self-awareness is a property of the personality and, further, that the personality's capacity for self-reflection can only manifest itself through the material self (the mortal intellect) unless and until the seat of personal identity has been transferred to the soul by virtue of evolutionary growth. Augustine could never have envisioned the idea of an unconscious mind that was the locus of the immortal soul.[68]

Finally, for Augustine the soul was not evolutionary. It was not able to improve itself, for example, by unaided moral action or through a Platonic contemplation of higher ideas. Even a soul filled with grace could not evolve toward God. After death, the immortal soul would abide in an incorporeal state until it was reunited with

---

[68] According to my own interpretation, only first circlers are soul-identified, that is, stabilized in soul-consciousness. Because of their advanced status, they have direct access to the contents of the soul, which for the rest of us is hidden away in the unconscious. (In other words, they would need no life review later on.) However, the *UB* alludes to the idea that the soul and Indwelling Spirit can communicate in the superconscious mind.

the body on the occasion of the general resurrection of souls at the end of time.

Following Paul, Augustine, and other early teachers, Christians thought of the soul's heavenly existence as unchanging. There were no educational encounters or higher stages of personal growth in the afterlife—only the eternal bliss of heaven, or the pain of eternal hell. (An important exception, however, is the Catholic idea of Purgatory.[69]) Only much later, in the fourteenth century, did the poet Dante envision an active life in the heavenly estate, but it was not until the visions and revelations of Immanuel Swedenborg in the eighteenth century that the heavenly life came to be seen as involving moral progression and relationships with others, in ways that were akin to *The Urantia Book's* rich conception.

Many fascinating depictions of the afterlife have arisen in modern times, including the teachings of Spiritualism and of those of advanced psychics such as Rudolf Steiner and Edgar Cayce. Mormonism and Seventh Day Adventism also have certain affinities with the teachings of the Urantia Revelation about the soul and the afterlife. Plus, the findings of advanced researchers such as Fredrick Myers and the hypnotist Michael Newton have culminated in the varied maps of the afterlife that students of NDEs are now compiling. It is my hope that others can pick up my thread and provide additional comparative analysis. Because of its beauty, coherence, plausibility, and rich detail, it is my view that the *UB's* descriptions of the destiny of the soul are now the standard against which all other models should be compared.

---

[69] According to this tradition, which dates back to the eleventh century, there exists an intermediate place or state of mind in which purification of the soul may occur before its entrance into heaven. But this option is only available to those whose sins are *venial* (forgivable by God in the afterlife) as opposed to those who committed mortal sins on Earth and did not repent before death. Such souls are routed to hell with no appeal possible, according to Catholic thought. But it is said that no one on Earth can definitively ascertain the final state of another individual's soul; that is a private matter between that person and God.

CHAPTER 6

Gnosticism, Eastern Christianity, and the *The Urantia Book*

Light the lamp within you.
Knock on yourself as on a door.
—*from the Nag Hammadi library*

In the last chapter I surveyed some of the influences that shaped Western religious ideas about self, soul, and spirit. But this great tradition was also shaped by its omissions. In this chapter I will survey important ideas that were marginalized or suppressed in premodern times, but which are now worthy of reconsideration in the light of the Urantia Revelation. I'll review in particular two vivid cases. First, we'll survey Gnosticism, the early Christ-centered movement that was destroyed by opponents who later claimed the mantle of "Christian orthodoxy." Then I'll offer a summary of the neglected mystical teachings of Eastern Christianity, which happens to be the tradition I was brought up in. Both of these historic trends contain notable affinities with important aspects of the cosmic spirituality of the Urantia Revelation.

The ancient Gnostics prefigured, at least in mythopoetic form, the core teaching of Jesus in *The Urantia Book* about the Indwelling

Spirit, not to mention certain aspects of *UB* cosmology and history. Because of their overlapping doctrines, it is not entirely unfair when fundamentalist Christian critics denounce the Urantia Revelation as being Gnostic. In addition, my findings about Eastern Christianity reported in this chapter indicate that its theological formulations and esoteric spiritual practices clearly incline closer to certain *UB* teachings about self and soul than can currently be found in Western Christian practices and beliefs. This association leads one to infer that—in addition to the direct impact of Greek philosophy and culture—the Eastern Church must have been influenced by the Gnostic environment of its birth, as well as by some tenets of Asian religions that I briefly cover in the concluding section of this chapter.

Gnosticism and Christian Heterodoxy

A treasure trove of lost Gnostic gospels was accidentally discovered in 1945, the very year that the finishing touches were put on *The Urantia Papers*. They were discovered among the famed Nag Hammadi texts, thirteen leather-bound papyrus codices found in a large sealed jar by a peasant in Upper Egypt. What we especially learn from these texts is that the ancient Gnostic movement had developed a powerful counternarrative to the emerging orthodox Christian myth.[70]

Gnosticism offered a wide range of alternative views of the meaning of Christ's life and teachings. It presented a rather different picture of the role of humankind in history, the nature of the cosmos, the angelic hierarchy, and the ascension in the afterlife. In particular, or at least for our purposes, Gnosticism highlighted the idea of an Indwelling Spirit. The orthodox consensus focused instead on attaining salvation through *belief in the fact of Jesus's life, death, and resurrection*, while at the same time directing its adherents away from the rising belief throughout the Mediterranean world

---

[70] This discussion especially follows the argument of *Gnosticism: New Light on the Ancient Tradition of Inner Knowing* (Quest Books: 2002), by Stephan A. Hoeller, PhD, who is described by Robert Elwood, emeritus professor of religion at University of Southern California, as "the preeminent exponent today of Gnosticism as a living religious practice." Elwood calls this book a "splendid interpretation."

in the reality of a divine indwelling and its implications for spiritual life. This and other widely held Gnostic ideas and practices were stamped out, often with violence—especially after the seminal Christian doctrines we know of today were adopted by the First Council of Nicaea in 325 AD. As is well known, the convening of this council of bishops from around the Mediterranean was an act of political intervention by the Roman emperor Constantine, who issued the invitations and even funded the travel and the proceedings.

In effect, Constantine legalized a new orthodoxy that gave us today's versions of Christianity. But what is less understood is that in the previous three centuries, a disorganized Christian heterodoxy was the rule. During these early centuries, crucial teachings about selfhood, human history, and the cosmos circulated widely in the Christian world, only to fall into obscurity after they were suppressed by the politically sanctioned Church. Certain features of these ancient Gnostic ideas resurfaced occasionally in the teachings of secret societies or schismatic sects in later centuries, never again gaining wide acceptance until their emergence in many new forms in postmodern spirituality, esotericism, and New Age thought—of which the Urantia Revelation is but a small part.

Inspired by the story of Jesus, innumerable teachers, visionaries, and prophets who were Gnostic in orientation spontaneously arose throughout the Roman Empire. We've known this fact for centuries because of the writings of their orthodox critics, most notably St. Iranaeus of Lyon, whose works not only survived but have ever since been considered almost canonical. Yet the depth, richness, and variety of the heterodox ideas of the Gnostics became much more evident upon the discovery of the Nag Hammadi texts.

While we contemplate the newly unearthed facts about Gnosticism, we must also bear in mind that amid this great flowering of creative Christian ideas was a common core that early Christians of all tendencies accepted. From the beginning, the narratives and letters attributed directly to the Apostles or their immediate students were the central texts of the entire community. What later became the four canonical Gospels of the New Testament, plus the epistles of Paul, Peter, and John, were in wide circulation by the first century, so the basics of the gospel story were well known.

But the often-persecuted Christian movement was several centuries away from having an established canon. Extant were other well-regarded texts, many of which were also attributed to Apostles or key figures. The most important among those discovered in Egypt in 1945 include the Gospel of Thomas, the Secret Book of John, the Gospel of Philip, and the Gospel of Truth.

The Nag Hammadi codices (and several related scrolls independently discovered in the previous two centuries) reveal that the Gnostics were concerned with creating an all-encompassing *psychocosmic myth*, with Jesus as its central figure. And it is a fact that their historical and cosmological framework comports with certain features of the *UB*'s teachings on prehistory as well as the Urantian ascension cosmology, inclusive of its teaching about the Indwelling Spirit.[71]

The Gnostics depicted a multileveled cosmos, with our own world subsisting at its lowest level. Humankind was seen to be isolated at the greatest distance possible from the world of pure spirit, and languishing in a slumbering or unconscious state. Further, at least according to my own interpretation, the Gnostics intuited the deeper meaning of the effects of the so-called Lucifer Rebellion and its aftermath in the Fall of Adam and Eve (prehistoric events covered just below), offering an interpretation that harmonizes better with the *UB*'s story than the biblical accounts of these events. And it turns out that this alternative understanding of history had significant implications for the Gnostic conceptions of human spirituality.

Although humankind was seen as being "trapped in matter," the Gnostic vision also had a hopeful aspect. The benign forces of the world of spirit were engaged in a constant effort to awaken and liberate us from our fallen state. If we would only turn toward the divine light within, the *pneuma*, it would lead us on a step-by-step ascension through increasingly rarified levels of the cosmos all the way back to our true home—which, as in the *UB*, was conceived by some Gnostics as a "mother universe."

---

[71] But of course these ancient teachings could never have envisioned the modern idea of cosmic evolution that makes possible the ancillary idea of an evolving soul.

Among the early Gnostic thinkers who were later declared heretics was Valentinus, who was probably born in Carthage around 100 AD. Valentinus was a poet, teacher, and visionary who must have possessed outstanding leadership abilities. A staunch follower of Apostle Paul (who in some respects was a hero to Gnostics because he had received direct revelation from Christ), Valentinus became a resident of Rome, where he achieved prominence in the Christian community. According to historians, he was so well regarded by his peers that he missed out being elected the bishop of Rome by a narrow margin. In other words, the renowned Gnostic teacher Valentinus almost became the pope! Although this position was far less prestigious and powerful than what it became a few centuries later, we can only wonder how different things might have become if he had won the election.

Gnostics like Valentinus pondered the question of why humanity had arrived at its fallen and apparently hopeless state at the bottom of the celestial hierarchy. Why was the world pervaded by such outrageous suffering, violence, and ignorance? In answer to such questions, the Gnostic masters devised an original myth. This story had as its foundation two key factors, among others: a novel interpretation of the biblical story of the Fall of Adam and Eve, and a stark repudiation of the Christian attempt to merge Judaic doctrines with Christian belief, which was spearheaded by Paul and St. Iranaeus.

Gnostic Myth and the *UB*'s Revealed History

Ancient Judaism attributed the world's fallen state to the belief that the parents of all humankind had rebelled against the divine order. Such teachings were entrenched in the minds of the early Jewish converts to Christianity. And because Jesus was a teacher and prophet to the Jews, it was only natural that beliefs from his own tradition would make their way into Christian thought. In particular, the biblical story of Adam and Eve became central to emerging Christian thought in the first century because of the outsized influence of Apostle Paul, who reframed the old Genesis story into the radical new doctrine of original sin and the blood atonement of Christ.

But the Gnostics, as a movement, asserted an alternative vision of prehistory. Generally, they taught that *intermediate celestial beings*—and not the mother and father of humanity—were the cause of our rupture with the higher worlds.

And here is a significant instance in which we find an affinity with the cosmology and spirituality of the Urantia Revelation. The *UB* also provides an account of a far-distant planetary default, but one of even wider implications than that found in Genesis. It teaches that more than two hundred thousand years ago an intermediate-level angelic being, Lucifer—the chief celestial administrator of our local system of inhabited planets (the *UB* defines a local system as an aggregation of one thousand worlds), precipitated an extremely rare event in a local universe: a system-wide rebellion. The manifesto of the Lucifer Rebellion denied the very existence in humans of the sacred triad (the evolving soul, personality, and the Indwelling Spirit) and repudiated the reality of the universal plan for ascension to Paradise; amazingly, Lucifer and the millions of angels who followed him denied the very existence of God. The Luciferians took over the angelic administration of Earth, and among other calamities caused the destruction of the mission to our planet of Adam and Eve, which we're told occurred around 37,000 BC.[72]

---

[72] I realize that at first glance the *UB*'s story of Lucifer *itself* sounds like an ancient Gnostic myth. Nevertheless, here's a full outline: In the *UB* we read that Lucifer, along with his lieutenant, one named Satan, launched an angelic rebellion that negated the very idea of the existence of a Creator Father. They denied the reality of the evolving soul and the Father's gifts of personality and the Indwelling Spirit. They propounded the so-called Doctrine of the Liberty of self-will and self-assertion as their creed, rather than the divine way of love, forgiveness, and compassion. A total of 37 local planets supported the rebellion, and our chief celestial planetary administrator, named Caligastia, himself became a fervent Luciferian. The majority of the angelic host of our world followed him into perdition. (See Paper 53, "The Lucifer Rebellion"; Paper 54, "Problems of the Lucifer Rebellion"; and Paper 67, "The Planetary Rebellion.") The deeds of Lucifer and Satan (who are conflated into one being in Abrahamic scripture) are alluded to in the Bible and the Qur'an in a few cryptic passages, but the *UB* account offers about twenty pages of lucid material. We read there that Lucifer's followers on Earth usurped the benign celestial governance of our world. They precipitated the unwitting default of Adam and Eve—who we are told were real beings with a mission to upstep human biology. And the rebels wrecked other divine missions. As a result, they plunged our world into darkness and quarantine.

These misguided beings dominated the celestial administration of Earth until they were deposed by Jesus while he was present on Earth. The *UB* indicates that Caligastia

Compare the outlines of the *UB*'s purported revelatory account of prehistory with the propositions of the old Gnostic myth:

- Our world had somehow been created by an evil, deceptive, and secondary spirit being. (In the *UB* story, Lucifer was not the literal creator of the planet, but his actions did generate the abhorrent conditions that dominated planetary life up to the time of Jesus.)

- This subsidiary creator, said the Gnostics, was not the high God, but only a "half-maker," or *Demiurge*, that had interposed itself on Earth. (In the *UB* version, Lucifer and Satan were "midlevel" spirits who broke universe protocols by coming here to recruit, with great success, followers of the rebellion from among the angelic administration of Earth.)

- As a result, said the Gnostics, both the world and the human beings in it were in an absurd situation, and the only remedy was gnosis. (We've seen that the Urantia Revelation teaches a modern form of gnosis: soul-evolution, self-perfection, and ascension to Paradise.)

And now, here's the Gnostic punchline: for the most part, this subordinate deity, the Demiurge, revealed itself in the Old Testament as *Jahweh*, the traditional deity of the Hebrews. Jahweh was depicted by the Gnostics as tyrannical, violent, and heartless. Gnostics were the first in a line of critics who have pointed to the incompatibility of Judaism with the teachings of Jesus.[73]

---

was not technically removed by Jesus, but only shorn of his powers pending his adjudication in the highest heavenly court. However, the angels on our world who followed Caligastia into rebellion were removed from the planet on the occasion of Pentecost. The *UB* clearly states that Caligastia remained relatively free up until the appearance of the Urantia Revelation and afterwards, and has been available to conspire with followers on Earth who desired his presence. I accept the Urantian account of these events because it is embedded in an otherwise intellectually plausible and scientifically sound evolutionary cosmological worldview. Incidentally, in the Special Supplement near the end of the book, I summarize the evidence of archeological support for the *UB*'s story of Adam and Eve.

[73] Perhaps chief among these critics was Marcion, a leading early teacher whose influence is said to have matched that of Valentinus. Although once a bishop and a famous Christian preacher in Rome (ca. 150 AD), Marcion split with the emerging mainstream

Gnosticism had many variations and no central authority that fixed its doctrines. Gnostics were great mythmakers, and they were not shy about creating their own liturgies, rites, symbols, sacraments, and even priesthoods. But Marcion, Valentinus, and other leading teachers such as Simon Magus and Basilides of Alexandria all taught the same radical counter-myth: Adam and Eve's purported sin against the Hebrew God was not the cause of our suffering and the tragic quality of our life on this world.[74]

In other words, humanity was not a perpetrator of sin, but rather a cosmic victim. It had not chosen and then inherited some sort of collective guilt because of a "fall." Consequently, there was no need for God's only son to be sacrificed to save humanity from its sinful nature. Once again, we find agreement with the Urantia Revelation, which teaches that the doctrine of the atonement through the shedding of Jesus's blood was entirely erroneous. The *UB*'s critique of this idea is epitomized in this passage, which is strong medicine:

> When once you grasp the idea of God as a true and loving Father, the only concept which Jesus ever taught, you must forthwith, in all consistency, utterly abandon all those primitive notions about God as an offended monarch, a stern and all-powerful ruler whose chief delight is to detect his subjects in wrongdoing and to see that they are adequately punished, unless some being almost equal to himself should volunteer to

---

Church and formed a breakaway sect of his own, developing a network of churches throughout the Roman world, many of which lasted into the fifth century. His chief contribution was a critique of the canonical Gospels as being impure, claiming that various sections were fabrications (as is now believed by some biblical scholars). It was especially his view that the Hebrew God was not the loving Father of all and not the God that had been proclaimed by Jesus. Jahweh was the God of the Law, who mingled with matter to create our fallen world. At his best, said Marcion, Jahweh was a God of justice—but he could in no way be seen as allied with the high Father, the Good God taught by Jesus.

[74] They taught that instead, Adam and Eve had hoped to recover their divinity, their *imago dei*, by eating from the Tree of Knowledge. This act had angered Jahweh, who cast them out of the Garden of Eden. And further, according to the Gnostics, the original Garden was not a paradise. The world was not first created pristine and perfect, after which there was a great fall into sin that must now be passed on to each generation. Instead, the world was *radically fallen from the beginning*. It must be remembered that they believed that our world had been created by a lesser God, an impostor, in its own flawed image. The universe we see was impaired from the start and designed to deceive. The material world was a "matrix" in which we were caught.

suffer for them, to die as a substitute and in their stead. **The whole idea of ransom and atonement is incompatible with the concept of God as it was taught and exemplified by Jesus of Nazareth**. The infinite love of God is not secondary to anything in the divine nature. [188:4.8]

The Gnostic story continues: there were intermediate worlds or heavens and at their highest point was an "upper world"—an utterly transcendent source-universe of light, sometimes known as the *pleroma*, or "fullness." This was the abode of the high God of transcendent unity, the place from which Jesus himself had come. And this benign force of the highest heaven was engaged in a constant effort to contact us. This true God was trying to rescue us from our imprisonment in a material world where we lived under the aegis of the Demiurge.

This compassionate Deity was trying to reach us in two ways: by dispatching divine teachers from the upper world directly into ours—the chief of whom was Jesus—and also by sending us a gift, a pure and literal part of itself, a pure spirit. And this was a core teaching; Gnostics uniformly taught that each of us is indwelled with a "fallen spark" gifted upon us from the highest cosmic level.

Valentinus in particular, much like the twentieth-century existentialists, taught that the world is absurd—but unlike most of them, he also taught that this life is rendered meaningful by gnosis, or knowledge of the inner spark. One wonders how, with the great currency of Gnosticism in the early centuries, this idea could have been so roundly eclipsed.

In his comprehensive study of Gnosticism, Stephen A. Hoellner summarizes this teaching about the inner light in this way: "[Gnostics believed that] a human being consists of physical and psychic components, which are perishable, as well as a spiritual component, which is a *fragment of the divine essence*, sometime called the divine spark [emphasis mine]."[75] The *UB* uses similar language, as we've seen, also calling the divine gift a fragment. We are also told in the Urantia text that this divine fragment is imprisoned (see chapter

---

[75] Hoeller, p. 18.

9)—the same metaphor used by the early Gnostics who, according to Hoellner, preached that these "sparks of transcendental holiness slumber in their material and mental prison." But we are called to *awaken* to the inner spark.

This view of Gnosticism is complemented by the work of Elaine Pagels, perhaps the world's leading scholar in this field, in her luminous work *Beyond Belief: The Secret Gospel of Thomas.* Pagels details a provocative theory of an open conflict between those who believed in the veracity of the Gospel of John, and those who held that the Gospel of Thomas was a more accurate reflection of Jesus's life and teachings. Their dispute caused a fatal bifurcation in the early Christian community. This split had the effect of turning Western Christians away from the path of gnosis—or, as the Eastern Christian mystics called it, *the way of divinization, or deification*—and instead toward a mistaken juridical emphasis on the idea that "God so loved the world that he gave his only begotten Son, that whosoever believeth in him should not perish but have everlasting life." (John 3:16)

Eastern Christianity and the Path of Deification

The Gnostic emphasis on the *pneuma* survived in a sophisticated new form in Eastern Christian thought and practice, which in its mystical theology taught that we could be perfected, or deified, through an inner communion with God. With the notable exception of these deification teachings, the Christian soul was usually not depicted as evolving by one's own decisions, let alone progressing toward perfection. This omission has long been the case in Western Christianity until quite recently, despite several powerful pronouncements in the Gospels in which Jesus seems to refer to deification.[76]

---

[76] Of course, there were many exceptions among the Western mystics. Some of the medieval Catholic mystics allude to stages of unfolding, notably St. John of the Cross and especially St. Teresa of Avila, who walks her readers through the "mansions" of our inner being, which she called "the Interior Castle." In addition, the sixteenth-century founder of the Society of Jesus, St. Ignatius of Loyola, taught in his *Spiritual Exercises* that one must "conquer oneself and regulate one's life in such a way that no decision is made under the influence of any inordinate attachment." The Jesuit aspirant was taught

We saw how the emerging mainstream Western Church repelled the Gnostic emphasis on an indwelling divine spark. As Christian theology and culture evolved through the line of Paul and Augustine, the point of Christian life—at least outside of the monasteries—became the quest for *salvation from sin and a path to heaven by grace, through belief in the Lordship of Christ*. If one had professed belief in the Creed and been baptized, salvation could be sustained by penitence, recitation of prayers, taking the sacraments, and by living a life of charity and good works. A Christian was a member of an ethical fellowship of believers in a religion *about* Jesus—not the practitioner of the self-regenerating experiential religion *of* Jesus based on a personal relationship with God. The *UB* makes a big point of this distinction.

In the enthusiasm of Pentecost, Peter unintentionally inaugurated a new religion, the religion of the risen and glorified Christ. The Apostle Paul later on transformed this new gospel into Christianity, a religion embodying his own theologic views and portraying his own *personal experience* with the Jesus of the Damascus road. **The gospel of the kingdom is founded on the personal religious experience of the Jesus of Galilee; Christianity is founded almost exclusively on the personal religious experience of the Apostle Paul**. Almost the whole of the New Testament is devoted, not to the portrayal of the significant and inspiring religious life of Jesus, but to a discussion of Paul's religious experience and to a portrayal of his personal religious convictions. The only notable exceptions to this statement, aside from certain parts of Matthew, Mark, and Luke, are the Book of Hebrews and the Epistle of James. Even Peter, in his writing, only once reverted to the personal religious life of his Master. **The New Testament is a superb Christian document, but it is only meagerly Jesusonian.**" [196:2.1]

---

to train his mind—with the help of prayer and self-examination—to be free from his own likes and dislikes, in order to better discern God's will. This training was eventually extended to the laity and has become popular in certain Catholic circles today.

Philosophic confusion resulted from this overemphasis on the person of Jesus as the only path to salvation, not to mention the theological contrivances of Paul. The possibility of a clear distinction between soul (*psyche*) and spirit (*pneuma*) soon fell away. The underdeveloped concept of the human soul that remained in the West became conflated with basic capacities of the intellect such as reason, reflection, and will—as we earlier noted in St. Augustine's writings. It was not a far distance from here to the dualism of Descartes, which conflated mind and soul into an otherworldly entity that stands above and apart from the body.

What's more, the human will is helpless without the grace of the sacraments, according to the pessimistic Western Christian position—at least that was the juridical Pauline and Augustinian view that later came to dominate Catholic doctrine and was greatly reaffirmed by Luther and the Protestant reformers. Through our faith in the glorified Christ who "died for our sins," a measure of grace was released that freed the depraved the will from original sin. This formula contributed to the cathartic or "silver bullet" form of salvation later promoted worldwide by evangelical Protestants, with its singular emphasis on being "born again."

By contrast, the Eastern Church saw salvation, much as *The Urantia Book* does, as a continual *growth in grace* by choosing the will of God again and again. According to the *UB*, Jesus taught his followers to engage in a "glorious progression, to become perfect, even as your Father in heaven is perfect." [142:7.13]

In part due to the Greek and Gnostic matrix out of which it was born in the Eastern Mediterranean, Eastern Orthodox Christianity did not hold to the view of a broken and utterly dependent human will. The Byzantines adopted the more optimistic idea that, although the human will is weak, it can still be a reliable partner with God's will. According the great Eastern theologian St. Maximus, "Our salvation finally depends on our own will."

Passages that hint at the potential for divinization are sprinkled throughout the New Testament, but all of them are cryptic. The Eastern theologians picked up on these powerful epigrammatic statements that were often ignored in the West and slowly developed the doctrine, building especially upon the monastic experience of the

Desert Fathers that first sprang up in Egypt beginning in the third century. Favored passages included Jesus's teachings in Luke 17:21, "The kingdom of God is within you"; "Is it not written in your law, 'I said, *you are gods*?'" (John 10:34); Peter's statement "so that . . . you may become participants of the divine nature" (2 Peter 1:4); and Paul in Romans 8:16, "It is that very Spirit bearing witness with our spirit that we are children of God." The result in the Eastern Church was the claim that the ultimate aim and purpose of human life was *theosis*, a Greek word that is translatable as "deification" or "divinization." In a definitive scholarly study of this theme in contemporary Christianity, Stephen Finlan and Vladimir Kharlamov conclude that "the Eastern Orthodox Church has retained *theosis* as a concept for theological reflection, while the Western churches . . . have dropped it." They call this doctrinal omission in the West a "serious loss for Christian thought and hope."[77]

The survival into modern times of the Eastern Church's deification doctrine offers an important bridge to the *UB*'s teaching about levels of circle-making that lead to God Fusion. The teachings of the great Eastern practitioners, especially as collected in the *Philokalia* (a five-volume compendium of monastic writings compiled over many centuries), speak of a progression from "purification of the body" (ascetic practices, including stillness of the body and mind) to "illumination" (perception of the presence of Christ through prayer of the heart), and finally to "union" (formless oneness with the "energies" of God).

Through the centuries, the goal of deification through union has always been described in the East in *apophatic* terms. Apophatic theology is the mystical way of the negation of all concepts—and even non-concepts—of God, because God is absolutely transcendent to all possible qualifiers. God is not simply One as opposed to the many; not simply Being as opposed to nonbeing; not even Spirit as opposed to nature. The essence of God cannot be appropriated through specific techniques that involve ideas, feelings, movements, images, or even the human will. Such things were seen as subtle idolatry.

---

[77] Stephen Finlan and Vladimir Kharlamov, *Theosis: Deification in Christian Theology*, vol. 1 (Wipf & Stock, 2006), p. 8.

The Eastern Christian mystics arrived instead at the stance that it was necessary for the *entire* person to present himself to God. There was no royal road to union through any one of the human faculties. The whole self would be nakedly disclosed to God in the "divine darkness." Partaking in the sacraments, singing hymns, reciting the name of Jesus, and heart-centered breathing could focus the mind to prepare the practitioner. But all this was preliminary. The point was to surrender into contemplation, taking a leap beyond all doing and into a state of resting in the unknowable divine presence in utter stillness (known by the Greek term *hesychia*). This mobilization of the entire self toward a formless but ceaseless worship beyond thought (or even beyond non-thought) is not unlike the *UB*'s idea of faith—if such a state of faith-filled awareness is seen as an existential liberation of the whole person into transconceptual spiritual receptivity.

Hesychastic heart-spirituality did not pose a dichotomy between the body and the spirit as developed later in the West. The Eastern mystics did not privilege any aspect of the human organism as being closer to the divine than any other. Instead, they depicted all elements of the human person as equally fallen in the face of God's utter transcendence and incomprehensibility, and thereby all parts of the self—compositely represented as "the heart"—could equally benefit from the gifts of grace conferred upon the believer practicing hesychia.

But even in states of union, the contemplative never contacts the *essence* of God. The hesychast was only able to participate in the "uncreated" energies of God, as the great fourteenth-century Byzantine theologian St. Gregory Palamas explained when challenged by Western theologians. At best, we would be granted a vision of the "uncreated light" of God, much as the Apostles Peter, James, and John were granted during the transfiguration of Jesus on Mount Tabor. (Such was the teaching of St. Symeon the New Theologian in the tenth century.[78]) And even this notion comports with the Urantia Revelation, which states that we increasingly

---

[78] According to the great Russian theologian Vladimir Lossky, St. Symeon represents the apex of Eastern Christian mysticism. Lossky's writings were a crucial guide for writing this section.

participate in divine glory but do not contact the essence of God until far, far into the ascent—only on Paradise. "Though you cannot find God by searching, if you will submit to the leading of the Indwelling Spirit, you will be unerringly guided, step by step, life by life, through universe upon universe, and age by age, until you finally stand in the presence of the Paradise personality of the Universal Father." [2:5.5]

Thus, according to Palamas, God *energetically* descends to minister to humanity in response to our aspiration and need, especially in the person of Jesus, but this Palamite teaching does not mean that God shares with us the fullness of his divine *essence*. Through this distinction, Eastern Christian theology believed it preserved the ineffable transcendence of the Father.

As a final note, it should be remembered in this connection that St. Athanasius of Alexandria's central argument, which convinced the Council of Nicaea to adopt the creedal formulation of the doctrine of the Incarnation, provided a philosophic basis for the later teaching of theosis (perhaps unwittingly, given Athanasius' forceful opposition to Gnosticism). The great theologian declared that if Jesus is not both fully God and fully man, then we cannot logically share in the divine nature. His famous line about the Incarnation epitomizes the Orthodox concept of theosis: "He became man so that man might become God."[79]

Asian Ideas of Self and Soul

As we complete our global survey of the wisdom traditions, let us turn for a moment to Asia to trace some of its unique ideas about soul, spirit, and personhood. Hinduism and Buddhism do have some mild affinities with Gnosticism and Greek Christianity, so we conclude this chapter with an all-too-brief survey of their views on these matters.

It is fair to say that the ancient Vedanta adepts penetrated to inner depths unprecedented at that time in humanity's religious

---

[79] For much more on this subject, see my essay "Eastern Orthodox Christianity: Hesychia, Theosis, and *The Urantia Book*" at: http://urantia-book.org/archive/sfj/orthodox_christianity_urantia.htm.

history. Doing so meant casting aside the symbolism and ceremonialism of the Brahmin priests, then plunging into a devoted effort to directly experience the hidden truth that lies beneath the world of flux. Deep within every person, these sages concluded, exists an eternal, incorporeal, and *impersonal* Self. This entity alone, it was said, is ontologically real, while the contingent personal self, the struggling human ego, is ultimately illusory. The esoteric branches of Hinduism have ever since taught that the Indwelling Spirit-entity constitutes the existential presence of a nonpersonal Deity, while the particular bearer of the Self (the living and embodied personality) is caught in a dream of existence. This idea resolved itself into the concept of the indwelling *atman*—the microcosmic Self that corresponds to *Brahman*, the macrocosmic essence of the Absolute. "A liberated person sees no difference between his own *atman* and *Brahman*, and between *Brahman* and the universe" (*Adhyatma Upanisad*).

On the surface, this conception is not unlike the *UB*'s notion of the Indwelling Spirit, which we've defined as a prepersonal fragment of the Universal Father. But one's cosmological and theological assumptions make all the difference. Unlike the idea of the God Fragment, the Hindu atman was not the gift of a loving Divine Parent. The Self had no interest in guiding or conserving human experience, or in cocreating and then perfecting a human soul. "*Atman* can be defined only through negating any personal attributes. Although it constitutes the existential substrata of human existence, *atman* cannot be the carrier of one's 'spiritual progress,' because it cannot record any data produced in the illusory domain of psycho-mental existence."[80]

In other words, the absolute was not interested in human progress. The Vedanta cosmos was static and impersonal; concepts of evolution would not penetrate Hindu thought until the twentieth century, when it arose especially in the work of Sri Aurobindo, a contemporary of the revelators who authored *The Urantia Book*.

Yet there *was* a conception of a metaphysical record of sorts that kept track of human behavior. Somehow attached to the Self was

---

[80] See http://www.comparativereligion.com/reincarnation.html.

a *subtle body* that kept the atman in bondage to the law of karma—
and from which the atman had to free itself through the practice
of yoga. Karmas and life impressions (*samskaras*) were deposited in
the subtle-body reservoir, but this repository was not a uniquely
personal and experiential soul; it was not an immortal asset of the
evolving universe as conceived in the synthesis hypothesis. One's
deposit of karmic debt (as a result of choices and behavior in the
world) merely contributed to the operation of a mysterious, impersonal mechanism—the inexorable law of karma. Its function was to
generate the characteristics of one's next incarnation through the
impersonal operation of cause and effect.[81]

In classic Vedanta, no unique and sacred personhood was
present in the human incarnation, exercising its free will. Only
the atman was truly real; the illusory personal ego would dissolve
upon the achievement of liberation from bodily existence, when the
aspirant "got off the wheel"—the ultimate return of the atman to
Brahman, likened to a drop of water returning to the ocean. This
was enlightenment, or *moksha*, according to the Upanishads. The
practitioner was now liberated from suffering and reincarnation,
but this freedom *entailed the extinguishment of selfhood*. Sadly, this
result is not unlike the *UB*'s depiction of the return of both the
God-given personality and the remnant of the human soul to the
Supreme Being that occurs when a person rejects eternal life—the
ultimate failure of the conscious self.

Thus, in traditional Vedanta teaching, the virtuous effort of an
aspirant did not yield any new value in an evolving universe. It did not
generate a personal soul that contributes to cosmic evolution while

---

[81] "As a necessary aid in explaining the reincarnation mechanism, Vedanta adopted the
concept of a subtle body (*sukshma-sharira*) which is attached to *atman* as long as its
bondage lasts. This is the actual carrier of karmic debts. However, this 'subtle body'
cannot be a form of preserving one's personal attributes, i.e., of any element of one's
present conscious psycho-mental life. The facts recorded by the subtle body are a sum
of hidden tendencies or impressions (*samskara*) imprinted by karma as seeds that will
generate future behavior and personal character. . . The reservoir of karmas is called
karmashaya . . . This deposit of karma merely serves as a mechanism for adjusting the
effects of karma in one's life. It dictates in an impersonal and mechanical manner the
new birth (*jati*), the length of life (*ayu*) and the experiences that must accompany it
(*bhoga*)." Ibid.

at the same time immortalizing the spiritually significant choices of a unique personality (according to our synthesis hypothesis).

It is worth pointing out that these teachings also differed from classical Platonism, which asserted the preexistence of an immortal soul in a celestial world and its fall into a human body. Plato never conceived of a "subtle self" containing traces of one's previous life that would determine the conditions of the next incarnation or a heavenly ascension.

For his part, the Buddha added what he considered to be a profound corrective to Vedanta concepts of the atman: he did not deny the existence of the moral, intellectual, or volitional aspects of this entity, but he stumbled at the notion of an eternal, unchanging atman; for him there was a *functional* self, yes, but not an ontological soul or spirit (or Self). The attributes of the atman might be immaterial, but immateriality in no sense meant permanence; all possible attributes of this atman were to be considered ephemeral. Buddha believed that his predecessors had harbored a psychological delusion, a subtle attachment to a reified "it" of selfhood that obscured the prospects of a deeper penetration into pure consciousness.

But it is important to note that the later Buddhist doctrines of an indwelling Buddha-nature may have marked the return of the classical atman in a new and much improved form. And we should note well that the Urantia Revelation praises this very concept (see 94:11) as one that closely approximates its own teaching about the spirit-self, an indwelling gift of God that is not exactly impersonal but will one day gain personalness through its dramatic fusion with both the soul and the personality. We return to this important feature of Buddhism in chapter 9.

Allowance was made within classic Buddhism for the transmigration of moral characteristics into the next life—actions lead to consequences—but there is no ultimate actor. Of course, in Buddhism, atman is not identical with Brahman—Buddha found no evidence that either was ontologically real. To believe in an eternal Self or Godhead, he taught, is to hold to an artificial and ignorant construct.

Not unlike in the West, the great traditions of origin in India resolved themselves on the one hand into a substance dualism (the atman versus the illusory ego-self), and on the other to various renditions of a Buddhist monism—which shares characteristics of Aristotle's monism.

In chapter 7, I'll trace how Ken Wilber and his colleagues in the integral movement have created an impressive philosophic edifice that highlights essential truths of the world's wisdom traditions that we have surveyed so far, and then goes on to correlate these ideas with the findings of modern thought. A great convergence of integralism with important teachings of the Urantia Revelation is one of the results of this heroic effort.

Self and Soul in Modernity and Beyond

The earth is but one country, and mankind its citizens.
—Baha'u'llah

Traditional Western Christianity originated as, and remains, a religion based on *faith in revelation*—the good news *about* the death and miraculous resurrection of the redeemer of all mankind. This Pauline gospel exalted a powerful but only partial truth— the Lordship of Christ—while grafting onto the new religion the ancient idea of blood atonement. The ultimate effect was the subordination of the religion *of* Jesus—Jesus's noble teachings about the brotherhood of humankind, the ethics of the Golden Rule, non-resistance to evil, the forgiveness of one's enemies, the individual's experience of the presence of God, and the Father's unconditional love. The New Testament also offered a perplexing description of self and soul that was embedded in a primitive cosmology and a garbled sacred history. Yet the Judeo-Christian mythos, along with its compromised institutions, was potent enough to launch an enduring civilization and prepare humanity for a new dispensation.

Waiting in the wings, of course, were some needed corrections. Europe's most courageous thinkers would rightfully reject—in the name of reason—the Church's claims on a monopoly of truth. And what was at first a trickle of dissent and nonconformity eventually became the tsunami we now call modernism. Understandably, because of its epochal struggle with the Church, the modern mind remains deeply skeptical of any claim of supernatural revelation.

Ironically, *The Urantia Book*—itself purporting to be a supernatural revelation—endorses the modernist critique of the traditional Christian worldview. And it goes on to audaciously present a new version of faith in revelation—the inner disclosures of truth by the Indwelling Spirit to each son or daughter of God.[82] While the *UB* urges us to live a life based on the insights born of faith, its very teaching about faith is framed in the language of *philosophic reason*—also rather ironically. It is a remarkable fact the Urantia Revelation uses categories borrowed (in part) from modernist thought in order to surpass the limitations of modernism.

Many new readers of the Urantia Revelation are disappointed when they realize that it lacks the visionary, metaphysical, or poetic qualities they are familiar with in other scriptures or prophetic texts, and reads more like a gigantic university course in the philosophy of spiritual living. Its biography of Jesus offers many thrilling narrative passages in the course of providing a revolutionary new depiction of the religion *of* Jesus—his superb life of faith in the loving presence of God—yet his longer discourses come across in strikingly philosophic language.[83] The *UB* is rich throughout with philosophic syllogisms, and while it resorts to the use of existing philosophic categories, *The Urantia Book* goes so far as to attempt to rehabilitate philosophic reason. It shocks many readers with the

---

[82] What the Catholic Church calls private revelation is an exception to my statement. This is the charism of personal revelation that helps believers live by the existing precepts of divine revelation—the complete Word of God as found in the Bible and sacred tradition. Such private revelations, while sometimes authentic, can never supersede the content of divine revelation (also known as public revelation). St. Thomas Aquinas taught that all new public revelation ended with the death of John the Apostle.

[83] See, for example, his discourses on soul, mind, and science in Paper 133. Other philosophic discourses by Jesus cover these topics: religion, reality, time and space, good and evil, truth and faith, wealth, the family, mercy and justice, forgiveness, and spiritual freedom.

assertion that all previous metaphysics "has proved a failure." But then the text hardly skips a beat, declaring in the same passage that "revelation authoritatively clarifies the muddle of reason-developed metaphysics on an evolutionary sphere." [103:6.8] This statement provides yet another challenge for future research into the deeper implications of the Urantia Revelation.

In the traditional Christian mindset, faith in revelation meant holding fast to creeds and doctrines based in part on a series of mythic narratives established by ecclesiastical authority.[84] By contrast, the Urantia Revelation urges us to exercise faith in *personally revealed truth*, while at the same time using for orientation a revelatory reference text framed in philosophic and modern scientific language that offers a futuristic argument for a new cosmic spirituality.

All this is another way of saying that with the advent of *The Urantia Book*, the possibility of faith in revelation has returned in the postmodern era, but at a much higher level of sophistication. In the words of Jesus from his "Second Discourse on Religion":

> Your religion shall change from the mere intellectual belief in traditional authority to the actual experience of that living faith which is able to grasp the reality of God and all that relates to the divine spirit of the Father. The religion of the mind ties you hopelessly to the past; **the religion of the spirit consists in progressive revelation and ever beckons you on toward higher and holier achievements** in spiritual ideals and eternal realities. [155:6.4]

If we turn to the Urantia Revelation, we find that our personal spiritual experience is now sovereign. It is no longer subordinated

---

[84] Of course, the Bible also contains much factual content that has been verified by archeology and historical research. And strikingly rich wisdom and inspired ethical teachings appear in many books of the New and Old Testaments. The intent of this discussion is to call attention to the stark contrast between the demythologizing thrust of *UB* and the often mythopoetic quality of the Bible, which is characteristic of its pre-modern cultural pedigree.

to the authority of the traditions of the past, however benign they may be, nor is it subject to institutional requirements.[85]

In the final analysis, the teachings of Jesus presented in the *UB* are about a life of genuinely free religious experience, the joy of soul-making based on our own creative choices, and the thrill of developing a philosophy of living that arises from personal interpretations of the values of truth, beauty, and goodness.

Modernism and Its Discontents

With the authority of scripture and the Church in retreat, many in the educated classes of early modern Europe turned their attention away from the things of faith in favor of scientific reason based on material facts—and this new focus quickly yielded the material blessings of the modern age. In the face of this new materialism, what could now be done to retrieve some notion of an immaterial soul and an afterlife?

According to the leading philosopher of the European Enlightenment, Immanuel Kant, philosophic reason and scientific inquiry would never suffice to answer this question. In an effort to save this great ideal, he declared in his *Critique of Practical Reason* (1788) that we should simply *assume* the reality of the soul's existence because of its immense moral value to society.

Kant would likely agree with the *UB* that we are dependent on revelation for true knowledge about the soul and of God. And in his time and immediately thereafter, new claims of revelation began to fill the vacuum; a movement of the modern zeitgeist toward post-biblical revelation began to gather momentum. At first it took the form of the personal revelations of Immanuel Swedenborg in the eighteenth century and the aspirations of the Idealist philosophers who followed after Kant. Then came the visions of the Romantic poets of the early nineteenth century, such as William Blake. The

---

[85] There is no official Urantia church or priesthood; students of the *UB* can interpret its revelatory guidance as they see fit without the pressure of official interpretations handed down by an ecclesiastical hierarchy. *UB* adherents can (in theory) live "the religion of the spirit" because the text does not purport to be inerrant and its teachings always appeal to philosophic reason.

trend culminated later in the nineteenth and early twentieth century with the claims to revelation by movements such as Christian Science, Seventh Day Adventism, New Thought, Theosophy, and Anthroposophy—and in the Islamic world with the revelations of *Baha'u'llah*, the founder of the Baha'i Faith. In our time, revelatory NDEs have inspired a renewed faith in unseen metaphysical realities, and channeled works such the Seth Material, *The Law of One*, and *A Course in Miracles* have proliferated.

I believe that the Urantia Revelation tops off this movement with an *epochal* outpouring of revelatory grace, this time with a special focus on how to integrate science and philosophy with a cosmological vision of the human self and soul. In this chapter I argue that a new cultural paradigm that is generally friendly to such an integrative methodology has arisen that can support the futuristic teachings of the *UB*. The insights of integral theory are already assisting the Urantia Revelation in making its proper contribution.

Unfortunately, the prevailing cultural memes of our time are unfriendly and even outright hostile toward both of these two meta-narratives of integration and synthesis. Under the sway of modernist secularism, human consciousness and selfhood have been reduced to by-products of brain biochemistry, inherited genetics, and the influences of one's environment. Modernity has made numerous positive contributions, but its often amoral strivings have blighted the planet with war, environmental destruction, and inequality. And while it is true that the secularist revolt freed up energies for economic growth, its attack on the excesses of traditional religion created, in turn, its own excessive reliance on science, technology, political control by technocratic elites, and profit-driven global capitalism.

Arising after World War II with a critique of these growing maladies was the boomer generation, the postmodernists. Theirs was a double revolt—against both the negative effects of modern materialism and the authoritarian religious traditions of the West. But like the modernists, postmodernism was also constructive. The postmodern meme has contributed environmentalism, multiculturalism, sexual frankness, and egalitarianism. Its educators have produced thousands of articulate advocates for cultural pluralism and tolerance for minorities. Especially for our purposes, we can add to this list the postmodern innovations known as New Age spirituality, interfaith dialogue, and the interspirituality movement, each based in part on the desire to reframe and package esoteric ancient wisdom in an updated and popular format. In particular, postmodernists drew from nineteenth-century occultism and spiritualism and from living masters of Buddhism, Hinduism, and Taoism who had migrated to the West.

While this effort to reenchant the world and advocate for social reform has been a gift, postmodernism has also had the effect of propelling global civilization into even more conflict than the earlier division between traditional culture and modernity. The traditionalists upheld the truths of ancient scripture and the modernists celebrated scientific truth, but the postmodernists declared *any* claim to truth to be suspect. Truth was merely "truthiness" (to quote comedian Stephen Colbert). It was little more than an assertion of the powerful, or a transient interpretation of cultural artifacts by whatever system of thought happened to be in fashion. To launch a new "truth," said the postmodernists, one needed only to establish a hegemony that allowed one to control the institutions of its expression. The old verities—such as the values of truth, beauty, and goodness—did not exist in some transcendental space waiting to be discovered by noble thinkers; such ideas were an *invention* by society based on arbitrary rules of language and cultural convention. And the cultural supremacy that resulted was all backed up by naked political power.

When postmoderism came to dominate academia in the 1980s, the tide turned. Professors of the humanities and social sciences taught a generation of students that the interior life is embedded—and in fact, smothered—in contingent cultural assumptions. Individuals, they said, are largely unaware of their conditioning. Every value they hold dear is a product of passing cultural agreement, and almost none of it can be considered transcendent or revelatory.

Politically, this meant that no particular culture or religion could be considered to be superior to any other—because all were fungible, all were a fiction of the moment. Postmodernist deconstruction went so far as to cast doubt on the facts and truth-claims of science, to the dismay of modernists. Even the findings in physics and biology were distorted by hidden political agendas and cultural biases.

The result we now face is today's all-too-familiar cultural fragmentation, where three primary and divergent worldviews—premodern, modern, and postmodern—coexist uneasily alongside one another and sometimes even fall into open warfare. Each culture believes that it alone has a monopoly on what is real and relevant.

The Irish poet William Butler Yeats foresaw this result in his prophetic 1919 poem "The Second Coming," which I quote in part:

> Things fall apart; the centre cannot hold;
> Mere anarchy is loosed upon the world,
> The blood-dimmed tide is loosed, and everywhere
> The ceremony of innocence is drowned;
> The best lack all conviction, while the worst
> Are full of passionate intensity.
> Surely some revelation is at hand . . .

The Coming of the Integral Age

Quietly into this predicament came the Urantia Revelation, now "at hand" (to quote Yeats). To a war-torn world whose "centre cannot hold," the *UB* offers the revelation of a divine spark centered in the heart of each person and a loving Creator at the center of the cosmos. It provides an inspiring vision of philosophic coherence, evolutionary synthesis, and universal unity.

In the late twentieth century, the *UB* has initiated a many-sided mission of correction that is already catalyzing the epochal changes to come. But what has been urgently needed to support its proper utilization has been a comprehensive map of the whole that consolidates the evolution of consciousness up to the present moment—now that we are several generations after the publication of the Urantia Revelation. This is now available in the form of what philosopher Ken Wilber, our chief source in this chapter, calls the *Integral Map*, which offers a multiperspectival model for all of life and cosmic reality.

Integral culture, by definition, *transcends but includes* the best features of the three historic cultures we've been discussing: traditionalism, modernism, and postmodernism. Integral theory provides for a new set of universals, and may set the stage for the reception of a new revelation as prophesied by Yeats.

It is fascinating to note that some of the intellectual objectives of the Urantia Revelation relate directly to the integral movement. As with integral theory, *The Urantia Book* provides a blend of the best of the enduring values of the three competing cultural paradigms we've been discussing. Below I briefly summarize how *The Urantia Book* harvests and reframes some of the best features of the three competing worldviews that were first distinguished by integralists:

1. **Pre-modernism:** The crucial premodern concepts of the soul, the Indwelling Spirit, and the intrinsic divinity of selfhood (the *imago dei*), as well as panentheism and Trinitarian theology, are "recycled" and rehabilitated in the Urantia text, but are now understood in the light of critical philosophy, universal evolution, and a scientific cosmology.

2. **Modernism:** The *UB* embraces the best features of modernist thought, including scientific method, physical and biological evolution, human rights, the importance of trade and industry, and democratic government. For example, in Part III, "The History of Urantia," the opening fifty-page section describes the evolution of life on Earth over the last five billion years and reads like a modern science textbook. It even describes in detail the operation of continental drift (now called *plate tectonics*), a cardinal feature of today's geophysics that was not proven until 1969. In addition, three entire papers (70 –72) discuss various features of democratic government, modern industry, and even issues like labor relations.

3. **Postmodernism:** The *UB* highlights key ideas associated with this worldview, including pluralism, cultural tolerance, gender equality, social justice, global citizenship, and interfaith dialogue. Various versions of these concepts can be

found spread out through the four parts of the text, but especially in the 62 papers of Part III. I believe that a case can be made that certain crucial ideas of postmodernism found their first-ever systematic presentation in the *UB*.

But the Urantia text is not merely integrative in relation to the cultural ideals of our more immediate past, thereby "transcending and including" the best of these values. While its teaching bridges the three cultures that now compete for influence in the world, it also pushes beyond them into the far-distant future of religion and high civilization, as well as into the far-distant past of prehistory. In doing so, the revelators fill in breathtaking gaps in our understanding. Consider this list of elements:

- **The distant future:** The Urantia Revelation stuns the reader with its descriptions of the inhabitants of the perfect central universe; and it also offers a glimpse of the perfecting civilizations of other planetary cultures in our galaxy, some of which are millions of years ahead of ours. ("You would instinctively describe such a realm—could you be suddenly transported to a planet in this stage of development—as heaven on earth." See Paper 54, "The Spheres of Light and Life.") Notably, the citizens of such advanced worlds are masters of the cosmic spirituality described in this book.

- **The distant past:** We noted in chapter 6 that *UB* also propels us very far into the deep past, explaining why our dilemmas—especially the problems of racism, exploitation, and the tendency of humankind to war and polarization—have deep roots in prehistory, from the days of the Lucifer Rebellion more than two hundred thousand years ago. While this topic is beyond the scope of this book, I refer the reader again to these key Papers: 53, 54, and 67.

Given its wide scope, the Urantia Revelation is obviously not reducible to being a species of either premodernism, modernism, or postmodernism, nor can it be assimilated into organized

Christianity.[86] But the *UB does* have important affinities with the integral worldview.

Integralism and the Urantia Revelation

Integral thinkers around the world are building an emerging culture based on an understanding of large-scale evolution and cosmic integration that has many characteristics similar to that of the Urantia Revelation. This new integralism has roots in holistic evolutionary philosophers such as G. W. F. Hegel, Alfred North Whitehead, and Sri Aurobindo. But today the field of integral theory and practice is led by Ken Wilber—one of the world's most inclusive thinkers and its most widely translated philosopher.[87]

Integralism scales up our understanding of evolution, cosmology, culture, psychology, philosophy, and spirituality in a way that complements the community of inquiry growing up around the *UB*. While these two systems may disagree about what exactly constitutes the errors and excesses of the previous three worldviews, at a minimum they seem to agree to the idea of adopting a transcultural and integrative stance in relation to all of them.

The *UB* and integral theory have something to teach the other. One on hand, *The Urantia Book's* revelations about psychology, theology, evolution, history, angelology, and cosmology widen the outlook of integralists. Its teaching about the purported real nature of the atman (the Indwelling Spirit of God) and the evolution of an immortal soul is compatible with an integral understanding of selfhood, and can provide new depths to integral psychology.

For its part, integralism provides an advanced template for an updated cosmic spirituality based on today's latest advances in developmental psychology, integral health and medicine, evolutionary

---

[86] My essay, "The Cultural Dilemma of the *UB*" (see Evolving-Souls.org/cultural-dilemma), provides my speculations on why the revelation cannot easily find a home in any of the cultural formations on Earth at this time, with the possible exception of the integral worldview. However, the lack of a cultural home for the *UB* does not mean that individuals can't in the meantime appropriate the many riches of the text.

[87] Among the close colleagues of Wilber's whose work informs my research for this book are Allan Combs, Sean Esbjörn-Hargens, Dustin Diperna, and Mark Gafni. Most have been members of Wilber's Integral Institute.

theory, integral philosophic method, and consciousness studies, all of which occurred after the publication of the *UB*.[88] These new disciplines have been embraced by integral theorists, and I believe that Urantia students, if they are to keep current, need to embrace these new developments as well.[89] In particular, it would be especially helpful if Urantians made use of the culturally neutral language of today's developmental psychology, which integral theory very effectively employs in its descriptions of human growth. I attempt to do so in the remainder of this chapter—as one illustration of the benefit of using integral theory to assist in the exegesis of the Urantia Revelation.

Furthermore, just like the *UB*, the emerging integral worldview is super-interdisciplinary. And in addition to harvesting disciplines almost unknown at the time of the *UB* revelation, integral theory provides an advanced protocol and methodology for the integration of all of these disciples, which Wilber calls the *Integral Operating System* (IOS).[90] I cover the IOS in a rudimentary way in the next section. For a beginner's overview of Wilber's system as it relates to the themes of this book, please see Appendix C.

Ken Wilber's integralism arose from his own heroic and extensive cross-cultural research that sifted through the entire spectrum of partial truths of the world's great wisdom traditions and today's psychospiritual teachings. With the help of scientific psychology, the integral perspective has pruned many errors or limiting perspectives, giving us a model of human development that purports

---

[88] I would also include paranormal studies (such as NDEs) to this list, but to date this field has not been widely embraced by integralists or Urantians.

[89] It is worth adding here that the theory of *integral politics* advocates inclusive solutions of likely interest to Urantia students. Modernism gifted us with markets and the rule of law; postmodernism gave us more advanced arguments for justice, equality, tolerance, and pluralism; and integral politics points us to a dialectic that goes belong left and right factionalism toward a higher synthesis, including the advocacy of world unity through enforceable global law and planetary democracy—which the *UB* generally teaches as well. The *UB* goes even further, audaciously putting the advocacy for world federation in the mouth of Jesus (see 134:3), and providing a cosmological and futuristic context for global politics as well as "exopolitics" that integralists can learn from. See also in this connection the book I coauthored, *One World Democracy* (Origin Press, 2005).

[90] For those entirely new to Wilber's IOS, I recommend *The Integral Vision: A Very Short Introduction to the Revolutionary Integral Approach to Life, God, the Universe, and Everything* (Shambhala, 2007).

to transcend but include the best elements of them all. This is not unlike the work of the revelators of the Urantia text, who surveyed and analyzed the best human knowledge at the time that the revelation was compiled. They selected the most suitable human ideas and sources and wove entirely new revelatory facts and ideas around this humanly derived conceptual scaffolding.[91]

"Showing Up" with Multiple Perspectives

What is perhaps most compelling is the fact that Urantians and integralists can find common ground in regard to the basic assumptions of each system. Allow me to offer a brief comparison, beginning with a look at the fundamentals of the integral vision.

At its most basic, integralism entails a willingness to recognize three irreducible perspectives on the real. These are the domains of *self*, *culture*, and *nature*, and the disciplines related to them. To acknowledge and use these perspectives is to "show up"—a simplifying phrase that Wilber coined. These core elements of *that which is real* can be defined as follows:

- **Self:** the interior or *subjective* world of one's felt experience, the first-person point of view of the "I."

- **Culture**: the *intersubjective* or collective interior domain, the relational second-person perspective of "you" as well as the moral consciousness of the group—the "we."

- **Nature:** the exterior or *objective* world of nature—the material facts and natural systems studied by the sciences; this is the third-person perspective viewpoint of the "it" (or "its") domain.

According to Wilber, if one wants to "show up" in order to identify with the real, taking all of these perspectives to heart is essential. And if one wants to show up in a more scholarly way, one

---

[91] A case could be even be made that Ken Wilber's synthesis, plus contributions by his colleagues, fills in some of the vacuum left in our generation's worldview due to the stalled project of the dissemination of the Urantia Revelation in our time.

engages in an interdisciplinary fashion with science, philosophy, and religion—as exemplified, for example, in Wilber's classic *The Marriage of Sense and Soul* (1999).

In this connection, recall from chapter 1 that life reviews in NDEs are also multiperspectival, in that they display one's soul record as seen from the contrasting points of view of the self, significant others (including divine beings), and even the wider society. The heavenly world itself seems to be ratifying the idea that holistic and integrative awareness is essential to soul evolution.

Also in this regard, I find it helpful when Wilber renders the three irreducibles into his "Three Faces of God" concept: (1) God in first person refers to the actual phenomenological encounter with spirit, our own felt experience of mystical or ecstatic states of consciousness; (2) God in second person is traditionally defined as the "I-Thou" relationship; and (3) God in third person is often described as the divine "It," the "great web-of-life," or the evolving universe as a whole.

As noted in chapter 4, the Urantia Revelation also recognizes three reality domains as primordial, calling our relationship to them the fundamental forms of our God-given capacity for reality response. We noted that our response to the real is based on three core insights or cosmic intuitions that we are told are *inherent* in mind itself. "These scientific, moral, and spiritual insights, these cosmic responses, are innate. . . . The experience of living never fails to develop these three cosmic intuitions; they are constitutive in the self-consciousness of reflective thinking." [192.5])

The *UB* arranges this same triad in numerous edifying ways, as can be seen in this passage:

> There are just three elements in universal reality: fact, idea, and relation. The religious consciousness identifies these realities as science, philosophy, and truth. Philosophy would be inclined to view these activities as reason, wisdom, and faith— physical reality, intellectual reality, and spiritual reality. We are in the habit of designating these realities as thing, meaning, and value. [196:3.2]

Urantians can also find common ground with the integralists with respect to another crucial triad—the good, the true, and the beautiful. Wilber calls these the Big Three, while we earlier noted that the *UB* calls this trio *the comprehensible elements of Deity*. The *UB*, in fact, provides more than eighty references to this primal set of values, in what amounts to one of the most replete set of definitions of the Big Three to be found anywhere.[92] Here's one rendition I especially like:

> All truth—material, philosophic, or spiritual—is both beautiful and good. All real beauty—material art or spiritual symmetry—is both true and good. All genuine goodness—whether personal morality, social equity, or divine ministry—is equally true and beautiful. Health, sanity, and happiness are integrations of truth, beauty, and goodness as they are blended in human experience. Such levels of efficient living come about through the unification of energy systems, idea systems, and spirit systems. [2:7.11]

Assuming that you can accept this comparison as a general demonstration of an alignment of assumptions in the two systems, let's move on to the deeper meaning of the idea of *showing up*.

As a way of schematizing the primary elements of the real, Wilber took a momentous step that began with the publication in 1995 of his groundbreaking *Sex, Ecology, Spirituality*. The result was *integral perspectivism*—a methodology now used worldwide by thousands of thinkers and professionals in a myriad of settings. In fact, I have used this approach for two decades to help me better understand the spirituality of the Urantia Revelation.

The basic idea is as follows: We will want to enact each of the three elements of universal reality if we are to truly show up in our world. To facilitate putting this triad into action, Wilber resolves it into four fundamental perspectives on any situation, which have to

---

[92] Rick Warren, "84 Truth, Beauty and Goodness Quotes." See http://www.integral-world.net/warren1.html. This piece is a rare case of a Urantia student in dialogue with followers of Wilber.

do with either *the inside or the outside of the individual or the collective* on any given occasion.[93]

As we can see in the illustrations below, each of these four points of view subsists in its own domain. By blending these vantage points in our experience and in our research, we fully exercise our relationship to the three irreducible reality domains, thereby enhancing selfhood reality. Wilber's four primary perspectives are now known as his famous "four quadrants," shown in Figure 1.

	INTERIOR	EXTERIOR
INDIVIDUAL	**UPPER LEFT** I Intentional (subjective)	**UPPER RIGHT** IT Behavioral (objective)
COLLECTIVE	WE Cultural (intersubjective) **LOWER LEFT**	ITS social (interobjective) **LOWER RIGHT**

Here is a brief overview of Figure 1. We can perceive phenomena either by looking from the inside out—in a search for intentional experiences based on the felt values of the self (the upper left quadrant)—or by looking from the outside in, as we investigate individual facts with the help of the senses (upper right quadrant). We can take the standpoint of investigating the *systems* of external facts at hand (lower right quadrant) or else take on the collective aspect of the interior view of shared felt experiences—the perspective of human culture (bottom left quadrant). In short, any given

[93] We can go from three to four perspectives because the so-called objective exteriors in the right-hand quadrants, i.e., the verifiable facts of a situation, can be either singular or plural. For example, we can start with a singular artifact, such as an individual subway train (an "it"), but if we expand our scope we discover the network of "its" that comprise the subway *system*.

occasion has four perspectives: *either the inside or the outside of either the individual or the collective.*

In a similar fashion, the *UB* calls for us to assume an interior *and* an exterior view on any phenomenon—that is, to distinguish subjective experiences from the objective facts. Of course, when we do so, these observations will greatly diverge, since we are opening to the *felt experience* of spiritual realities (the interior view) at the same time that we are making an objective assessment of the material world (the "outside looking in" approach). So what does one do with this split? How do we get an integrative grasp of both as one? The revelators tell us that we *converge* the disparate truths found in each domain. This entails cultivating the crown jewel of a life of meaning, *philosophic awareness*, which yields true wisdom: "From outward, looking within, the universe may appear to be material; from within, looking out, the same universe appears to be wholly spiritual. Reason grows out of material awareness, faith out of spiritual awareness, **but through the mediation of a philosophy strengthened by revelation**, logic may confirm both the inward and the outward view, thereby effecting the stabilization of both science and religion." [103:7.6] My added emphasis points to the fact that revelation adds strength to the difficult work of using philosophic truth-perception to harmonize interior or exterior perspectives.

Surprising as it may sound, the *UB* depicts Jesus himself as a teacher of such an integrative philosophic awareness to his more advanced disciples. Jesus calls this approach to life "truth-coordination" and "wholeness of righteousness" in this unusual presentation to the apostles and a group of evangelists in Galilee (emphases mine):

> In all that you do, **become not one-sided and over-specialized**. . . . Consider the Greeks, who have a science without religion, while the Jews have a religion without science. And when men become thus misled into accepting a narrow and confused disintegration of truth, **their only hope of salvation is to become truth-co-ordinated**—converted. Let me emphatically state this eternal truth: If you, by truth co-ordination, **learn to exemplify in your lives this beautiful wholeness of righteousness**, your fellow men

will then seek after you that they may gain what you have so acquired. [155:1.4-5]

Wilber and the *UB* on "Growing Up"

Things become even more interesting when we realize that each of Wilber's quadrants *themselves* show development and evolution. Acknowledging the fact of growth in all domains is essential, of course, because in today's post-Darwinian world, we know that everything evolves—except, of course, that which is revealed to be transcendent to space and time.

All things, ideas, and relationships "show up" (or "tetra-arise," as the integralists say) in at least four dimensions or perspectives. But we can also observe that each domain, within its own space of evolving activity, progresses toward higher levels of complexity and consciousness. Especially when applied to individual persons (the upper left quadrant), Wilber and his colleagues call this the process of "growing up."

It turns out that we've already spent time with an example of growth within a single quadrant: the progression through traditionalism, modernism, and postmodernism discussed earlier in this chapter. This sequence of stages belongs in the lower left quadrant of the *collective interior*. But to maintain our focus on personal spirituality, let's correlate these cultural levels with the evolving stages of growth of *individuals* in the upper left quadrant, which tracks their felt experience of their own evolution to the highest stages of personal growth.

To illustrate, let's say you identify yourself as a member of the Baha'i Faith and you live in Tehran. Almost by definition, a typical Baha'i is culturally postmodern, yes? So now the question becomes: where does your cultural identification place you in terms of your personal progress? To answer this, you would look to the upper left quadrant to locate the *individual interior* correlate to the Baha'i cultural worldview as depicted in the bottom left zone.

Wilber's culturally neutral and generic terminology helps us out here: as individuals grow in their ability to include wider spheres of humanity in their awareness, they evolve from *egocentric*, to *ethnocentric*, to *worldcentric*. This sequence is a natural progression of consciousness, according to today's developmental psychologists. (One might also call these stages *preconventional*, *conventional*, and *postconventional*.)

Now, given that you're a Baha'i, we very likely can't describe you as an egocentric crime boss who is out for your own enrichment. Nor can we locate you as someone who is dominated by ethnocentric consciousness—for example, exclusively identified with being an ethnic Iranian. The "altitude" of your awareness (to use another Wilberian term) is also likely to be higher and more inclusive than the mentality of even a nationalist. For example, the worldview of a modernist Iranian businessman is probably nationalist, as it likely goes beyond ethnocentrism to embrace minority ethnic groups whom he sees as legitimate members of the nation (or neighboring nations) and equally worthy to do business with.

As a Baha'i, you are aware that your founding prophet, Baha'u'llah, taught his followers to be far more inclusive than mere nationalists. So you are multicultural and worldcentric, or at least you aspire to be. Your individual awareness is pluralistic and tolerant. You are open to the truths of all the cultures and religions of the world and, because of your religious faith, you aim to bring peace and harmony to them all. Your faith even advocates reforming the United Nations to create a democratic world government.

Growing up to such higher levels, it turns out, can occur on its own, with or without explicit beliefs about spirituality. At first, we start out as egocentric children. But if we receive a decent modern education, we naturally progress from ethnocentric to nationalistic to worldcentric as we attain more advanced awareness of the greater realities of cultures around the world. Of course, when we achieve worldcentric status in our thinking, our soul-making will be all the more advanced.

Based on sociological research by other colleagues, Wilber points to a profound modification that usually occurs at the worldcentric stage. Individuals at that stage can suddenly move beyond the assumptions of the postmodern stage to become *post-postmodern*. The data shows that these people make a great leap to the stage of *integral consciousness*, which aims to transcend yet include the best values of *all* previous cultural levels (traditional, modern, and postmodern). Such people no longer see their particular cultural level as the only valid one; they realize that each level of the spiral of cultural progress has activated essential values that contribute something vital for all subsequent levels. The entire spiral of the evolution of consciousness begins to occupy and function *within their own being*. They honor and learn from all that has come before.

We can add still more advanced stages beyond worldcentric/ integral if we include awareness of human life on off-planet cultures.[94] If we operate at this even more advanced level, we are *universe citizens who practice cosmic spirituality* based on universal compassion, just like some of our extraterrestrial counterparts, who are actually described in the *UB*. (See, for example, Paper 72, "Government on a Neighboring Planet" and especially "The Spheres of Light and Life," Paper 55.) Expanding our ethical awareness to include the millions of inhabited planets in the local universe (and beyond) was the prophetic stance of the Urantia Revelation decades before the *Star Trek* series and today's movement for UFO disclosure. By the way, Wilber makes general reference to universe-centric awareness with his coined term *kosmocentric*.[95]

Let's not forget that there are other perspectives that are pertinent to our example. The lower right quadrant has to do with the social system in which one happens to be embedded. If you are a Baha'i in Iran, where this religion is discouraged and often persecuted, you will have a different growth path than that of a Baha'i living in Chicago, for obvious reasons. In each case, you can locate

---

[94] At John 10:16 Jesus said, "I have other sheep, too, in another fold. I must bring them also." Christians correctly infer that this refers to Gentiles as well as Jews, but the *UB* makes clear that Jesus is referring to citizens of other planets in the local universe of his own creation. At 165:2.9 the *UB* offers this restatement by Jesus: "But I have many other sheep not of this fold, and these words are true not only of this world. These other sheep also hear and know my voice, and I have promised the Father that they shall all be brought into one fold, one brotherhood of the sons of God. And then shall you all know the voice of one shepherd, the true shepherd, and shall all acknowledge the fatherhood of God."

[95] This term has also been used by integralists to refer to one's identification with all of reality or with all sentient beings in all worlds, or the ability to tap into the field of collective consciousness.

where the evolutionary level of the social, economic, and political system you are embedded in might fall in a detailed lower right quadrant chart (which can be viewed online). These are the *collective exterior* elements of your life, and they are also essential. These aspects of social infrastructure don't determine your attainments in the left quadrants, but they certainly condition your opportunities to evolve and your pace of growth. And finally, we must also have a discussion of the religiocultural components that condition your awareness, which can be mapped in the lower left quadrant.

All that said, we now thank you, Baha'i friend, as we move on to other adventures in integral analysis and the *UB*. For the question now arises, where might the *UB*'s depiction of soul evolution fit into this scheme of quadrants that evolve, especially the upper left? This brings us to a brief discussion of the different *lines of development* and especially to the *integral psychograph*.

The Lines of Human Development

In chapter 4 I introduced the *UB*'s seven levels of circle-making, which are also referred to by the slightly daunting phrase "self-perfecting." You'll recall that attaining your circles entails *progress of the totality of the self* as you slowly ascend (in the afterlife as well as in this life) toward the great goal of God Fusion. Much more research is needed here, but let's make a stab at tracing how this Urantia-based conception of *cosmic individuation* might fit into Ken Wilber's map, keeping in mind that I follow up on these issues in Part IV of this book.

You cannot fuse with the divine source of reality if your personal growth and your identifications are less than reality-centric—or lopsided, to put it colloquially. To enter into an irrevocable union with the source of Allness, you need to have engaged with *all* the elements of selfhood progression and thereby achieve a sublime symmetry in your personal development. In Wilber's terms, you must have at least shown up as a conscious participant in each of the four perspectives or quadrants, and you will need to have been fully engaged with the Big Three values of truth, beauty, and goodness as you achieve higher levels of consciousness in the upper left quadrant.

In the *UB*'s simplest terms, you must have grown up with regard to the two great dimensions of soul growth, the quantitative and the qualitative. Doing so prepares you for attaining the highest circle (the first psychic circle), which allows *direct and reliable communication with the Indwelling Spirit of God*, as you will recall from chapter 4. We noted there that Jesus is depicted in the *UB* as the ideal model of this sort of growth in all of these respects, having ascended to this status due to his unequaled faith as well as his seasoned wisdom. That's why the text often describes Jesus as a unified person.

> It is altogether possible for every mortal believer to develop a strong and unified personality along the perfected lines of the Jesus personality. The unique feature of the Master's personality was not so much its perfection as its symmetry, its exquisite and balanced unification. . . . Jesus was the perfectly unified human personality.

The section where this statement can be found, "The Acme of Religious Living" (see 100:7), goes on to provide a long list of his qualities that illustrate his personality unification and unprecedented balance of virtues. I paraphrase some of these here:

> Jesus was . . . surcharged with enthusiasm, but never fanatical . . . emotionally active but never flighty . . . imaginative but always practical . . . courageous but never reckless . . . prudent but never cowardly . . . sympathetic but not sentimental . . . unique but not eccentric . . . pious but not sanctimonious . . . generous, but never wasteful . . . candid but always kind . . . courageous but never foolhardy.

With that overview of the evolutionary goal of those who follow Jesus, let's break these notions down a little more to see what more we can learn about circle-making and soul-making in terms of integral theory.

As a first step, I'll review the findings of today's academic research community with regard to human development, leaning, as we go, on Ken Wilber's summary of this vast subject. During the early decades of work in human development theory, various groups of relatively isolated researchers identified what they believed to be the exclusive indicators of the stages of adult maturation. For example, the pioneering French psychologist Jean Piaget thought that these stages had to do with improved *cognition*. A contrasting approach measured human development in terms of the growth of *faith*—that being the life work of James Fowler, the author of *Stages of Faith* noted earlier. Another important inquiry related to the ascending levels of value identification, an approach that happens to correlate directly to the three stages of cultural evolution that we already located in the lower left quadrant. This trend was led by Claire Graves, and was later refined especially by Don Beck, coauthor with Christopher Cowan of the seminal work *Spiral Dynamics* (1996 and 2005). And researchers have isolated still other, more particular types of intelligence that undergo growth and maturation. For example, you've likely heard of *emotional intelligence* (Daniel Goleman) and *moral intelligence* (Lawrence Kohlberg). Today we have data on more than a dozen human developmental processes that include kinesthetic, musical, mathematical, and aesthetic lines of intelligence. Figure 2 below depicts a typical selection of key lines in the upper left quadrant.

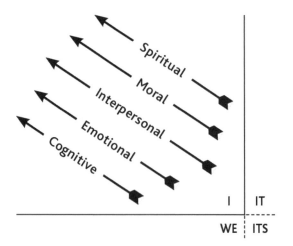

A further refinement of this chart depicts key lines in terms of our three cultural levels, which in effect maps the upper left (the interior of the individual) to the lower left quadrant (the interior of the collective). Figure 3 is known as an *integral psychograph*.

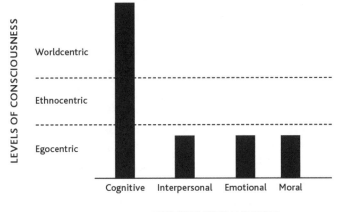

MULTIPLE INTELLIGENCES

Entire books have been written on the lines of development, notably *Multiple Intelligences* (2006) by Harvard professor Howard Gardner. Fortunately for us, Wilber and his associates have resolved this flowering of research into a few major lines that seem to organize all the others. One of the most prominent of these, it turns out, is the *cognitive line*—which relates logically to all other lines by its very nature (and not because many people involved with this work are overly cognitive types, as portrayed in the above chart).

Common sense tells us that you must actually be *aware* of something in order to engage with it along any one of the lines of intelligence. For example, you can't grow in musical intelligence unless you expand your basic knowledge about things musical by mastering the skill of reading music notation, learning about the various genres, studying the great composers, attending live performances, and so on. As Wilber puts it, "You have to be aware of something in order to act on it, feel it, identify with it, or need it. . . . Cognition delivers the phenomena with which the other lines operate."[96]

---

[96] *Integral Spirituality: A Startling New Role for Religion in the Modern and Postmodern World* (Integral Books/Shambhala, 2006), p.65

The *UB* conception, which precedes this research by half a century, ratifies the centrality of the cognitive line as well. For instance, recall our two key axes of self-perfecting: (1) qualitative growth in the ability to feel values—or the faith-discernment of the presence of God who is the source of all value, and (2) comprehension of meanings—growth in our cognitive understanding of the meaning of our experiences, which in the first place requires that we are *paying attention to what is arising in our experience.* This second axis, the line of quantitative soul growth, generally maps into Wilber's cognitive line. Progress on this line requires having numerous life challenges that force us to inquire, reflect, and *think*.

Two ordinary examples: A person might say to himself, "My wife seems to be acting distant from me this weekend—what can that possibly mean? What am I missing in our relationship?" Another may ask, "My boss insists that I perform tasks for which I have no training—how will I get these things done? And why am I even working for a company that makes such unfair demands?"

Recognizing and then solving such perplexing problems obviously requires the exercise of thought. So, while both of our axes (feeling and thinking) are essential to balanced growth, it turns out that cognition is almost always in the lead. For if we don't become cognitively aware of the dilemma we are facing in the first place, it's all moot; and yet, having at least identified the problem cognitively, if we fail to think through the challenge it poses and face it emotionally, we certainly can't exercise profound feelings of faith in relation to it. How much sense does it make to pray for the divine will if we haven't taken the time to understand the issues at hand before beginning to pray?[97] This distinction may explain an enigmatic statement in the *UB* that I have puzzled over for decades: "It is your *thoughts*, not our feelings, that lead you Godward" [101:1.3].

Some of us tend to admire simple-minded people (or politicians) who are oblivious to advanced meanings but who "trust their

---

[97] In this connection, see the powerful section in the *UB* called "Conditions of Effective Prayer" at 91:9. The first two of these "laws of prevailing petitions" are:
"1. You must qualify as a potent prayer by sincerely and courageously facing the problems of universe reality. You must possess cosmic stamina.
2. You must have honestly exhausted the human capacity for human adjustment. You must have been industrious."

instincts." We may even romanticize them—take the figure of Forrest Gump, for example, the simpleton who had his heart in the right place. On the other hand, powerful intellectuals may be utterly lacking in a basic feeling for humanitarian values, such as the men in the Pentagon who cooked up the Vietnam War. Both types miss the mark because they are cognitively deficient. Gump represents the sentimental fantasy that deep reflection, rigorous study, and worldly experience aren't necessary for success in life. And, war planners and policy wonks may have a imposing grasp of weaponry, military history, battlefield tactics, and power politics, but their compartmentalized thinking prevents any wider understanding of the issues at hand—which if properly identified and reflected upon would be certain to arouse moral feelings and lead to a crisis of faith.

Allow me to illustrate this further with the metaphor of eyesight. By meditating with "one eye single to the glory of God" (a phrase used in the *UB*), we can develop a rich interior feeling for higher values. But depth of feeling does not directly translate into solutions to the complex problems of daily life; such determinations require far-reaching practical experience and socialization, which yield the ability to think broadly and reflect deeply to solve the problems of the hour in the most practical way. Competent thinking of this sort requires a different kind of vision—the ability to see with the eyes of the mind, followed by the openness required to feel crucial values with the "eyes of the heart."

But in the final analysis we need to see with *both* eyes—the eye of feeling as well as the eye of cognition. And while employing such stereoscopic depth-vision, we can exercise a willingness to act that blends them both in soul-making decisions.

Which Line of Growth Is Central in Human Development?

Focusing in this way on the two axes of growth and their harmonious coevolution gives us a good start, but which line, if any, should be our greatest concern? In highlighting the cognitive line, Wilber points out that cognition is necessary but not sufficient to explain and motivate human growth. Researchers need to identify a line, he argues, that is even more universal than cognition, preferably one that does not refer to only one particular human faculty, such as thinking or feeling. And I believe that the revelators would agree with Wilber's assessment.

Wilber first tackled this issue in his *Integral Psychology* (2001), where he puts the "self" or "self-sense" line at the center of human development. This line has everything to do with the cultural identifications we earlier discussed, those cherished ideas and feelings that provide, more or less unconsciously, our immediate answer to the core question, Who am I? Infants see themselves as their body; teens identify or merge with their peer group. As we mature, we find that we widen the scope of our consideration and care. We go on to self-identify with our ethnicity, then with our nation, and then with the whole world, as shown in our Baha'i example.

Of course, the process of disidentifying with our previous level of self-awareness is always difficult, which is why so many remain stuck at their current stage of growth. Indeed, if we do find the courage to let go of our previous stage, the transition we face could entail feelings of anguish that some might call an ego death. Yet, in healthy human development, our faith is richly rewarded; we always find that a new "I" emerges on the other side of such a dark night of the soul. In this progression, we are not extinguishing ego-identifications entirely; we are simply engaging with more advanced and inclusive identifications.[98]

Impressive research has shown that one activity in particular can accelerate progress most effectively along Wilber's self-line: the noble endeavor of achieving deeper (or higher) states of consciousness, especially through meditation. These experiences are critical because in such altered states we energetically let go of our subjective identifications. What was once an experience felt from the inside out now becomes an *object* of present awareness that is

---

[98] Carl Jung pointed out that such a progression actually strengthens the ego and prepares it for the unifying and balanced identification with what he called the Self. I should add that engaging in *shadow work* is also a crucial component of this process of letting go and engaging in more inclusive identifications. It is my great hope that the understanding of psychopathology provided by integrally informed clinicians will become an essential enhancement to the growth path described in the *UB*. The Urantia Revelation only briefly alludes to such issues.

observed, as it were, from the outside looking in. We now have space around this previous worldview and its many fascinations and are free of its exclusive hold on us. I'll return in chapter 9 to this crucial idea of waking up to higher states of consciousness.

In his later thought on this issue, Wilber subtly changes his emphasis. He focuses instead on consciousness itself, harvesting the central Buddhist insight that consciousness should be defined as "openness" or "emptiness." Today Wilber argues that the most inclusive and important line is consciousness alone, because consciousness or awareness is the space in which all identifications and all other lines can arise. Consciousness as such has no content (according to Buddhist psychology at least), so the other lines of development can be observed to rise and fall as consciousness rises and falls—that is, as the clearing or the inner capacity for awareness-in-general opens or closes.

Wilber hasn't been called "the Einstein of consciousness" for no reason. But if he is not right, if consciousness is *not* the organizing vehicle for all the other lines of intelligence, what characteristic might play this role to instead?

To get at the *UB*'s possible answer, let's revisit the quantitative or cognitive line that I previously defined as *the growth of seasoned wisdom through wide-ranging life experience*. Growing up to become wise surely necessitates discriminating awareness, but one can agree with Wilber that neither basic cognition nor the refinements of feeling that results from profound thinking is sufficient to answer the question of what constitutes the central line of growth. However, because of the *UB*'s revelation of the nature of personhood—which is the subject of our next chapter—*Urantia Book* students are pointed in a different direction from that favored by Wilber.

The Urantia text (as well as common sense) tells us that growing in wisdom also entails *doing things*—the living experience of making decisions, acting on them, and then coping with the consequences. The *UB* coins two phrases to refer to this sort of action-oriented decisiveness: "decision-action" and "choice-experience."

In daily life, we think about and feel into what is relevant and worth acting upon; and we can support our conclusions by drawing on religious faith. But we must also *carry out* decisions based on such explorations. We must *do* something. And unfortunately (or perhaps fortunately for the sake of soul-making), all of this personal reflection—if it is truly sincere—may point to some rather risky choices for action. Engaging in such decision-action will, in turn, lead to the necessity of making follow-up decisions that will require mustering a new round of reflection on thoughts and feelings. And so it goes. Such is the nature of choice-experience. For example, think of Jesus's decision to rout the moneychangers from of the Temple, after which he dealt with a dramatic aftermath that included his painful night of prayerful deliberation in the Garden of Gethsemane a few days later.

In our personal lives, we not only *decide* to buy a house or raise a child, we must also muster the fortitude to engage in all of the subsequent decisions and actions that accomplish such serious commitments. In this light, I'd now like to suggest a third line not yet discussed: *the willingness to act*, or simply, *the line of will*.

Allow me to illustrate this further with a theological metaphor. In the vertical dimension of our relationship to the divine, our growing faith leads us to increasingly advanced levels of God-consciousness. But we can (and must) also experience a horizontal connection to the divine that is implicit in all of this depth of feeling or thinking. This aspect of our relationship to divine reality involves the willingness to carry out steadfast decision-actions in the material world based on our newfound convictions. And here is the crux: as uniquely revealed in the Urantia Revelation, this line of willing and acting directly measures our relationship to *evolutionary Deity*. A crucial passage from Paper 110 makes the point:

> The motivation of faith makes experiential the full realization of man's sonship with God, but **action, completion of decisions, is essential** to the evolutionary attainment of consciousness of progressive kinship with the *cosmic actuality* of the Supreme Being. Faith transmutes potentials to actuals in the spiritual world, but potentials become actuals in the finite realms of the Supreme only by and through the realization of choice-experience. [110:6.17]

We are here on Earth to actualize cosmic potentials through action—not just feel and think our way to self-realization. We were placed here to act on our convictions and thereby perfect the evolving universe, doing so through love, service, and creativity. And so I affirm that it is justifiable to add the faculty of will as a third line.

Does that mean that willingness to act is the central line of cosmic individuation? Should *will* be our main concern in soul-making and self-perfecting? In a teaching presented near the end of his ministry to his apostles and chief disciples, Jesus declared that "will is the determining factor" in our experience. This statement is listed as one of the "five cardinal features of the gospel of the kingdom" [see 170:4]. On balance, however, I believe that a wider understanding of the *UB* will arrive at the conclusion that *the trio of willing, thinking, and feeling* are essential and interdependent components; each is of equal import for personality unification.[99]

One indicator that brings me to this conclusion is the *UB*'s description of the first stage of the afterlife, which states that all ascenders will attend "the schools of thinking, the schools of feeling, and the schools of doing." Also, at higher stages in the ascent, Paradise pilgrims "enter the schools of philosophy, divinity, and pure spirituality." In regard to the lessons in these schools, the text further admonishes, "Those things which you might have learned on earth, but which you failed to learn, must be acquired under the tutelage of [heavenly teachers]. There are no royal roads, short cuts, or easy paths to Paradise. Irrespective of the individual variations of the route, you master the lessons of one sphere before you proceed to another; at least this is true after you once leave the world of your nativity." [48:5.6-7]

In this connection, you will recall that circle-making is said to be proportional to *personality reality*—the equivalent of personality

---

[99] Immanuel Kant worked with the categories of feeling, thought, and will, and esoteric philosopher Rudolph Steiner especially highlighted this triad in his writings and made it central in the pedagogy of his Waldorf Schools. Steiner wrote, "The three fundamental forces of the soul [are] willing, feeling, and thinking. . . . The success anticipated from a right education or fitting instruction is based upon the presumption that a connection between thinking, feeling, and willing, corresponding to human nature, can be established in the pupil." Rudolf Steiner, *Knowledge of the Higher Worlds and Its Attainment* (Anthroposophic Press, 1947), p. 215.

unification. To restate the quote from chapter 4: "The degree of selfhood reality . . . is directly determined by circle conquest. Persons become more real as they ascend from the seventh to the first level of mortal existence."

Our level of selfhood reality, in other words, is the yardstick of our cosmic circle achievement, and we also know that such achievement has to do with mobilizing the many powers of the human self to become *one balanced and unified power*. And so, based on my inaugural research, it seems clear that while willingness to act is a crucial line in the cosmic spirituality of the Urantia Revelation, it is not the central line. Feeling, thinking, and willing are *all* essential. Indeed, with every corner we turn, these three faculties of the self always rise together. Further, I surmise that *our circle-making level cannot rise higher than the level of most deficient line*.

Accordingly, I believe that in response to Wilber's illuminating theory, a *UB*-based approach would designate the central line as *the line of circle attainment*—the *composite* of all the elements of selfhood reality. Figure 4 below depicts a person whose highest line (cognition) is at circle 1, while his lowest line (will) is at circle 3. This person can be no more than a level 3 achiever at this point in development. In other words, all of his or her lines have achieved level 3, whereas their growth beyond that level is uneven. Their personality unification is currently consolidated at the third circle, and more growth in the feeling and will lines will be required for stabilizing as a first circler.

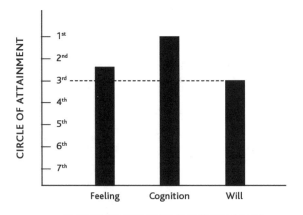

COSMIC INDIVIDUATION PSYCHOGRAPH

In more practical terms, it's best not to be an overly pious or sentimental person, a nerdy intellectual, or a hyperactive doer if you intend to attain true maturation according to the Urantia Revelation. Remember: "There are no royal roads, short cuts, or easy paths to Paradise." If you are unbalanced in any of the virtues, you will have just that much remedial work to do (in the afterlife if not before). You will need to scale up your weak axis to bring the short lines up to par with the others—that is, if you want to "become perfect as your Father in heaven is perfect."

In the final analysis, our degree of cosmic individuation depends not on consciousness alone but instead reflects the degree of personality reality that we achieve. And that leads us directly to "The Nature of Personality Reality," the first chapter of Part IV. Then I return to further consideration of the lines of thinking, feeling, and willing in chapter 9, "The Gift of the Divine Indwelling."

PART IV

Foundations of
Cosmic Spirituality

The Nature of Personality Reality

Always remember that you are absolutely unique.
Just like everyone else.
— *Margaret Mead*

The Urantia Revelation greatly expands the definition of what it means to be a person, revealing for the first time new rights, powers, and attributes of personality that are available to us on three levels: first, the prerogatives of personhood that we exercise as we evolve an immortal soul; second, the inherent legal and political rights and duties that belong to each person as a planetary citizen; and, finally, and perhaps most important, the cosmic level of personality expression—the right to an afterlife in which we unfold and perfect our personalities as cosmic citizens on the journey to Paradise.

At the level of the individual, the *UB* establishes each human personality as infinitely unique and directly sourced from the Father-Infinite, who confers upon each of us the God-like powers of free will and self-awareness. Because all persons are sourced from the Absolute Person, we are each loved unfathomably throughout our journey into eternity. This love manifests through the vehicle of the sublime partnership with our Thought Adjuster, a pure fragment of true God; the angelic ministers who catalyze our soul growth; and the Paradise beings who incarnate, sometimes at the risk of their own lives, to teach us higher truth. Personality is the greatest of all gifts, but these three complemental ministries make the original gift of personhood more meaningful and valuable.

At the planetary level, the *UB* exalts the supreme value of the individual by calling on us to expand our rights beyond the level of citizenship in a nation. It boldly advocates that humanity adopt a global bill of rights, a representative world legislature elected by the world's people, and individual accountability before global law.[100]

At the universe level, the Urantia Revelation enhances the definition of what it means to be person by proclaiming *our universal right to an eternal life* in the grand cosmos, supported by the provision of vast resources for education, socialization, and personal advancement along the way. Assets are generously supplied that enable us to perfect ourselves in our slow ascension through the superuniverse of our origin. Much later, we traverse the central universe, stand ecstatically in the literal Paradise presence of our Creator, and embark on cosmic adventures even beyond that. Along with such exalted privileges, we are individually accountable to this larger universe. It is our duty at each step to contribute to the growth of evolutionary Deity (the Supreme Being) as cosmic citizens, and ultimately it is our privilege to offer a life of endless service in other universes, as will be discussed in the coming chapters.

The Origin of the Idea of Personality in the West

For the sake of gaining perspective on the *UB*'s revelations about the nature of personality reality, let's start this inquiry with brief look at the earliest sources of the idea of personality in the West. At Exodus 3:14 we meet the mysterious Hebrew God who declares himself to Moses in a rather dramatic way. Moses asks for his name, and God answers, "I Am Who I Am. This is what you are to say to the Israelites: *I Am* has sent me to you." Not an easy assignment for old Moses! But it is not an exaggeration to say that his

---

[100] See Paper 134, section 3: "The Urmia Lectures."

obedience to Jahweh's commandment made possible our modern ideas of personhood.

Clearly, this newly announced Hebrew God was *relational*. He displayed unmistakable personal qualities. He took the initiative with Moses. He entered into a give-and-take dialogue and even used a show of fire to get his point across. Further, Jahweh's phrase "I Am Who I Am" conveyed that he was a self-aware and self-caused being, not a mere abstraction or metaphysical principle. As the Hebrews were soon to learn, this independent and powerful God had *feelings and ideas and plans*. He had will and intention. He was a living and personal Creator who communicated with his people through his prophets.

If Jahweh was their true God, then who were the Hebrews? They, as God's own people, could rightly envision themselves as thinking, feeling, and choosing persons—each one a mini *I Am*. Every one of God's people was a true individual in God's eyes; they were the offspring of the original *I Am*, who made man "in our image and likeness" (Genesis 1:26). And this notion later became a bedrock doctrine of Christianity.

Similar ideas had emerged in other ancient venues, especially in Greek philosophy. In democratic political traditions based on principles that go back to ancient Greece and Rome and that draw from the Old Testament, the status of personhood conferred certain inalienable rights on citizens who could now be described as free and sovereign individuals. Slaves were the exception because they were not defined as persons under ancient law, but Christian thinkers later arrived at a splendid concept of personhood that eventually led to the abolition of slavery. We are *all* the children of a loving Father, and each one of us is precious—all the more so because God loved us enough to incarnate as one of us. "There is neither Jew nor Gentile, neither slave nor free, nor is there male and female, for you are all one in Christ Jesus." (Galatians 3:28)

In ancient and medieval times, the dignity of personhood and the rights of citizenship also entailed duties to the state. These rights and duties were clearly spelled out at first in Roman law. They were later codified by modern democracies in their constitutions and elevated to even higher status in the United Nations Declaration of Human Rights in 1948.

The Riddle of Personhood—Ancient and Modern

The revolutionary teachings of the *UB* arrived with barely a whisper in 1955, unknown and unacknowledged in a world swirling in doubt and turmoil about the dignity of personhood.

Communism and fascism had been built upon a critique of individualism and a frontal attack on the classical ideal of the free, sovereign, and rational self that is endowed with inherent rights by God; the state—the collective of all the people—was the locus of genuine rights. Nietzsche and his followers declared that the Western idea of self was a fictional construct, buffeted about by the arbitrary conventions of language and culture—seminal ideas that later became the foundations of postmodernism. Freud and Jung depicted the personal ego, the conscious self, as a small boat on the vast ocean of the unconscious that could capsize as a result of stress or trauma.

A generation later, transpersonal psychologists and New Age thinkers influenced by Eastern religion taught that the belief in a separate self was a sign of "negative ego" and a source of pain and conflict. The impressive findings of neuroscience in the past few decades led scientists and philosophers to deny the ontological or even the psychological reality of the personal self, instead reducing our thoughts, feelings, and choices to mere biochemical operations of the material brain.

Clearly, the idea of personhood is in trouble today—both as a concept and in terms of the protection of human rights on the world stage. But long before the modern turn to the idea of a fragmentary or fictional self, or a "protean self," the idea of the insubstantiality of selfhood already had a distinguished pedigree in the venerable teachings of classical Buddhism.

The earliest texts of the Theravadan school of Buddhism in particular negate the idea that we are each uniquely personal beings, calling this idea the primary source of *dukkha* (dissatisfaction and suffering). The current Dalai Lama often restates this classical view, which is that that *our belief in an independent self is the root cause of all suffering.* He has even embraced the findings of neuroscience to support the Buddhist notion of the emptiness of ego-bound selfhood.

What we believe to be the self, says Buddhist psychology, is merely an aggregation of ever-changing attributes, such as sensations, perceptions, wishes, and shifting states of awareness called *skandhas.* Such mental events may appear to have unity, but on closer inspection reveal no stable organizing center or enduring continuity of consciousness. This disquieting observation—this idea that the self or soul lacks any cohesive quality—has its own lineage in the modern West, represented, for example, by the writings of the eighteenth-century skeptical Western philosopher David Hume. Hume famously argued in his "bundle theory of personal identity" that if we pay attention to our raw experience, we can readily perceive the lack of unity of selfhood in our ordinary daily life.

Of course, many of us chafe at such radical claims. We insist on our "me-ness" as a matter of common sense, and we prefer to leave it at that. Yet the great mystical traditions persist in asking: just where or how is this sense of "I" or "me" to be located?

The Buddhists had a firm answer. Their disciplined methods of introspection practiced over several thousand years provide no direct evidence of any enduring artifact of selfhood. The Buddhist and other nondual schools teach that a quality of awareness (or self-awareness, as with the so-called witness) does seem to abide *behind* the typical mental parade of thoughts, feelings, and images. But on even closer inspection, the practitioner discovers that this subjective awareness, when fully deconstructed in deep meditation, is empty and featureless, as we noted in the last chapter.

Ah, but we in the West—we hold out hope for an identity we can do business with in practical life. Most of us no longer believe in traditional Christianity but feel there must be some feature of the self that stands for the biblical "I am," something familiar that can provide a comfortable feeling of constancy amid the flux. So we've come up with answers such as these in modern times: "I am an immaterial thinking self" (René Descartes, eighteenth century). Or "I am my feeling heart!" (Romantic poets, nineteenth century). And "I am a coherent set of electrochemical transactions in my brain" (the materialists of today).

I submit that none of these depictions of the self is stable and reliable across time, not even in one twenty-four-hour cycle—and especially not if we add to the equation our nightly surrender of selfhood to the dark world of dreams and deep, featureless sleep.

Can it be that devoted Buddhist meditation (and other forms of mysticism) has revealed the ultimate truth of the insubstantiality and impermanence of the self?

In the end, even Buddhism does not go there. As it grew in sophistication, later schools concluded that Buddha did not exactly hold to a settled doctrine of the no-self. Further, he did not respond to other crucial questions, such as whether there is an afterlife or if the universe is eternal. He merely denied that such questions could be usefully answered on psychological grounds, *if your goal is to end dukkha*. These issues are imponderable and indeterminate, he declared. To debate them is beside the point. The Buddha would say: "O monks, do not brood over such views. Such brooding, O monks, is senseless."[101]

So, which is true? The adamantine "I am"—the old Christian, Hebraic, and Hellenistic idea that we are unique and independent individuals with singular rights and duties, along with its many secularized renditions in the modern era? Instead, must we overcome any sense of separate selfhood through a quest for impersonal enlightenment, as taught in many mystical schools? Or might there be a third option: Buddha's teaching that to concern ourselves about this issue would be a distraction from the path to enlightenment, because the essence of personhood is unfathomable?

According to the Urantia Revelation, humans and even divine beings lack the cognitive capacity to penetrate this cosmic riddle. We can make observations about human behavior, but the fundamental nature of personality is unknowable unless and until clues about its reality are somehow revealed to us in a way we can understand or experience. Indeed, epochal revelation from above is required, such as the incarnation of a divine being or a gift like *The Urantia Papers*.

---

[101] This discussion especially draws from "The Atman and Its Negation: A Conceptual and Chronological Analysis of Early Buddhist Thought" by Alexander Wynne, Journal of the International Association of Buddhist Studies (vol. 33, pp. 103–171).

According to Christianity, Jesus was and is the living revelation of authentic selfhood, the very icon of personhood. This traditional Christian understanding of Jesus's divine personality (the branch of theology called Christology) is greatly clarified in *The Urantia Book*. And as far as I am aware, the Urantia text also goes beyond any previous conception of personhood in *any* category of human thought—including theology, philosophy, or psychology—laying out many heretofore unknown aspects of the mystery of personality in Paper 112, "Personality Survival."[102] In addition, the theology and cosmology provided in Parts I and II of the *UB* include an original philosophic teaching about the divine source and nature of personhood, to which we now turn.

Personality as Host, Unifier, and Systematizer

So what *is* human personality—even divine personality—to the extent that we can grasp it in this life with the help of revelation? According to the *UB*, human personhood is *gifted by divine fiat upon each individual*. This endowment confers powers of reflective awareness, self-determination, creative consciousness, relative free will, and the capacity for cosmic insight.

We also read that personality, in each instance, is both *utterly unique* as well as an *unchanging reality*, as declared in these imposing statements:

> Throughout all successive ages and stages of evolutionary growth, there is **one part of you that remains absolutely unaltered, and that is personality—permanence in the presence of change**. [112:0.1]
>
> **Personality is that part of any individual which enables us to recognize and positively identify that person as the one we have previously known**, no matter how much he may have changed because of the modification of the vehicle of expression and manifestation of his personality. [16:8:4]

---

[102] This unique Paper, whose rich content is in my opinion worthy of years of study, has no known human sources of the sort that are discussed in the Special Supplement at the end of this book. See Section 3 of the Supplement, "The Human Sources of the *UB*."

Personality is unique, absolutely unique: It is unique in time and space; it is unique in eternity and on Paradise; it is unique when bestowed — there are no duplicates; it is unique during every moment of existence. [112:0.12]

These strong statements seem to confirm our Western bias in favor of the independent and autonomous self, including even the old biblical notion of the "I am" created in the image of God. On closer inspection, however, we find that the *UB*'s full depiction of personality is much broader and deeper—and also richly paradoxical.

Personhood is stated to be "unique in eternity." But we soon come across this disconcerting statement, which declares that *personality has no identity*: "Personality, while devoid of identity, can unify the identity of any living energy system." [112:0.7]

How can both of these be true? How can something that is utterly unique have no specific identity?

Can it be that personality "holds the space" so that a *provisional* identity may appear and evolve as we make our freewill choices? Might it also be possible that, in so doing, our unique personality *conditions* the mode of manifestation of our transient identity in any one moment—doing so behind the scenes but always with a consistency that never changes? And how might this description comport with Ken Wilber's self-line that we encountered in the last chapter?

Try on this thought experiment: There's that consistent *something* about you. Those who feel its presence as something precious and unusual are attracted to it, so they come closer to you. The closer they approach and the more they get to know your unique and unchanging qualities, the more likely that they will come to truly love you. And behold—you now have a spouse or a loyal best friend! But things can now change drastically. As your relationship develops, your psychological identifications are (ideally at least) moving on an upward path. You are growing from ego-centrism toward soul identification, and onward to more advanced levels of personality reality. And so also is your spouse or best friend, we would hope.

But what happens now to that *something special* about you? I submit that the cosmic task of your personality is to provide an unchanging container, a sacred space, in which your identity can evolve according to your life choices while still *remaining recognizable* to those who know you today. I hypothesize that your personality can impart a certain unchanging flavor or a consistent look and feel in each edition of your identity that emerges over time. Otherwise, how would your loved ones keep track of you as the wonderful and quirky you they have loved in the past?

Personality may not be the *determiner* of your identity or your psychological identifications, but it is the *unifier* of the ingredients that comprise your ever-changing identity. Consider this statement:

> But the **concept of the personality as the meaning of the whole of the living and functioning creature means much more than the integration of relationships; it signifies the** *unification* **of all factors** of reality as well as co-ordination of relationships. Relationships exist between two objects, but three or more objects eventuate a *system*, and such a system is much more than just an enlarged or complex relationship. This distinction is vital, for **in a cosmic system the individual members are not connected with each other except in relation to the whole and through the individuality of the whole.** [112:1.17]

Personality, it would seem, is a cosmic systemizer. Its essence is transcendent and unchanging, yet it dynamically unifies the constituent parts of the evolving self. It harmonizes the ever-changing elements of the contingent self (that is, our body, mind, and soul) by updating their energetic configurations on the fly. Truly, your personality *is* your self-system. And it is like an operating system that never needs to be updated. As a divine fractal bestowed from the highest source, it always and without error provides the same superb functionality, even while remaining both unique and *self-similar*.[103]

---

[103] Paradoxes abound here, of course, and it should be made clear that the *UB* only implies the fractal nature of personality. In fractal theory, if the replication is exactly the same at every scale, it is called a self-similar pattern. I think of personalities as identical

Personality does its level best to bring coherence to our very partial identifications, our many imperfections, and our evolving sense of self; it must do so for small children, harried single mothers, men hailing taxis for the next meeting, or elders reminiscing in rocking chairs. It lets us stand tall as individuals, ready for concerted and single-pointed action in any given moment—despite the fact that we are immature cosmic citizens. Our self-awareness and self-presentation may continually change and our choices may often fall short, but something confers unity and stability on this ever-changing constellation of elements. This unity will also encompass features of the self that are unconscious—what Jung called the personal unconscious as well as the contents of the evolving soul.

I would further speculate that when one of the ingredients in our self-system becomes flawed, the selfhood-systematizing function known as personality will precipitate out this flawed feature. It will spin out clues that show up in our self-presentation. An adept psychologist (or a spouse, good friend, or a judge in court) will be able to pick out this inconsistency, which sometimes will betray itself in a single "frame." If such a self-systematizer were not in place, this radically out-of-place part might never be revealed against the backdrop of the individuality of the whole person.

I hope these interpretations are helpful, but we must always remain humble before the majesty of personality. Consider yet another revelatory assertion: "The type of personality bestowed upon Urantia mortals has a potentiality of seven dimensions of self-expression or person-realization." [112:1.9] In this same passage, we learn that only *three* of these dimensions are finite! These three finite dimensions are *direction*, *depth*, and *breadth*, we are told. And the higher dimensions of personality aren't even named. The upshot is that *personality chiefly operates from outside of space and time.* This means that personality quietly carries out most its functions outside of any possibility of human awareness. The nature of this other-than-finite activity, rooted perhaps in God's absolute personality, must remain a mystery.

---

in their *function* in all humans at any stage of life, while at the same time being existentially unique in their pattern of manifestation in each of us, at any scale. But these ideas are merely a speculation that I hope will spur further research.

Personhood *is* largely unknowable. Yet, as noted above, it does have a subset of dimensions in the finite realm—enough that we can fall in love with the manifested personalities of other persons. But what about the *science* of personality? How do we begin to identify and describe the *direction*, *depth*, and *breadth* of personhood in human behavior? I leave that question for the psychologists of the future who are intrigued by the *UB*'s revelations about personality and its relationship to the inner triad.

More Paradoxes of Human Personality

But now we face another problem. We've glimpsed the idea that personality is absolutely unique, so how is it that we are also utterly equal before God, who is "no respecter of persons"—the biblical idea that God shows no partiality toward people according to race, class, gender, or so on? How is it possible that we are nothing special from the perspective of the divine infinitude—a truth that Eastern religions also highlight—yet we are at the same time "unique in eternity"?

It turns out that *The Urantia Book* finds a way to advocate all three of our possible positions in this regard: uniqueness (the general Western view); selflessness or "nothing-special-ness" (the Eastern understanding that also shows up in the Bible); and imponderability (as in Buddha's warning to his students). But how can all three be true?

It turns out that we can map these three positions into the fundamental gospel teaching of Jesus as provided in Part IV of the *UB*: *the fatherhood of God and the brotherhood of man* (or, the parenthood of God and the siblinghood of humankind). "The gospel of the kingdom *is* the fact of the *fatherhood of God*, coupled with the resultant truth of the sonship—the *brotherhood of men.*" *[190:0.4]*

Let's take a tour of this core *UB* teaching:

First and most foremost: God is our loving parent, attending to us and our needs as if we were God's *only* child. We are uniquely adorable in God's eyes, and each of us is indwelt by God and specifically guided to carry out a singular life purpose that has been gifted upon us.

On the other hand, any apparent differences between you and me pale in comparison to our enormous cosmic distance from divine perfection. The eternal and infinite God regards us all to be of equal status in the cosmic economy, a truism also found in Bible: "He maketh his sun to rise on the evil and on the good, and sendeth rain on the just and on the unjust." (Matthew 5:45). The *UB* expresses the idea this way: "As . . . different classes of mortals appear before the judgment bar of God, they stand on an equal footing; God is truly no respecter of persons," says Jesus. [133:0.0] And, as stated more philosophically in Part I of the text: "The Fatherhood of God and the brotherhood of man present the paradox of the part and the whole on the level of personality. God loves *each* individual as an individual child in the heavenly family. Yet God thus loves *every* individual; he is no respecter of persons, and the universality of his love brings into being a relationship of the whole, the universal brotherhood." [12:7.8]

Offering an additional revelatory enhancement of such wisdom, the *UB* tells us,

> Personality . . . is unique in relation to God—he is no respecter of persons, but **neither does he add them together, for they are nonaddable—they are associable but nontotalable.** [112:0.12]

In other words, two great principles apply to personality, and they are stark opposites that only God's infinitude can unify: the reality of our individual uniqueness ("they are nonaddable") and the abiding truth of our utter equality before the divine throne as God's immature children ("he is no respecter of persons"). In the face of such a paradox, the *UB* goes on and makes clear that our personhood is also *unfathomable*—even for a Divine Counselor who wrote the following words, speaking on behalf of his exalted order of being.[104]

---

[104] "These Trinity-origin beings are the counsel of Deity to the realms of the seven superuniverses. They are not *reflective* of the divine counsel of the Trinity; they *are* that counsel." [19:3.1]

Personality is one of the unsolved mysteries of the universes. We do not fully comprehend the real nature of the personality itself. We clearly perceive the numerous factors which, when put together, constitute the vehicle for human personality, but we do not fully comprehend the nature and significance of such a finite personality. [5:6.2]

Evidently we are falling down a slippery slope toward imponderability, which the Buddha warned us about.

Revisioning Personhood with the Urantia Revelation

Epochal revelation unveils the fact that personality has key features that operate outside of time and space. And, much like the Thought Adjuster, our unique personality is a deeply mysterious extension of infinitude into the realms of the finite. Consider: On the one hand, a portion of the infinite personality of the Father is somehow gifted to animal-origin humans, and *this endowment of personhood is truly divine*. But the converse is also true: *That which is divine is also essentially personal* (although it has nonpersonal dimensions as well). And if these two propositions are both true, this means that *personality is the primal manifestation of the infinite*.

According to this understanding, infinity inherently personalizes as the Father of all. In turn, the Father personalizes as his eternal coordinates (the other persons of the Trinity), and thereafter as his children in the central universe and in the evolving universes. Nonpersonal manifestations of divinity—Paradise, gravity, space, the galaxies, the planets of evolving universes, and so on—all are made available in the service of personality, both eternal and evolutional.

But the *UB* now goes on to say even more about personality, declaring it to be *the very essence of Deity, and God's chief attribute*. These astonishing statements make that clear:

Without God and except for his great and central person, there would be no personality throughout all the vast universe of universes. *God is personality.* [1:5.7]

Personality, in the supreme sense, is the revelation of God to the universe of universes. [1:5.13]

We noted earlier that the *UB* is a personalist teaching. Some interpreters even contend that the ontological reality of personality is the *central revelation* of the Urantia text. The statements above point us in that direction.

The Foreword to *The Urantia Book* can be notoriously difficult, but a brief encounter would help us understand this point. These opening pages purport to reveal the fundamental definitions and a priori principles of cosmic reality. Right from the outset we learn of the primary division within universal reality—the primeval distinction between realities that are "deified" and those that are not—"undeified realities." Next we learn that all deified realities are by definition personal, since God *is* personality. Here again we see the equation of divinity, personality, and reality.

Now, if we limit our purview to the evolving universes, we discover that the primary distinction within the space-time domains is also between personal and nonpersonal realities: "Personality may be material or spiritual, but there either is personality or there is no personality. The other-than-personal never attains the level of the personal except by the direct act of the Paradise Father." [5:6] In other words, no one can evolve a personality. It is either gifted to a being or it is not.

These are crucial ideas, but they don't exhaust our subject. While the Urantia Revelation does not and cannot offer a systematic or complete definition of personality, it reveals in Paper 112 a numbered list of fourteen characteristics of personality. I will summarize and expand the central ideas in this chapter by highlighting a selection of ten of these, expressed as aphorisms. My list is paraphrased or otherwise derived from many other statements in the *UB* in addition to the fourteen attributes, and I have also added a few inferences and speculations:

1. The Infinite Father inserts into evolution the gift of personality—which is changeless—in response to the readiness of his evolving creatures.

Personhood is a direct bestowal from God into the stream of evolution. But personality does not evolve as does the human soul, and it can't be enhanced (in the sense that the Thought Adjuster can be) by virtue of its experience of indwelling a human mind. Personality is either present or it is not present; it is also changeless, yet paradoxically it also has functions to perform. Personhood is existential and incomputable; it has no measurable units, unlike material and morontial forms of energy. Personality is largely transcendent to time, but the capacity for creatures of time to *receive and embody* the gift of personality—to become self-aware persons—is an evolutionary attainment. Far back in the story of humankind, slowly evolving hominids achieved a certain evolutionary readiness that triggered the heart of Deity, after which they achieved what the *UB* calls *will dignity* through the gift of personhood. (This story is told in Papers 58–63.) Since those far-distant times, all of us have duly received the mysterious grant of personality.

2. All persons are encircuited in the indivisible personhood of the Father.

The Divine Person is One and indivisible, and all of his bestowals participate in this unity.[105] Human personality—as a manifestation of this indivisible unity—is inherently encircuited with the Divine Person through the Father's *personality circuit*. An exclusive revelation of the Urantia Papers, this circuit enables the Father to maintain simultaneous contact with *all* persons:

> We cannot fully comprehend the methods whereby God is so fully and personally conversant with the details of the universe of universes . . . [but] through the personality circuit the

---

[105] Here and throughout this section I draw special inspiration from George Park, independent philosopher and author of the very helpful essay "Personality and Man," which first appeared in *Urantia Fellowship Herald* (2007). See http://urantia-book.org/archive/newsletters/herald/. Among his many profound findings, Park's research has led him to infer from various statements in the *UB* that personality is bestowed at birth, or possibly at conception.

Father is cognizant—has personal knowledge—of all the thoughts and acts of all the beings in all the systems of all the universes of all creation. Though we cannot fully grasp this technique of God's communion with his children, we can be strengthened in the assurance that the 'Lord knows his children.' [32:4.8]

3. The gift of personality confers self-awareness and creative freewill on each individual; when they operate effectively, these powers reflect their divine origin.

Although personality is a universal mystery, we are offered many clues about it. Among these are the revelation that human personality possesses—though in a limited way—two powers that are intrinsic to Deity's inherent nature: self-awareness and will. "Creature personality is distinguished by two self-manifesting and characteristic phenomena of mortal reactive behavior: self-consciousness and associated relative freewill." [16:8.5] These two attributes of human selfhood are a priori signs of the divine origin of personhood. Our efforts at self-perfection are guaranteed to succeed when the divinely gifted personality freely chooses to follow the infallible guidance provided by the Indwelling Spirit, which inherently seeks union with our personality. In light of these statements, Lucifer's denial that personality is a gift of the Universal Father becomes truly staggering. [See 53:3.]

4. We can show gratefulness for our free will by letting go of limiting identifications so that we can choose the will of God—which is true freedom.

The bestowal of personhood naturally evokes a grateful human response. We can respond in kind by letting go of limiting identifications, thereby releasing the divine gift of free will from the mechanical grip of material obsessions and trivial distractions. Continued spiritual growth liberates our will to consistently choose the way of God. Indeed, the divine will becomes self-evident to us when our limiting identifications drop away. *A Course in Miracles* correctly teaches that, *our deepest will is God's will.* By identifying with the impulses of the Thought Adjuster, we move toward Father

Fusion, the irrevocable decision to live permanently in the joy and freedom of always choosing God's will.

5. Personality lets us rise above incoming stimuli; it allows us to be creative and reflective by freeing us from being helplessly reactive to past events.

Personality allows *interiority*. In connection with our endowment of mind, personality opens an internal space in which we are relatively free from the past. "[Personality] is not wholly subject to the fetters of antecedent causation. It is relatively creative or cocreative." [112:0.5] In other words, our inner life offers us a province of free choice in which we're not helplessly reactive to external stimuli, unlike most animals. Only personal beings are self-observing or self-reflective, that is, able through effort and intention to focus their thoughts and feelings and mindfully choose a particular direction of action. Human personalities have, at least in potential, the internal spaciousness and intellectual capacity required to think, plan, evaluate, and choose among options that are soul-making.

6. When human personality operates through the vehicle of spirit, it is always superordinate to other parts of the self and all other forms of energy.

Personality is primal in all universes. The Divine Person is antecedent to and all powerful in relation to all things, including spirit. "Personality is superimposed upon energy." [0:5.4] Human personality has the potential to control all domains of energy-reality when it operates through the vehicle of spirit, the highest form of energy. Otherwise expressed, personhood has prerogatives that are logically prior to all other attributes and energies of the human self (body, mind, soul, or spirit). "When bestowed upon evolutionary material creatures, personality causes spirit to strive for the mastery of energy-matter through the mediation of mind." [112:0.6] Personality confers the precious power of freewill choice, allowing the mortal intellect to choose among higher values originating in our spiritual impulses.

7. Personality has no identity but is rather the *host* of identity; it *unifies* and *systematizes* the elements of selfhood around chosen identities.

Personality is a transcendent function that unifies and systematizes selfhood at any level of its identifications, high or low. At the highest level, where persons are spirit-identified, they can achieve the superb personality unification and symmetry of selfhood that we witness in Jesus.[106] At lower levels, persons who are confused, misguided, traumatized, or disassociated block the efficient operation of the unifying powers of the personality; these individuals appear untrustworthy and unreliable in their self-presentation to others.[107] Their self-system "precipitates" disunity and asymmetry. But unified persons are those who reflect on their life purposes and goals in prayer and introspection in ways that allow the personality to do its primary job: the systematic work of unifying and balancing their living energy system around a chosen identity. The theological basis of this function is the premise that *God is unity*; God is one in existential perfection. Out of love and regard for us, the eternal God invites us into this divine unity and perfection, which is ours to achieve as a attainment made possible by the intrinsic attributes of personality. God's gift of personality is able to confer increasing unity and symmetry on such an evolving being. "The purpose of cosmic evolution is to achieve unity of personality." [112:2.15]

8. We are social creatures who crave to belong; personality is spontaneously sensitive to the presence of other persons.

"Personality responds directly to other-personality presence." [112.0.13] Our personhood is nonlocal—it's embedded in a unified field that envelops us as God's *personality circuit*. Once we cross the threshold into this nonlocal field of personal selves, we—as persons—find that each individual we encounter is lovable in their own

---

[106] As a reminder, I cite again this statement: "The unique feature of [Jesus'] personality was not so much its perfection as its symmetry, its exquisite and balanced unification." [100:7.1]

[107] In other words, these divided persons are unable or unwilling to integrate their life experiences. This problem likely points to a key purpose of life reviews in the afterlife (as reported by NDEers)—to find the resources required to be able to identify, "own," and make peace with all of one's decisions and actions while on Earth.

unique way. Each reflects the beauty of the Divine Person—who is the source of all these unique personalities. The participation of every one of us in the unified field of personality makes us inherently sensitive to and appreciative of the personality-presence of others. Especially when we encounter those we care about, we don't merely observe the details of face, age, body type, dress, demeanor, speech, or behavior; we take in the whole person. We may find that we adore their entire personhood just as it is, intuiting the beauty of the transcendent unity of their unique personal presence. Personality, then, is a like a cosmic version of the law of attraction. When you are near me, I resonate naturally and immediately with you, over against the nonpersonal things or events in the room. This occurs not because you may be useful to me but simply because you are a *fellow personality*. In moments of prayer, worship, or celebration, you and I may fall even further into this delightful domain of our sacred oneness.

9. Personality is an end in itself; love is the highest expression of the realization of that truth.
Love is the mutual regard of whole personalities. Loving other persons is a recognition of their irreducible and infinite uniqueness, their radiant personal qualities that ultimately point to—and inherently participate in—the Infinite Personality. Persons who love others personalities find their ultimate fulfillment in union with the Original Personality.

> **In the true meaning of the word, love connotes mutual regard of whole personalities, whether human or divine or human *and* divine.** Parts of the self may function in numerous ways—thinking, feeling, wishing—but only the co-ordinated attributes of the whole personality are focused in intelligent action; and all of these powers are associated with the spiritual endowment of the mortal mind when a human being sincerely and unselfishly loves another being, human or divine. **All mortal concepts of reality are based on the assumption of the actuality of human personality**; all concepts of superhuman realities are based on the experience of the human personality with and in the cosmic realities of certain associated spiritual

entities and divine personalities. **Everything nonspiritual in human experience, excepting personality, is a means to an end**. Every true relationship of mortal man with other persons — human or divine — is an end in itself. And such fellowship with the personality of Deity is the eternal goal of universe ascension. [UB: 112:2:7–8]

10. Each personality is unique in eternity; the proliferation of unique human persons on billions of worlds provides God with the richest possible access to his evolving creation.

Each personality is absolutely unique. But what can explain the ongoing explosion of unique, experiential beings who increasingly populate Earth and all other inhabited worlds? The singular perspective supplied by each new person must have ultimate value. It must have a transcendental purpose. As I have shared previously, human personhood allows the existential God—an infinite and perfect being who exists outside of space and time—to acquire something impossible to obtain otherwise: *a replete experience of the experiences of his evolving creatures.* We might say that God desires to have an "all-experience" and therefore brings forth a virtually infinite diversity of experiencing subjects, each of whom provides him with access to their idiosyncratic viewpoint. The Divine Person encompasses and transcends cosmic evolution and all evolutionary beings. We can't get outside of his circle of eternity, but we can allow God to dwell *with us* in our evolutionary home of personality expression through God's gift of personality—as well through as the additional gift of the Thought Adjuster, the subject of the next chapter. And all of this, indeed, is a love supreme.

> **Nothing in the entire universe can substitute for the fact of experience on nonexistential levels**. The infinite God is, as always, replete and complete, infinitely inclusive of all things except evil and creature experience. God cannot do wrong; he is infallible. **God cannot experientially know what he has never personally experienced; God's preknowledge is existential. Therefore does the spirit of the Father descend from Paradise to participate with finite mortals in every bona fide experience of the ascending career**; it is

only by such a method that the existential God could become in truth and in fact man's experiential Father. The infinity of the eternal God encompasses the potential for finite experience, which indeed becomes actual in the ministry of the Adjuster fragments that actually share the life vicissitude experiences of human beings. [108:0.2]

The Gift of the
Divine Indwelling

*What a mistake to dream of God far off in the skies when
the spirit of the Universal Father lives within your own mind!*
—*The Urantia Book* 5:2.3

The Father Fragment is a charter member of the inner triad that we have discussed many times before. In the next two chapters, I introduce more advanced ideas concerning this priceless gift, our eternal partner in soul evolution and self-perfection. Throughout this discussion, what we discover again and again is that the scope and purpose of the divine indwelling is simply staggering.

Papers 107–111 describe in unprecedented detail the reality of this divine presence within us. The more I plumb these writings, the more I agree with other veteran students of the Urantia text that this section may be its most magnificent revelation.[108] In particular, Paper 110 ("Relation of Adjusters to Individual Mortals") explains the levels of self-perfecting, and Paper 111 ("The Adjuster and the Soul") offers a full presentation of the dynamics of soul-making;

---

[108] Decades of searching have turned up *no* human sources for this series of papers other than one insignificant source at 111:4. See http://urantiabooksources.com/index.php/part-iii/.

these revelations form the basis of the core argument of *Your Evolving Soul*. Because of their central importance, I'll quote extensively from these Papers.

The *UB* describes at least four types of high endowments, each corresponding to a reality domain of one of the personalities of the Trinity. (These were first described in chapter 2, and are summarized in an essay at my website entitled, "The Four Primary Gifts to Humankind.") In this chapter we dive more deeply into the most important of these divine offerings to humanity.

All of the gifts and influences we have discussed so far are synergetic, and our personhood is their unifier, but the Divine Indweller orchestrates this sublime harmony of influences because of its unique capacity to act as the "center within"—as a Deity fragment that lives in the heart of the human mind: "Mortal man has a spirit nucleus. The mind is a personal-energy system existing around a divine spirit nucleus and functioning in a material environment." [12.9.6]

This gift of a literal portion of Deity that indwells our mind comes directly from God as Primal Father. And it is worthy of note that the Father and the Eternal Son sharply differ in their ability to self-distribute through this mystery of fragmentation: "The Eternal Son is not thus fragmentable; the spirit of the Original Son is either diffuse or discretely personal." [107:1.7] The Second Person of the Trinity primarily ministers to us through dramatic incarnations, so his influence on our spiritual life comes from the "outside."[109] But the Father reserves to himself the prerogative of entering directly into the interior viewpoint of the creature, eventually to *become* the creature's subjective viewpoint on the universe after the event of fusion.

> Even though the spirit of a Son be poured out upon all flesh, even though a Son once dwelt with you in the likeness of mortal flesh, even though the seraphim personally guard and

---

[109] As already noted, the Eternal Son also ministers to us through the universal diffusion of what is known as spiritual gravity, which operates via the *spirit-gravity circuit* to control the energetic realms of spiritual values (see 7:1). This influence is supplemental to the ambient presence of the Spirit of Truth, and both of them influence our thoughts and feelings from the outside working in, as also do the incarnations of "Sons of the Eternal Son" such as that of Jesus.

guide you, how can any of these divine beings of the Second and Third Centers ever hope to come as near to you or to understand you as fully as the Father, who has given a part of himself to be in you, to be your real and divine, even your eternal, self? [12:7.14]

Because the indwelling God Fragment is more intimate than any other influence, the effort of receiving and feeling its guidance is our most powerful spiritual practice. Attunement with this divine entity is also our "great challenge" and "greatest adventure," we are told [196:3.34].[110] The degree of our receptivity to the leadings of the Divine Indweller determines the course of our soul evolution and conditions the degree of our cosmic individuation.

A Grand Meeting of Opposites

Let's revisit the integral view of the self that I presented earlier. On the one hand, the objective view of the self-system reveals the variegated parts of the self (the sacred triad) and their many vital functions. A replete discussion of these features from "the outside looking in" is a chief preoccupation of the Urantia Revelation, simply because these metaphysical realities are unknowable in their essence unless divinely revealed to us. On the other hand, the inside-out viewpoint reveals a subjective awareness that measurably "wakes up" and "grows up" but does not display easily identifiable metaphysical components. We can turn to the mystics and masters of all human wisdom traditions if our aim is to understand such phenomenological realities as reported from the first-person point of view—depicted, for example, in the lyric poems of Shamseddin Hafiz, the teachings of Ramana Maharshi, or in the *Confessions* of St. Augustine. These descriptions offer no pretense of being objective or revelatory.

---

[110] "The great challenge to modern man is to achieve better communication with the divine Monitor that dwells within the human mind. Man's greatest adventure in the flesh consists in the well-balanced and sane effort to advance the borders of self-consciousness out through the dim realms of embryonic soul-consciousness in a whole-hearted effort to reach the borderland of spirit-consciousness—contact with the divine presence."

But what a majestic meeting of opposites is involved in the divine indwelling—regardless of the perspective we may adopt on the self. This spirit-entity is described as "the gift of the absolute God to those creatures whose destiny encompasses the possibility of the attainment of God as absolute." [107:1.6] In other words, our Creator traverses a vast cosmic distance to partner with us lowly creatures of the material worlds, for sole the purpose of empowering us to achieve the absolute.

"It is indeed a marvel of divine condescension for the exalted and perfect Adjusters to offer themselves for actual existence in the minds of material creatures, such as the mortals of Urantia, really to consummate a probationary union with the animal-origin beings of earth." [108:6.1] Over the course of several billion years of evolution of life on Earth, primitive bacteria evolved to bring forth hominids approximately a million years ago, who slowly mutated into the befuddled humans we are today. And yet, we somehow qualify to receive not only unique personalities but also a portion of the perfect divine light that descends from eternal Paradise.

> Although the Universal Father is personally resident on Paradise, at the very center of the universes, he is also actually present on the worlds of space in the minds of his countless children of time. . . . **The eternal Father is at one and the same time farthest removed from, and most intimately associated with, his planetary mortal sons.** [107:0.1]

This free offer of a spirit of God comprises, as New Agers might say, our higher self, in contrast with our lower self or ego. And as a lover of philosophic beauty might put it, this intimate association is the most dramatic encounter possible of that which is highest with that which is lowest.

> The [Indwelling Spirits] are the actuality of the Father's love incarnate in the souls of men; **they are the veritable promise of man's eternal career imprisoned within the mortal mind; they are the essence of man's [perfected] personality, which he can foretaste in time** as he progressively masters the divine technique of achieving the living of the Father's will,

step by step, through the ascension of universe upon universe until he actually attains the divine presence. [107:0.1]

The world's great religious teachers have always been intuitively aware of the grandness of the meeting of opposites implied by our endowment with such a heavenly gift. For example, ancient Chinese philosophy envisioned a convergence of "heaven, earth, and man," and Confucius especially taught that our effort to harmonize these tremendous opposites becomes the source of health, good fortune, and happiness. The ancient Gnostics taught that the high Gods looked down upon us, saw that we were trapped in the prison of the Demiurge at the lowest level of universal existence, and in mercy bestowed on us a "divine spark" so we could find our way back safely to Paradise. And Carl Jung celebrated this great meeting of dust and spirit as the *coniunctio oppositorum* (conjunction of opposites)—the primal encounter of creature and Creator.

The fact that we act as the host for such a tremendous meeting of opposites allows us to achieve the dialectical synthesis that yields evolutionary progress—as the philosopher Hegel famously put it. And this is the very same process that I have called soul-synthesis.

This gift of infinity to humankind, conferred in love on the finite mortal mind, keeps on giving its riches—unto the zenith of our attainments in eternity.

Naming and Describing the Inner Divinity

While many truth revealers of the past have left us with cryptic teachings about an abiding inner light, the *UB* offers us more specific descriptions than we have ever enjoyed, while also providing new names for the Indwelling Spirit that seem more serviceable in the postmodern era. Consider these unambiguous portrayals of the divinity within:

To say that a Thought Adjuster is divine is merely to recognize the nature of origin. It is highly probable that such purity of divinity embraces the essence of the potential of all attributes of Deity which can be contained within such a fragment of the absolute essence of the Universal presence of the eternal and infinite Paradise Father.[107:4.1]

They are fragmentized entities constituting the **factual presence of the infinite God.** [They] are undiluted and unmixed divinity, unqualified and unattenuated parts of Deity; **they are of God, and as far as we are able to discern,** *they are God.* [107:1.2]

These are radical and stark pronouncements. But again, we've seen that such notions are not unfamiliar if we search the scriptures of our traditions. In Asian thought, the idea of a pristine spirit-self can be found in the concepts of the atman or Buddha-nature. We've also seen that the divine presence within was envisioned in the deification teachings of Eastern Christianity, which built upon the Greek philosophic legacy that goes back to Socrates, who often spoke of the *daimon*—the inner divine presence that told Socrates what *not* to do.

In the centuries after the Axial Age (more than twenty-five hundred years ago), the world's leading religions reached a plateau of understanding regarding a divine spark within. Their conceptions rose to greatest clarity in monastic or mystical enclaves in which, typically, elite groups of males were initiated into this truth in some form and then trained under the tutelage of a religious or cultic hierarchy.

Because the reality of an indwelling entity had been inferred through immense effort, humanity had surely earned an expansion of understanding. Wherefore the *UB*'s revelators stepped forward to make the concept of the inner divinity *democratically available to all of humankind* in the form of a printed book with no human author. Such an approach to providing revelatory information is not so easily controlled by a religion, a sect, or a cult leader.[111]

I believe that the *UB*'s revelations about the divine indwelling are designed to supersede our humanly evolved nomenclatures and

---

[111] An exception that perhaps proves the rule has been the Quakers, who in their meetings for over three centuries have practiced a meditative stillness that enables them to feel the presence of the divine spark. Their practice is unmediated by a hierarchical priesthood and is open to all.

religious structures, tied up as these are with the political and cultural baggage of centuries of tradition. And while the historic consensus about an inner divine presence is notable, we saw in Part III of this book how the world's wisdom traditions diverge on many crucial technical points regarding the nature and function of our psychospiritual endowments, with each of these issues needing philosophic resolution. On that basis, let's proceed to examine the *UB*'s teachings on these questions that, I believe, can lead us into a new era of understanding.

In this passage, the revelator—a high being of direct origin from the Infinite Spirit—almost laments about the difficulty of finding an appropriate name for the indwelling spark of God:

I doubt that I am able to explain to you just what the Adjusters do in your minds and for your souls. I do not know that I am fully cognizant of what is really going on in the cosmic association of a divine Monitor and a human mind. It is all somewhat of a mystery to us, not as to the plan and purpose but as to the actual mode of accomplishment. And this is just why we are confronted with such difficulty in finding an appropriate name for these supernal gifts to mortal men. [108:5.7]

The phrase "Father Fragment" was coined to vividly convey the idea that a factual portion of "God-ness" indwells us. The word "fragment" is meant literally and not as a metaphor. But in the descriptions we are given, we learn that a piece of something that is absolute remains but a *portion* of the Father's absoluteness, paradoxical as that sounds; for the God Fragment is not the allness of Deity in its fullness. You and I are not the Creator God who resides at the center of all things and pervades all universes (although many cult leaders do arrive at such conclusions). Nevertheless, the Spirit Fragment within us *is* absolute in its divinity nature. We read that "in extensiveness [the God Fragments] are limited, but in intensiveness of meaning, value, and fact *they are absolute*." [107:4.2]

Further, because it is factually absolute and of origin in the Primal Father, the God Fragment is by definition *pure spirit and pure energy*. That's because, as described earlier, God as First Source and Center is ancestral to the divergence of spirit and energy that characterizes the evolutionary realms.

> We know that Thought Adjusters are spirits, pure spirits, presumably absolute spirits. But the Adjuster must also be something more than exclusive spirit reality. In addition to conjectured mindedness, factors of pure energy are also present. **If you will remember that God is the source of pure energy and of pure spirit, it will not be so difficult to perceive that his fragments would be both.** [107:6.4]

In other words, if God as Father is understood as *the existential One*, then spirit and energy must be understood as one in undifferentiated unity in the domains of eternity. But in the galaxies of space, the two diverge until they are "synthesized" through the ministry of mind and by the techniques of evolution ordained by the God of Mind, the Infinite Spirit—the divine minister of love and mercy *applied* in time and space. And such a voyage to unification is possible because humans already have within them a fragment of unified spirit-energy that is lighting the way. The God Fragment's overlighting function guarantees that, if we desire to make the trip, we shall return to the very origin of energy and spirit that first descended to indwell us while "trailing clouds of glory," as the poet Wordsworth once put it:

> Our birth is but a sleep and a forgetting:
> The Soul that rises with us, our life's Star,
> Hath had elsewhere its setting,
> And cometh from afar:
> Not in entire forgetfulness,
> And not in utter nakedness,
> But trailing clouds of glory do we come
> From God, who is our home.[112]

---

[112] Excerpted from William Wordsworth's "Ode: Intimations of Immortality from Recollections of Early Childhood." Like his contemporaries, Wordsworth does not clearly distinguish spirit from soul, but we can allow him poetic license, a favor we can't extend to philosophers.

The odd phrase *Mystery Monitor* points to a different aspect of the Divine Indweller's work. With the most benign intent possible, the Monitor searches for impulses and ideas that are soul-making, tracking by some mysterious technique all of our activities at all times and without interruption. The Monitor maintains an observer position until the "indwellee" becomes adequately responsive to his gentle leadings. Then he "resigns" from this role to become our private tutor, offering a never-ending stream of insights and guidance. If he could speak, he might say something like this:

> I dwell within you and partake of your every living moment—either as a mere observer or as a more involved partner. You are the one who decides which level you take our relationship to as I patiently wait for you to initiate each step. As I witness your touching efforts to include me in your life, I come out of what is perceived by you to be my hiding place—my aloofness. But I am not the one who is elusive, for I am totally committed to bringing you back with me to the glory of Paradise.

But the most important term in the Indwelling Spirit lexicon is *Thought Adjuster*. The Indweller adjusts our ideas and feelings toward the highest possible value-choices, fine-tuning our thoughts so that we engage in soul-making activities. The "TA" does this through a variety of unknown techniques that it quietly employs in the superconscious mind. These exquisite but largely unknown operations are described with affection in this well-known passage by the celestial author of Paper 110:

> I wish it were possible for me to help evolving mortals to achieve a better understanding and attain a fuller appreciation of the unselfish and superb work of the Adjusters living within them, who are so devoutly faithful to the task of fostering man's spiritual welfare. These Monitors are efficient ministers to the higher phases of men's minds; they are wise and experienced manipulators of the spiritual potential of the human intellect. These heavenly helpers are dedicated to the stupendous task of guiding you safely inward and upward to the celestial haven of happiness. These tireless toilers are consecrated to the future personification of the triumph of divine truth in your life

everlasting. . . . They are the careful custodians of the sublime values of creature character. I wish you could love them more, co-operate with them more fully, and cherish them more affectionately. [110:1.2]

The Inner Betrothal Day

You may ask, when does our engagement with such heavenly helpers begin? I've already shared in chapter 4 that the Thought Adjuster is bestowed on each normal child around the age of six. You'll recall that this moment initiates the child into the *seventh psychic circle*, the first of the circles of cosmic individuation. Significantly, the Indwelling Spirit arrives at this juncture because of a *decision to do something*—not as a result of a mere thought or feeling.

[Adjusters] are **not actually assigned until the human subjects make their first moral personality decision**. . . . Adjusters reach their human subjects on Urantia, on the average, just prior to the sixth birthday. In the present generation it is running five years, ten months, and four days; that is, on the 2,134th day of terrestrial life. [108:2.1]

The unsuspecting child directly triggers a cosmic response because of a simple but life-changing decision. We read further:

When such a moral decision has been made, this spirit helper assumes jurisdiction. . . . **There are no intermediaries or other intervening authorities or powers functioning between the divine Adjusters and their human subjects**; God and man are directly related. [108:2.4]

We're told later in this section that the child's first moral choice is "automatically indicated [and] registers instantly" in the central universe headquarters of Thought Adjusters. The child's gift of *personality* has already been conferred from outside of space-time, arriving without fanfare, just as does the God Fragment. These important statements tell us, very touchingly, that all children on all worlds are lovingly monitored from the heart of the cosmos.

With a bit of skepticism, I have heard reports from some Urantia students that they can recall this delicate event in their childhood. But here is one case I found compelling.

> I was about five years old and I was playing alone in the hallway of our family's new home. Sometime during the prior week, feeling excited because my brothers and I had just been watching *Zorro* on TV, I had scrawled several *Z*s on the baseboard of the new wall cabinets, in imitation of my hero carving his initial everywhere with his sword. But my mother was not at all pleased with my crayon work, and she scolded me for it. As I sat playing in front of those cabinets again and saw the marks I had made, I remembered what she had said. I realized that it would be kind to my mother if I did what she asked, so I decided I wouldn't write on the baseboards again. Suddenly, distinctly, I felt the presence of God coming upon me. I remember saying to myself, "This must be the same thing as when my parents and the people in church talk to God."

We are told in the *UB* that the vast majority of cases, the reception of the Thought Adusters by youngsters is unconscious. Regardless, our very first moral choice elicits a very conscious response from on high. But in line with the interpretations I offered in chapter 3, such a decision doesn't have to be the "correct" one. A child's first decision doesn't have to be "right" or "wrong" as an adult might see it; the point is that the youth is now capable of moral discrimination— the elementary ability to identify a set of options, evaluate them, and select one course of action. The Thought Adjuster is primarily interested in evidence of independent decision-making. The human soul is an immortal record of our lifelong trial and error learning process, and the impulse to experiment with and explore new realities is, after all, the essence of cosmic evolution. The evolving soul attests to our oftentimes awkward but sincere efforts to "learn the steps" as we dance with complex universe realities.

The first receipt of the Divine Monitor is the child's Inner Betrothal Day, so to speak. It initiates an auspicious but highly uneven friendship, one between a perfect entity and a very imperfect child. And that's why a transforming love is essential to arouse and inspire a child's virgin mind to take the first baby steps of soul-making.

> As far as I am conversant with the affairs of a universe, **I regard the love and devotion of a Thought Adjuster as the most truly divine affection in all creation**. . . . The Paradise Father has apparently reserved this form of personal contact with his individual creatures as an exclusive Creator prerogative. And there is **nothing in all the universe of Universes exactly comparable to the marvelous ministry** of these impersonal entities that so fascinatingly indwell the children of the evolutionary planets. [110:0.1]

The Monitor has taken up residence at the nucleus of the child's mind and a devotional relationship of the sort celebrated by poets like Rumi has now begun. This interior lover's only object, its "marvelous ministry," is to motivate the growth toward perfection of the beloved. "The indwelling Adjuster individualizes the love of God to each human soul." [2:5.10]

To illustrate this liaison of love, I've adapted the story of Cupid to help describe how the child's receipt of an Adjuster initiates a relationship like no other. Perhaps you'll remember how the old myth goes. When Cupid spots a candidate who feels a new affection for someone, he shoots this person with an arrow of love that arouses a fiery desire for the beloved. Compare this to the reception of the Thought Adjuster. God spots a precious child who is a newly emergent "moral agent" desires to arouse ever-more responsive love in this innocent youngster, so he picks an arrow of pure spirit from his quiver, pulls back his bow, and fires into the child's heart a shaft of pure spirit sent directly from the infinite source of love.

This is a grand initiation, because the reception of this God Fragment also activates the child's evolving soul. The initiated child can now—on its own—assume the role of Cupid. In the story, Cupid shoots *himself* with the arrow because he adores Psyche, whose name in ancient Greek literally means "soul." The upshot, in our story, is that the child self-initiates its soul journey. This youngster—already a bearer of freewill personhood—is potentially *an agent of evolutionary love* in the space-time cosmos. "The urges of social service and the idealism of altruism," we read, "are derived from the direct impulse of the divine spirit indwelling the human mind." [103:5.1]

But what if, for whatever reason, the decisions being made by the growing youth fall far short of the ideal of serving others? The Heavenly Guide remains steadfast, regardless: "The endowment of imperfect beings with freedom entails inevitable tragedy, and it is the nature of the perfect ancestral Deity to universally and affectionately share these sufferings in loving companionship." [110:0.1]

This kind of unconditional affection is all the more poignant when we consider that the effort of a troubled young person to emerge from dire circumstances can yield an especially rich harvest of soul-making. That's because the tireless toiler is always cheerleading, even for the worst of the worst offenders. And it almost always succeeds. Once the two beings are betrothed, their long engagement is likely to be consummated, regardless of the possibility of severe challenges along the way. This inner marriage is the great goal of the fusion of the soul and personality with the Adjuster—the achievement of irrevocable immortality.

We saw in chapters 4 and 7 that the long path to fusion requires the harmonious mobilization of the powers of the totality of selfhood. We noted that the self's abilities are many, but that they can be broken out into three primary governing faculties: *feeling, thinking,* and *willing* (or *doing*). In the rest of this chapter and the next, I'll revisit these three lines of development in terms of our attunement to our ultimate spouse, the Thought Adjuster. Let's start with the line of feeling.

The Felt Experience of the Inner Light

"Be a lamp unto yourselves," declared Sakyamuni Buddha to his disciples as he lay dying. "Seek no external refuge; let the dharma be your island and your only refuge." According to the Urantia Revelation, our God Fragment *is* this inner lamp and our true refuge. Its light provides the luminosity that "lights every man who comes into the world" (John 1:9). As we allow it to light us from within, we progress along the qualitative, or feeling, line of soul evolution.

But the Buddha was ruthless about epistemology—the question of what we can really know about the lamp. As we saw earlier, he felt that his Hindu predecessors had harbored religious delusions in their teachings. In particular, they were dogmatically attached to a reification, a reduction of raw spiritual experience down to a lifeless "it" that they called the atman—the inner counterpart to the transcendent abstraction they called Brahman. Because Buddha wanted to free his students from all such doctrinal presumption, he exhorted his followers to achieve ever-deeper and ineffable experiences of the dharma beyond the limits of any humanly derived ideas *about* this inner reality.

In this regard, Buddha was a prophet for our time. We can have theories derived from a revelatory text such as *The Urantia Book*, but these ideas are quite secondary to our actual experiences of the inner lamp. Settled theological beliefs may or may not point us in the right direction. We can easily become blind to the *felt reality* of God-consciousness if our interior experience is dominated by incorrect theories, unexamined assumptions, fixed ideas—or in fact any form of discursive thought.

Esoteric Buddhist teachings, especially in the Zen and Dzogchen traditions, teach that what we can feel in our spiritual experience cannot be captured in words and concepts. Along the same line, in his masterwork *The Varieties of Religious Experience*, William James proclaims, "I do believe that feeling is the deeper source of religion, and that philosophic and theological formulas are secondary products, like translations of a text into another tongue."[113]

For its own part, the *UB* incessantly speaks of the centrality of personal spiritual experience—the imperative of *feeling* the divine

---

[113] William James, *The Varieties of Religious Experience: A Study of Human Nature* (Random House, 1902), p. 422.

presence. Here are just a few typical statements sprinkled throughout the text:

> Quality—values—is felt. [111:3.6]
>
> The world needs more firsthand religion . . . the experience of knowing the presence of God. [195:9.8]
>
> Many of your brethren have minds that accept the theory of God while they spiritually fail to realize the presence of God. [155:6.4]
>
> The secret of [Jesus's] unparalleled religious life was [his] consciousness of the presence of God. [196:0.1]
>
> It is not so important that you should know about the fact of God as that you should increasingly grow in the ability to feel the presence of God. [155:6.13]
>
> The indwelling Thought Adjuster attaches the feeling of reality to man's spiritual insight into the cosmos. [102:3.12]

Similarly, early Buddhism taught "transconceptual" experience with a minimum of doctrine. This emphasis fostered a vital stream of firsthand religion in Asia that was enhanced by its early contact with esoteric Taoism in China. The later-appearing doctrine of an indwelling Buddha-nature marked a return to the classical doctrine of the atman, but in the much more subtle and paradoxical form of understanding. The Urantia Revelation praises this evolutionary achievement in a memorable passage: "[Later Buddhist] philosophy also held that the Buddha (divine) nature resided in all men; that man, through his own endeavors, could attain to the realization of this inner divinity. **And this teaching is one of the clearest presentations of the truth of the indwelling Adjusters ever to be made by a Urantian religion.**" [94:11.4]

Realizing this inner divinity requires a still mind, or so taught the Buddha. Buddhist meditation entails the conscious cultivation of a focused state of mindful and relaxed alertness, a practice that remains so potent that mindfulness techniques are becoming a staple in corporations and even some hospitals. In Buddhist religious settings, practitioners are supported by the *sangha* (the community of practice), and claims of enlightenment require scrutiny by "a community of the adequate"—elders who have mastered higher states and levels of consciousness and have conformed to the other practices of the Eightfold Path (right views, intention, speech, action, livelihood, effort, mindfulness, and concentration).

In a comparable way, believers and monastics who practiced hesychia—noetic stillness and prayer of the heart—were given priority of place in the Eastern Christian traditions. We've already noted that Eastern Orthodox theology is based to a greater extent than Latin theology is on the spiritual experiences of the mystics of the Church, in strong contrast to the more rationalistic emphasis of the West. As I also noted in chapter 6, the mystical theology of the Eastern Church was apophatic, not unlike the Buddhist emphasis on transconceptual experience.

To better understand the prominence of meditative worship and prayerful reflection in all esoteric traditions, consider this metaphor: Our minds can be compared with a container of water that, when turbulent, reflects and refracts the sun's light in many directions. But when stilled by devoted meditation, the water (a symbol for our minds) transmits the pure light of God (symbolized by the sun) to consciousness.

According to the *UB*, Jesus himself used various meditation techniques in his practice of the presence of God. We learn about this from Rodan, a Greek philosopher from Alexandria who met with and came to believe in Jesus. As exclusively revealed in the *UB*, Rodan depicts Jesus as a man fully devoted to a "habit" of "worshipful meditation." In this important passage, Rodan is in conversation with the apostles Nathaniel and Thomas.

> The greatest of all methods of problem solving I have learned from Jesus, your Master. I refer to that which he so consistently practices, and which **he has so faithfully taught you, the isolation of worshipful meditation.** In this habit of Jesus' going off so frequently by himself to commune with the Father in heaven is to be found the technique, not only of gathering strength and wisdom for the ordinary conflicts of living, but also of appropriating the energy for the solution of the higher problems of a moral and spiritual nature. . . . **I am**

deeply impressed with the custom of Jesus in going apart by himself to engage in these seasons of solitary survey of the problems of living; to seek for new stores of wisdom and energy for meeting the manifold demands of social service; to quicken and deepen the supreme purpose of living by actually subjecting the total personality to the consciousness of contacting with divinity. [160:1.10]

Later in this passage, Rodan explains that this practice involves a bodily and mental discipline: "[Jesus meditates] with an eye single to the glory of God" and "breathe[s] in sincerity [his] favorite prayer, 'Not my will, but yours, be done.'" (See 160:1.11.) Of course, an emphasis on breathing ("breathe in sincerity") and mental concentration ("an eye single") can also be found throughout the world's meditative traditions. Further, such practices also yield a profound relaxation, as today's scientific research proves. "This worshipful practice of your Master brings that relaxation which renews the mind. . . . The relaxation of worship, or spiritual communion as practiced by the Master, relieves tension, removes conflicts, and mightily augments the total resources of the personality." [160:1.12] I might add that this relaxation confers improved health on the body as well.

Such results are possible because, as the *UB* reveals, the "lamp of God" actually shines on us *from within the center of the mind*. The tranquil and devoted mind—the purified and transparent consciousness—opens an inner portal to the God Fragment. Once it is made receptive, our mind becomes congruent with the energies of divinity, as does our body. We overflow with the desire to love, and that's why the true mystic regards others as God sees them, resolving to treat them with an agape love that asks nothing in return.

Let's continue to follow this fruitful metaphor of light.

It is helpful to regard the qualities comprising love as being derived from the coherence of divine light. We know, for example, that natural white light refracts into the full spectrum of colors. More specifically, when the three primary colors (blue, yellow, and red) are combined in various ways, they produce the entire array of visible colors. In the same way, philosophers have pointed out that the light of God "refracts" into a set of three primary values—truth, beauty, and goodness.

A very helpful evocation of these "intrinsic values of evolution" is provided in Steve McIntosh's book *The Presence of the Infinite: The Spiritual Experience of Beauty, Truth, and Goodness* (2015), where he explains how the value-triad of truth, beauty, and goodness are like rays emanating from the radiance of the Infinite. As we metabolize these values through reflective practices and appreciative relationships, we achieve ever-more refined states of awareness, writes McIntosh, thereby accelerating the evolution of consciousness and culture.

Wilber's theory of integral spirituality systematizes the idea that our being evolves upward through such felt experiences. We ascend from *gross* to *subtle* to *causal* to *nondual* stages of consciousness as we stabilize ourselves in increasingly more refined states of awareness.

Following the lead of the *UB*, I have labeled this "the feeling line," and in chapter 7 I distinguished it from thinking and willing. It's now time to launch into a deeper look at the latter two developmental lines. Our hypothesis remains: *circle-making comprises all three lines* as we head toward the perfection and unification of the totality of self.

CHAPTER 10

Cultivating Contact
with Spirit

By faith Enoch was translated that he should not see death;
and was not found, because God had translated him.
—*Hebrews 11:5 KJV*

Seeds of the good, the true, and the beautiful are sprouting everywhere in the space-time universes. The grace and love of God
guarantees that experiences of these divine values will always be
plentiful for us all. This all-pervading presence of divinity catalyzes
soul-synthesis and motivates our journey to God Fusion as pilgrims
on the trail first blazed by Enoch.

By Creator design, our souls naturally evolve in response to
the budding presence of genuine values in daily life. Soul evolution doesn't require that we pursue a highly conscious path. Natural
beauty especially attracts our full attention—while requiring a minimum of conscious effort. Tourists gasp in awe the first time they
peer over the edge of the Grand Canyon. Dads cry for joy when
they witness the birth of a son or daughter. Such exquisite experiences can generate higher feeling-states of consciousness—even if
our usual energetic center of gravity is somewhat lower. We didn't
have to admire that adorable infant, but the choice to do so was
obvious and easy. I cite these examples to illustrate how elementary

soul-making decisions can bring about modest progress in the feeling line of consciousness development.

For some of us, even these small steps loom large in the soul. Recall the NDEr in chapter 1 whose simple experience of cupping a small flower in her hands was revealed during her life review to be the greatest single event of her life. Although the encounter happened by chance, her *choice* in that moment for a pure and undiluted experience of beauty was indeed a soul-making event. Her sidewalk epiphany advanced her ability to feel the presence of divinity. But imagine how this same woman might have evolved and how much richer her life review might have been had she spent her life *consciously* cultivating such peak-state experiences, as well as pursuing excellence in her other lines of development.

The Path and Fruition of Disciplined Meditation

Author and researcher Dustin Diperna makes especially clear in his work how such cultivation of higher states of consciousness is vital to spiritual progress. Diperna's findings follow closely in the footsteps of his mentors Ken Wilber and Daniel P. Brown.[114]

Practitioners on almost any path understand that we can consciously engage in disciplines that produce higher states. But according to Brown's schema as built upon by Wilber and explicated by Diperna, when such awareness practices are repeated often enough and carried out with devotion and intention, we can turn these passing states into established *vantage points*. These plateaus of awareness, once stabilized through persistent cultivation, become our new self-sense; they constitute the felt awareness that infuses our experiences of our world.

---

[114] See Diperna's *Streams of Wisdom: An Advanced Guide to Integral Spiritual Development* (Integral Publishing House, 2014). His mentor, Daniel Brown, PhD, is an associate clinical professor of psychology at Harvard Medical School and is the author of fourteen books, including *Pointing Out the Great Way: The Stages of Meditation in the Mahamudra Tradition* (Wisdom Publications, 2006). Brown is also a translator of Tibetan texts who has maintained close relations with teachers of the Tibetan major lineages for more than thirty-five years. *Pointing Out the Great Way* has been called "a valuable synthesis of more than a thousand years of meditation instructions filtered through the author's understanding of Tibetan and Western ways of describing the mind."

For example, with enough mind training, our subjective center of gravity can move upward from a gross to a subtle vantage point. Once we have achieved an unwavering consciousness at this new level of subtle-realm awareness, that higher position becomes like a stepping-stone that we linger over before moving on to more inclusive vantage points. As we arrive and stabilize at each stone in the progression, that new platform becomes our state identity, or *state-stage*, as Wilber calls it.

We can see in this analysis how decades of cross-cultural, faith-neutral research into states of awareness have been fruitful. Most researchers now agree with Brown (and many others) that at the baseline of consciousness, our thoughts and feelings are fused with our awareness. In other words, we are so identified with our mental chatter that we are unable to distinguish it from the general field of our experience—that is, we can't distinguish the forest of awareness from the trees of thought, so to speak. It is this confused and egocentric state that Wilber designates the *gross level of consciousness*, following the long-established stage theory inherited from Vedanta and Buddhist adepts as well as the descriptions of some Western mystics.

If the gross stage is our vantage point, our primary spiritual task becomes disidentifying with the flow of our thoughts and feelings, allowing us to untangle their incestuous relationship with awareness. Awareness is, by definition, inclusive of all cognizable mental events. Through intention, we can cultivate a higher state of consciousness that renders this flow of events as *objects within awareness*. Awareness itself now moves to the foreground and thoughts fall to the background; pure awareness as such becomes the seat of our subjectivity. This state (which Brown simply calls awareness) now becomes our new vantage point; Wilber and Diperna call it subtle-state awareness, as indicated above in our example.

Of course, we can progress further. While it is true that our flow of thoughts (ideas, images, sensations, and feelings) at this stage is now understood as merely the transient arising and passing of objects of awareness, it's now time for a new stepping-stone: the realization that *awareness itself* has hidden characteristics that color our perception. So the next step is to deconstruct the prejudices, opinions, and desires that color our awareness; we make *them* the objects of observation, surveying these forms of bias from an even higher place in awareness that Wilber calls the causal state. Of course, this activity can take many forms depending on one's religious tradition.

And on we go from there to more advanced stepping-stones.

Next, according to Diperna, the mystic will dismantle the assumption of a time-space continuum (Brown's phrase) that underlies awareness, thereby achieving a new vantage point beyond time and space. (Easier said than done, I might add.) The general result is that we dwell in the "eternal now" despite the outward appearance of flux. This level Wilber calls the witness.

But it turns out that the witness *itself* must also be deconstructed. Attaining the witnessing vantage point may place the practitioner above the fray in a state of serenity, but it still harbors an unnecessary duality. "The field of experience [still] appears to be other than the point of observation," writes Diperna, referring to the fact that the experiencer is still distinct from his or her experience. "The first step at this stage is to employ practices that see through this unnecessary duality." Diperna is referring here, of course, to the need to deconstruct the very distinction between subject and object in human consciousness.

Continuing along this line—if understood now in *UB* terms— the practitioner increasingly experiences a direct encounter with the Indwelling Spirit at the heart of consciousness. We progress toward a final identification with *its* vantage point—which, of course, is absolute. Diperna and hi colleagues call this stage non-dual realization.

In a breakthrough interpretation, *UB* scholar Robert Kezer has mapped onto this Diperna/Brown/Wilber model his understanding of Jesus's growth to perfection as narrated in the Urantia text. In this passage, Kezer especially links the *UB*'s discussion to the state-stages of Wilber's Integral Map.

According the Urantia Revelation, Christ **achieved permanent nondual realization in his thirty-first year** when he went into isolation for six weeks on the slopes of Mt.

Hermon for the purpose of completing the work of mastering his human mind. During this period, **he finished his "mortal task of achieving the circles of mind-understanding and personality control."** [134:7.6–7] In effect, this terminated the period of his mortal bestowal—the period of being known as the "son of man"—and in doing so **he met God's requirement of fully experiencing life as a mortal** [and demonstrated] **the qualities of a unified personality.**[115]

Soon after, Kezer continues, Jesus presented himself to John the Baptist on the shores of the Jordan. He is now "a mortal of the realm who had attained the pinnacle of human evolutionary ascension. . . . Perfect synchrony and full communication had become established between the mortal mind of Jesus and the Indwelling Spirit Adjuster." [136:2.2]

However, Jesus stopped just short of fusion at the moment of his baptism. He had a more far more important purpose: to serve humankind in his eventful public ministry. Fusion would have meant his complete and eternal identification with the vantage point of God—which, we have noted, is inconsistent with bodily existence on Earth, as Enoch first discovered.

God-Consciousness and Intellectual Self-Mastery

We know from our earlier discussions that the foregoing picture may be incomplete. Yes, of course, Jesus had fully immersed himself in God-consciousness like many other saints and mystics over the ages. But he was far more than a mystic adept, an otherworldly monastic, a fool for God, or a cultish zealot; he was a perfectly unified personality who had achieved his circles and was ready for Father Fusion. He had not only realized a superbly refined level of awareness along the axis of faith and feeling; he had also attained "quantitative soul growth through seasoned wisdom"—that being the other of the two axes of soul growth.

---

[115] "Integral Christ: Exploring the Kosmic Address of the Christ of the Urantia Revelation," by Robert Kezer, *Journal of Integral Theory and* Practice, vol. 5, no. 3, p. 168.

According to the Integral Map presented in chapter 7, the line of quantitative soul growth described in the *UB* corresponds more or less to the cognitive line highlighted by Wilber. We can also call it *intellectual self-mastery*. Jesus had "grown up" to gain mastery on this line because of his wide-ranging socialization, which included raising and supporting a large family, an extensive education that included world travel and the mastery of three languages, and his acquirement of advanced skills too numerous to mention. As a result, his level of cognitive attainment extended to worldcentric and beyond, whereas most of his contemporaries were little more than ethnocentric.[116]

But rather than explicate this aspect of Jesus's self-mastery with more theoretical analysis, allow me instead to illustrate it with two stories from his life. I earlier noted that during his "lost years," Jesus had visited Rome while working as a translator and tutor for a wealthy Indian merchant and his son who were traveling around the Mediterranean on business. We read that because the merchant carried with him special greetings from "the princes of India," the three were given an official audience with the Roman emperor, Tiberius. We pick up the *UB*'s narration here:

> The morose emperor was unusually cheerful on this day and chatted long with the trio. And when they had gone from his presence, the emperor, referring to Jesus, remarked to the aide standing on his right, "If I had that fellow's kingly bearing and gracious manner, I would be a real emperor, eh?" [130:0.1]

Tiberius had been one of Rome's greatest generals, having penetrated far into the frontier to establish the empire's northern boundary in the lands of "Germania." He was a cosmopolitan man who was the head of state for the world's great empire. Yet, next to him, Jesus stood out as kingly, even in the eyes of the emperor himself.

---

[116] This point of comparison holds true for most world-class mystics down through the centuries. The great Indian sage Ramakrishna had most likely achieved first-circle status and, to his great credit, even endeavored to break out of ethnocentric Hindiusm. But his quantitative soul growth as a monastic renunciant could not have been comparable to that of Jesus.

Something similar occurred in Jesus's encounter with Annas on the fateful night before his crucifixion. Annas was the high priest emeritus of Jerusalem, described in the Urantia text as "the most powerful single individual in all Jewry." (See the full account at 184:1, "Examination by Annas.")

It is not implausible that Annas or others among his contemporaries in the Sanhedrin had achieved high degrees of intellectual prowess and worldly wisdom. But the brief biblical account of this meeting—and more especially the *UB*'s detailed narration of it—shows just how Jesus far outranked Annas in faith attainment and intellectual self-mastery.

As we read the poignant description of their meeting, we realize that facing off with a man of far superior character proves too much for Annas to bear. Jesus outwits him with towering clarity and simplicity at each turn of the exchange—much as he had routed or refuted other challengers sent by the Sanhedrin to derail him with trick questions while he taught the common people.

Jesus's demeanor in the chambers of Annas at first startles the high priest. "Jesus was even more majestic and well poised than Annas remembered him," we read. As the examination proceeds, Jesus is undaunted and even "kindly" in the face of Annas's emotional abuse and vicious threats. By the end of the proceedings, the contrast of their two characters lays bare Annas's spiritual bankruptcy. Losing his equilibrium, Annas bolts from the room at the high point of their discussion. Clearly, he knows better than to condemn Jesus to death. But Annas is unable to face his own defective thinking and moral depravity, which are now all the more evident in the light of Jesus's regal demeanor. Ultimately, the high priest chooses self-enrichment and political expediency over "the light of God" that Jesus offers him. Annas would rather destroy Jesus than climb the difficult ladder of self-mastery that Jesus represents.

Divine Will Is Yoked to Human Will

The iconic example of Jesus helps us to better understand the developmental lines and levels of feeling and thinking in their relationship with the Divine Indweller. Indeed, the *UB* exhorts us on its final page to follow his example of balanced growth, saying, "Of all human knowledge, that which is of greatest value is to know the religious life of Jesus and how he lived it." [196:1.3] In this light, let's now turn to *willing*, the third of the trio of human faculties that encompass the circle-making enterprise of cosmic individuation.

Think of the faculty of will as the capacity for "decision-action" or "choice-experience"—shorthand phrases we met earlier that convey the import of being *willing to act*. Willingness in this sense can be defined as the resolve to engage in three fundamental steps of decision-making: (1) select a course of action from a set of options, (2) carry out this decision-action with sober and firm intention, and (3) face the wider consequences of this choice-experience by handling its outcomes with equivalent resolve.

Of course, there can be no doubt that clarity of thought and quality of faith are essential cofactors in the effective exercise of our human will. After all, our level of intellectual and emotional maturity governs what options have any chance of becoming available to us in the first place. For example, without Dr. Martin Luther King's advanced education and superb development of faith, he would have never been in a position to exercise those decision-actions that changed American history.

The story of Jesus's meeting with Annas illustrates Jesus's effective use of will in a manner that is *commensurate with his other lines of development*. His composure in the face of his accuser portrays a striking symmetry of self. In the final hours of his life, Jesus was at one and the same time the picture of deep thinking, superb faith, and wholehearted choosing of the divine will. This fact may not be clear to readers of the biblical accounts, but it is graphically portrayed in the *UB*'s narrative.

During the previous week, Jesus had faithfully marched through the outworking of a series of decision-actions that inexorably led him to the crucial encounter in the palace of Annas. This had included his triumphal entry into Jerusalem, his heroic decision to drive commercial trade from the Temple, his eloquent teaching to the throngs in the Temple, his daring public denunciation of the Jewish leaders, and his strategic withdrawal with the apostles for rest and their final meeting together—the Last Supper.[117] By now, Jesus knew he would be arrested by cowardly and unjust men. And then, while immersed in prayer in the Garden of Gethsemane, Jesus discovered that it was the Father's will that he *continue to experience the natural consequences of the decisions he had previously made* in these matters—much as would any other teacher of truth in the face of corrupt power, such as Socrates or Martin Luther King. There and then Jesus chose to further align his will with the divine will, which meant facing an appalling death at the hands of his enemies.[118] (See "Alone in Gethsemane" at 182:3.)

The Father's will, in this sense, is scalable—it adapts to a person's circle achievement as well as to the demands of the moment. High-quality thinking and feeling are crucial, but in the final analysis God needs willing and courageous workers. The divine will scales up as we become more willing to serve fearlessly in whatever circumstances challenge us. If we have the maturity to handle what may be needed for transforming a situation, the Father's requirements can potentially take us far out of any conceivable comfort zone. The Indwelling Spirit can and will stretch us to our limit, but if we decide to *not* "drink the cup" (I allude here to Jesus's statement on Gethsemane, "My Father, if it is not possible for this cup to be taken away unless I drink it, may your will be done." See Luke 22: 39.), the assignment will be transferred to others who *are* willing and who can be counted on to follow through with steadfast intent.

The Indweller's job, therefore, is the spiritualization of the human will so that we can "drink more cups" for cosmic evolution. Upon gifting itself to us when we were young children, the inner

---

[117] For those new to the *UB*, its narration provides vastly more information than the New Testament about the events of the final week of Jesus's life. The story that begins with his entry into Jerusalem and ends with his death fills sixteen papers and is 145 pages long (in the original edition of *The Urantia Book*).

[118] "The Father in heaven desired the bestowal Son to finish his earth career *naturally*, just as all mortals must finish up their lives on earth and in the flesh. Ordinary men and women cannot expect to have their last hours on earth and the supervening episode of death made easy by a special dispensation. Accordingly, Jesus elected to lay down his life in the flesh in the manner which was in keeping with the outworking of natural events, and he steadfastly refused to extricate himself from the cruel clutches of a wicked conspiracy of inhuman events which swept on with horrible certainty toward his unbelievable humiliation and ignominious death." [183:1.2]

Spirit of God faithfully monitors, adjusts, and inspires our willingness until we freely choose the divine will at the greatest scale possible for our native talents. To amplify this point, let's review four key qualities that the Indweller brings to this process: persistence, infallibility, respect, and love.

First of all, the Mystery Monitor never falters in its work. As a fragment of the absolute, it has unlimited energy to engage in this unique endeavor. "Thought Adjusters do not require energy intake; they are energy, energy of the highest and most divine order." [107:6.6] They unceasingly labor to reach us, even in our dream life.[119]

Second, the Indweller never makes mistakes: "The Adjuster is man's infallible cosmic compass, always and unerringly pointing the soul Godward." [107:0.6] Later we read: "*Adjusters never fail;* they are of the divine essence, and they always emerge triumphant in each of their undertakings." [110:3.3] In other words, our failure to survive in the afterlife can only be attributed to human error.

Truly, this divine "groom for our soul" possesses astonishing talents, skills, and assets that infinitely transcend those of the bride, the indwelled human. But upon closer inspection we find that the divine suitor comports itself with an amazing humility. And this is the third quality of his work within: though he displays an unwavering commitment to his flawless pursuit of the bride, he is *wholly subservient to her will,* as we have previously discussed. The Indwelling Spirit is constitutionally unable to coerce or cajole her into doing something she doesn't choose to do. He gives her all possible respect; accepting his love and guidance must be *her* idea.

---

[119] "During the slumber season the Adjuster attempts to achieve only that which the will of the indwelt personality has previously fully approved by the decisions and choosings which were made during times of fully wakeful consciousness, and which have thereby become lodged in the realms of the supermind, the liaison domain of human and divine interrelationship. While their mortal hosts are asleep, the Adjusters try to register their creations in the higher levels of the material mind . . . . [But] it is extremely dangerous to postulate as to the Adjuster content of the dream life. The Adjusters do work during sleep, but your ordinary dream experiences are purely physiologic and psychologic phenomena." [110:3.5]

In the final analysis, whatever the Adjuster has succeeded in doing for you, **the records will show that the transformation has been accomplished with your co-operative consent; you will have been a willing partner with the Adjuster in the attainment of every step** of the tremendous transformation of the ascension career. [110:2.2]

Fourth, the Adjuster naturally exudes a flavor of love, as already noted. Indeed, he inherently represents the divine will at any given moment, which always aims for and expresses love. The Indwelling Spirit is, after all, our divine GPS. He telegraphs the more loving and evolutional path to us through hunches, prompts, intuitions, symbols, dreams, and even via synchronicities arranged with angelic assistance. We are told that such offerings, if unheeded in the mind, can still enrich the soul superconsciously. But they become *experientially available* only to the degree that we are willing to receive, believe, and act on this guidance to serve—that is, to meet others right where they are and lovingly minister to their deepest needs. "Love is the desire to do good to others." [56:10.2]

When I survey my own life today, I sense that I am a willing agent of God's evolutionary love. And to become even more willing and available, I resolve to let pure and free awareness enter into the equation. I invite it to come to the foreground, and I let anxious thoughts recede into the background. I do my best to prepare myself so that the divine will can be conveyed to a still and pliable mind. Then I wait and watch; I hold fast to a vigil for spiritual input. The subtle influences of the God Fragment become more recognizable to me against the backdrop of this open field of receptive awareness.[120]

On the other hand, I know that many folks may prefer a more relational approach to discerning the divine will, as described in this important passage.

---

[120] Meditation lets the gross currents of the material mind drop away. Ideas based on fear, envy, anger, and other negative emotions drown out the input of the spirit-self, whose impulses often transcend ordinary ideation: "The realization of the recognition of spiritual values is an experience which is superideational. There is no word in any human language which can be employed to designate this 'sense,' 'feeling,' 'intuition,' or 'experience' which we have elected to call God-consciousness." [103:1.6]

The doing of the will of God is nothing more or less than an exhibition of creature willingness to share the inner life with God—with the very God who has made such a creature life of inner meaning-value possible. Sharing is Godlike—divine. God shares all with the Eternal Son and the Infinite Spirit, while they, in turn, share all things with the divine Sons and spirit Daughters of the universes. [111:5.1]

Communicating with our Divine Parent goes both ways, of course. I have found that when I am willing to share my needs and desires in prayer, the Indweller is willing to share its response to my listening mind—and this response *is* the will of God for me in that moment. This approach to seeking the divine will brings forward the more traditional I-Thou relationship in which God is understood in the second person as a loving and attentive Father and Mother. Along this line, the *UB* depicts the young Jesus as insisting on having "just a little talk with my Father in heaven" as a supplement to the rote bedtime prayers he had been taught by his parents. (See 123:7.3.)

Prayer, especially when it expresses gratefulness to God, has always been a healing and inspiring practice for me. Those who never share their lives in prayer may face a danger I call solipsistic rumination. Without an imagined "other" to converse with, their thoughts can spiral in on themselves, leading to fear, worry, obsession, or even addiction. To fill the vacuum, they insert their own self-derived notions without the benefit of peer review. They load useless speculation into the space in which prayerful sharing might have taken place. The better psychological choice for such folks is prayerful converse with a "near-by alter ego." And this ostensibly imaginary companion is no mere fiction, because it is the Divine Indweller who is being directly addressed.

Enlightened prayer must recognize not only an external and personal God but also an internal and impersonal Divinity, the indwelling Adjuster. It is altogether fitting that man, when he prays, should strive to grasp the concept of the Universal Father on Paradise; **but the more effective technique for most practical purposes will be to revert to the concept of**

a near-by alter ego, just as the primitive mind was wont to do, and then to recognize that the idea of this alter ego has evolved from a mere fiction to the truth of God's indwelling mortal man in the factual presence of the Adjuster so that man can talk face to face, as it were, with a real and genuine and divine alter ego that indwells him and is the very presence and essence of the living God, the Universal Father. [91:3.7]

So now we have come full circle. According to the argument of this book, cosmic individuation requires the balanced activation of the intrinsic faculties of the self as we move toward complete identification with spirit. The result is circle-making progress—the ultimate expression of our sacred triad with its God-given elements. But there is one final element that crowns the whole process: our God-given *purpose*.

The Inner Discovery of Life Purpose

We've noted that the Thought Adjuster works within to actuate our model careers. And that's because the Indweller is the literal seed-bearer of our ideal lives. Adjusters guide their human hosts throughout each day, but they also harbor a specific agenda—and they make every effort to impart this life plan to us over the course of our lives.

They arrive on the Day of Betrothal with a divine blueprint adapted to our genetic inheritance and the familial and social conditions we will encounter, we are told. The God Fragments operate within these parameters, perhaps in the same way that a human father might gently guide his child into an ideal profession because of his knowledge of the child's natural strengths and how they match the current marketplace. Such a well-meaning human father may be wrong about what is best for his kid, but the Father Fragment actually *knows* what is ideal. The plan it carries in its bosom is our transcendental life purpose. Because this plan has been designed and projected by perfect beings who minister to us from the eternal central universe, it is of great import for soul-making and self-perfecting. Nevertheless, we are *not* obliged to choose this model career.

When Thought Adjusters indwell human minds, they bring with them the model careers, the ideal lives, as determined and foreordained by themselves and [others]. Thus they begin work with a definite and predetermined plan for the intellectual and spiritual development of their human subjects, but it is not incumbent upon any human being to accept this plan. It is their mission to effect such mind changes and to make such spiritual adjustments as you may willingly and intelligently authorize, to the end that they may gain more influence over the personality directionization. [110:2.1]

Every single living person, proclaims the *UB*, has an ideal self in potential. Realizing this promise is the purpose of our soul-making and self-perfecting. Developing a unified and balanced personality is the royal road to that ultimate goal.

The Urantia Revelation clarifies for us that *the soul does not provide this model career*—the Indwelling Spirit *alone* conveys this life purpose.[121] And much is at stake in this distinction. True soul work entails the recognition, not the invention, of this unique aim of life. For most of us, our Thought Adjuster whispers news of our ideal career in childhood and adolescence. After a long series of increasingly accurate approximations, the model career may lodge itself in our soul. But if we conflate our idea of the evolving soul with the

---

[121] Possibly ratifying this idea is *The Soul's Code: In Search of Character and Calling* (Grand Central Publishing, 1997) by renowned post-Jungian psychologist James Hillman. In this important book, Hillman proposes what he calls the "acorn theory," according to which an individual's "life code" enters the child very early in life—which is not unlike the *UB*'s concept of predestination. The analogue, Hillman says, is that the oak tree is inside an acorn. The acorn will grow into an oak as long as it is *able* to grow. If it is not specifically thwarted, it will inevitably become an oak and not some other tree species. Hillman offers numerous examples to show how many people come in with "acorn-like" gifts that have no other explanation, because their talent manifests against all odds. His most vivid example is Judy Garland, but he cites innumerable other examples such as Charles Darwin, Henry Ford, Billy Graham, and Kurt Cobain. "I believe we have been robbed of our true biography," writes Hillman. "[It's our true] destiny that's written into the acorn—and we go to therapy to recover it. That innate image can't be found, however, until we have a psychological theory that grants primary psychological reality to the call of fate. . . . Repression, the key to personality structure in all therapy schools, is not of the past but of the acorn and the past mistakes we have made in our relation to it." I submit that the Urantia Revelation offers the kind of psychological theory that supports Hillman's discovery.

concept of the inner spirit, difficulties arise in our understanding of this crucial process.

Reincarnation on Earth Versus Purposeful Ascension

I am aware that many of my contemporaries, including some distinguished scientists, regard this matter differently. They believe that after we die our soul returns to Earth after having devised a life plan for its next incarnation. Many believe that the individual soul directs the action, along with input from other beings, perhaps after a review of the previous life. This evolving human soul chooses a new set of parents, a geographical location, and a new life mission—and then decides to reincarnate on Earth to learn new lessons and eliminate any karma debt created in its previous life or lives. But if the Urantia Revelation is right about the functions of the inner triad, this depiction of reincarnation can't be literally correct. In particular, the idea that a relatively inexperienced evolving soul chooses its own model career—its true life purpose—may be a serious fallacy.

In this book I have explicated the idea that the evolving soul is a unique synthesis of the energies of our imperfect material mind and the perfect Thought Adjuster. As such, the soul is energetically and ontologically distinct from the spirit and very different indeed from the unique personality. So let's bring these newly revealed ideas to bear in analyzing the ancient claim of reincarnation.

The *UB* teaches that the far-seeing Divine Indweller enters the budding mind of a newborn child with a special life plan that was formulated in eternity. This plan is the gift of the omniscient Father, who sorts and sifts the "personnel needs" of an evolving planet with the help of other divine agencies. The soul can never operate on its own in such matters, which are solely in the purview of the all-seeing infinite Creator and his coordinate Deities.

The picture of the overall role of the inner triad that we get from the *UB* is also far more intricate than the vague and varied descriptions we find in the lore of reincarnation. For example, the Indweller's decision to enter the mind of a particular child occurs long after the Father confers the gift of unique personality. And remember that the Divine Fragment is seeking union with the personality *and* the growing soul at the same time that it attempts to mold the indwelled child into a mature man or woman who embodies their unique life purpose.

For clarity, allow me to restate this complex issue in another way.

According to the account of "selfhood design" I offer in this book, all souls begin down here as virgin entities. The personality (which is also unique and new) operates during our life on Earth through the vehicle of the material mind and helps generate a fresh human soul in cooperation with the Divine Fragment. After death, none of these members of our inner triad return to the world of their first appearance. (But there is a big exception, explained below.) Indeed, there is no compelling reason for returning to the kindergarten of Earth; a vast multiverse is out there to be explored, and our benefactors are eager for us to advance to the first grade.

Remember that a magnificent ascension regime has been organized on our behalf. Our survival into the afterlife is like a matriculation into a gigantic cosmic university of ascension to Paradise. The educational charter of this universal school is to graduate self-perfected, God-identified souls. Our intense life on Earth is worthy of very careful review after our death, and the harsh lessons learned here will inform our personalized afterlife curriculum. The new lesson plan developed for us will require, in the first place, that we address our basic deficits in feeling, thinking, and willing. But the key point here is that the universe is progressive and evolutionary—we simply must move on. The principal of the elementary school of the grand cosmos doesn't need to keep recycling our souls back to a dangerous kindergarten on a lowly, crime-ridden, war-torn material planet.

As we go forward into the afterlife, we are given both individualized and group instruction. We meet other ascenders from millions of other worlds that have amazingly diverse forms of life and culture; later we can meet ascenders from other galaxies and even other superuniverses. Then we progress to the unspeakable grandeur of the central universe. As we socialize and ascend, our horizons grow immensely. We spend ages with beings of other orders who teach us and minister to us according to a course of learning unfathomable to educators on Earth.

All of this illustrates why cosmology is so crucial in this equation of soul evolution. Contemporary beliefs in reincarnation are almost all rooted in indigenous or pre-Copernican cosmologies that were cyclical rather than evolutionary. Most of these systems lack the theological sophistication and philosophic correction required to be serviceable in the integral age.

All that said, at least three factors listed in the Urantia text may explain why so many people, and in fact entire cultures, have come to believe that souls reincarnate:

1. Souls are nonlocal and thus are contactable. Research has established that human minds are capable of nonlocal activities such as clairvoyance, telepathy, remote viewing, distance healing, and many other psychic capacities. Accordingly, human souls are nonlocal as well. And if that is the case, I believe that it is a relatively simple matter for one's soul to resonate with another soul in the "field of all souls" called the Supreme Being. As Carl Jung clearly showed, the collective unconscious is constituted by the archetypal affinities among all the souls of the past. Childhood and adult experiences, and especially the dramas and traumas of life, may cause us to resonate with preexisting souls in the nonlocal field who have had similar or related experiences. After the surprising experience of feeling a psychic resonance with another soul, we may project onto this experience the idea that this other soul is *our own soul* from a previous life, simply because of a personal religious predisposition based on an outdated cosmology.

2. All human minds are derived from the cosmic mind. I've explained several times that mind is sourced from the unitary Absolute Mind of the Infinite Spirit, which in turn is the source of the cosmic mind that self-distributes segmentations of mind to all humans in space-time. We read in the following statement that as a result, minds can have uncanny affinities to other minds, which may also help explain how we gravitate to the souls of others: "The fact of the cosmic mind explains the kinship of various types of human and superhuman minds. Not only are kindred spirits attracted to each other, but kindred minds are also very fraternal and inclined toward cooperation the one with the other. Human minds are sometimes observed to be running in channels of astonishing similarity and inexplicable agreement." [16:6]

3. Some Thought Adjusters have indwelled other humans previous to the current indwelling. Although the *UB* teaches that neither the entity known as unique personality nor its associated soul can return to the Earth plane, it turns out that the Thought Adjuster *can* "reincarnate"—and this fact likely causes at least some of the confusion around the issue. The Adjuster is available to indwell another individual if the person formerly inhabited did *not* choose to survive to ascend in the afterlife. In addition, we are told that the soul and the personality of the nonsurvivor forever lose their associations with individualized consciousness; they become absorbed into the Supreme (the subject of the next chapter) as a contribution toward its evolution.

Thus, the Thought Adjuster of the nonsurvivor becomes a free agent who can indwell another person—*but always on a different planet than that of the original indwelling*. In other words, all personalities and all souls present on Earth are virgin, but this is not true of the God Fragments, who may have already inhabited a number of nonsurviving individuals. And I would not be surprised if many of you reading this book have been blessed with a spark of God that has already indwelled humans on other planets. These experienced Adjusters contain within themselves all the soul memories of the previous indwellee(s), and those records remain the eternal possession of that Adjuster. Such Adjusters do a better job in subsequent assignments because of their previous experience of inhabiting and adjusting other animal-origin human minds. If you are fortunate enough to possess such a veteran Indweller, it is plausible that if you received some intimation of a previous life (or lives), you could mistake it for a previous lifetime of your own. In other words, it is easy to confuse a past life on Earth with the actual life of some other personality on another inhabited planet.

Because so much is at stake, more research is needed beyond this rudimentary examination of the issue. And if we remember that the Indweller brings to us our ideal life plan, settling these questions becomes all the more important. That's especially because the Urantia Revelation makes it clear that we are all subjects of "predestination"—that is, a predetermined blueprint of a model career—if we are willing to actualize this unique life purpose. The opportunity is superb, but the choice is always ours.

> You are all subjects of predestination, but it is not foreordained that you must accept this divine predestination; you are at full liberty to reject any part or all of the Thought Adjusters' program. [110:2.1]

Evolutionary Deity and Cosmic Spirituality

Truth is to be found neither in the thesis or
the antithesis, but in the synthesis of the two.
—*George Wilhelm Friedrich Hegel*

In a scene near the end of the movie *The Grapes of Wrath*, the story's hero, Tom Joad, is about to flee a rural camp in California that is overflowing with migrant farmworkers, most of them displaced Oklahoma farm families. Company thugs have been beating up the Okies to keep them from striking, and now a posse is out searching for Joad (played by Henry Fonda). In the middle of the night Joad wakes up scared. Resolving to take flight, he goes to Ma to say goodbye. In this dialogue, she asks him what he'll do when he is on the run.

> **Tom**: Maybe I can do somethin' . . . maybe I can just find out something,' just scrounge around and maybe find out what it is that's wrong and see if they ain't somethin' that can be done about it. I ain't thought it out all clear, Ma. I can't. I don't know enough.

Ma: How am I gonna know about ya, Tommy? Why they could kill ya and I'd never know. They could hurt ya. How am I gonna know?

Tom: Well, maybe it's like Casey says. **A fellow ain't got a soul of his own, just a little piece of a big soul, the one big soul that belongs to everybody,** then . . .

Ma: Then what, Tom?

Tom: Then it don't matter. I'll be all around in the dark—I'll be everywhere. Wherever you can look—wherever there's a fight, so hungry people can eat, I'll be there. Wherever there's a cop beatin' up a guy, I'll be there. I'll be in the way guys yell when they're mad. I'll be in the way kids laugh when they're hungry and they know supper's ready, and when the people are eatin' the stuff they raise and livin' in the houses they build . . . I'll be there, too.

Ma: I don't understand it, Tom.

Tom: Me, neither, Ma, but—just somethin' I been thinkin' about.

This classic piece of Americana is reminiscent of Walt Whitman's idea of the collective soul and Ralph Waldo Emerson's *Over-Soul*. And Tom Joad is right, I think. Our evolving soul is not merely some private possession; it's actually "a little piece of a big soul." And if Joad lives from "big soul," he'll "be everywhere," as he puts it. (The collective soul is, after all, nonlocal.) The spirit of Joad will be out looking to spread justice, as well as fulfillment, to everyone.

Because injustice reigns on our world, "big-soul work" needs willing hands. Theologically speaking, there are righteous tasks to be done because the cocreative God of evolution—the evolving Supreme Being revealed in the Urantia Revelation—is an *incomplete* Deity-in-the-making.

The great oversoul evolves, but only when little souls contribute their "piece" to the big soul. As the *UB* puts it, "To the extent that we do the will of God in whatever universe station we may have our existence, in that measure the Supreme becomes one step more actual." (117:0.1) It's up to us and our divine collaborators, and that's why it's "somethin' we need to be thinkin' about."

The evolving God of time and space is *not* omnipotent. It is a tragic fact that war, crime, and atrocities can and do take place during the current phase of this unfinished God's evolutionary unfolding. And that's why the "God of this world"[122] may sometimes appear to us like the Demiurge of the Gnostics. (For a more thorough review, see chapter 6.) The ancient Christian Gnostics predated Darwin by eighteen hundred years. They simply could not envision an evolving universe, so they concluded that the material world—being so unfair and hellish—must have somehow "fallen" and was being held down by the malice of the Demiurge. Salvation, they thought, required escaping the illusory world of matter by uniting with the divine spark within that was provided by the high Gods in their merciful effort to circumvent the Demiurge.

Such is the cosmic escapism of Gnosticism. Its powerful logic has had a perennial impact on humankind, showing up in a variety of compelling teachings in the world's wisdom traditions. These sincere teachers of old, with a few possible exceptions such as the Egyptians, had no pathway for conceiving of an evolving soul. They could not help but miss the evolutionary imperatives of soul-making and the need for political and social transformation on Earth. At the high point of the Axial Age, it was widely believed that there was nowhere to go but "up and out" toward union with the One. Liberation from the "prison of matter" could only be accomplished by shedding material desires—letting go of all bodily and worldly concerns.

Many of today's teachers of monism and nondual spirituality, especially those following in the tradition of Ramana Maharshi, have successfully updated and restated for modern ears this classic preference for otherworldly bliss. But according to philosopher Steve McIntosh, nondualism of this sort misses what he calls "the evolutionary necessity of a spiritually real evolving soul." The nondualist

---

[122] "Satan, who is the god of this world, has blinded the minds of those who don't believe. They are unable to see the glorious light of the Good News. They don't understand this message about the glory of Christ, who is the exact likeness of God." (2 Corinthians 4 NLV)

teachings that are currently so popular, he points out, *conflate the Indwelling Spirit and evolving soul* into a static "Higher Self." (Of course, they don't distinguish the unique personality either.) The nondual practitioner's task, these new movements teach, is to dis-identify with our illusory ego and realize the "always-already" presence of spiritual perfection in an as the Self. McIntosh writes:

> **These teachings leave little room for the evident truth of the evolving soul that is growing out of the interplay of the Higher Self and the ego-identity.** . . . . But if our spirituality has no place in its teachings for an evolving soul—if our conception includes only the relatively unreal ego and the everlasting and unchanging absolute self (or no-self)—then the spiritual value of what is evolving in our consciousness goes missing. Stated another way, if the goal is simply to overcome our identification with the lower self and recognize that the always-already-perfect nature of the Higher Self is who we are, then **the spiritual reality of the "becoming" is collapsed or reduced to timeless "being" alone.**[123]

In the face of hard suffering, the impulse of the monist is to escape the pain and the darkness by collapsing the uncertainties of evolution into "timeless 'being' alone," which at a minimum implies that evolutionary decision-action is ultimately meaningless and val-ueless. This fallacy of impartiality misses the richness of the archi-tecture of evolutionary panentheism that, as McIntosh points out, maintains the creative polarity between time and eternity as well as a fruitful dialectic of the one and the many.

And the meeting point for this dialectic is the sacred triad within. On the one hand, the evolving universe *depends* on the human choice-experience that produces soul-making decisions. On the other, the Eternal Father cosponsors the effort through the gifts of the God Fragment and the unifying presence of the freewill personality. By revealing the hybrid nature of human selfhood—a self-system that is designed to be embedded in a God-centered evo-lutionary cosmology as an agent of change *and* continuity—the *UB*

---

[123] See *The Presence of the Infinite*, p. 177.

offers an essential correction to nondualism. This view of self and soul literally transcends but includes the monistic impulse, thereby correcting its tendency to nihilism.

But we don't need to lose sight of the fact that nondual spirituality offers essential truths, even if one sided. For example, imagine that a nondual practitioner sitting in *satsang* is able to dissolve the witness consciousness and allow her vantage point to become nondual. Achieving and stabilizing this advanced state represents a series of choices that are, paradoxically, profoundly soul-making for her. Her efforts can, at least potentially, harvest the creative tension between the arrow of time and the stillness of eternal being. The bliss of the spiritual energy that she liberates by her practice generates profound well-being in her life; but if this attainment were to be consciously informed by a sense of *evolutionary moral duty* (with the help of what McIntosh would call a "dialectical epistemology"), the very same energy could overflow into equally profound political engagement. Such was the *sadhana* of Mahatma Gandhi, for example.

Preserving the polarity of time and eternity also has great import for our understanding of the meaning of suffering and injustice. If we adopt the *UB*'s version of evolutionary panentheism, the presence of so much evil and darkness should not cause bewilderment. Instead, we can logically infer that the direct Creators of our world—while being of origin from the Paradise Deites—are also *nonperfect divine beings who are evolving right along with us*. Just like us, but on a vastly greater scale, they too have access to divine gifts provisioned by existential Deity. But they don't have the power to summarily remove evildoers and they do not and cannot, by divine fiat, create utopias. Instead, they must cocreatively evolve each imperfect planet by the technique of fostering creature choices in favor of the true, the beautiful, and the good. This profound quote sums up the point:

If man recognized that his Creators—his immediate supervisors—while being divine were also finite, and that the God of time and space was an evolving and nonabsolute Deity, then would the inconsistencies of temporal inequalities cease to be profound religious

paradoxes. No longer would religious faith be prostituted to the promotion of social smugness in the fortunate while serving only to encourage stoical resignation in the unfortunate victims of social deprivation. When viewing the exquisitely perfect spheres of Havona [in the central universe], it is both reasonable and logical to believe they were made by a perfect, infinite, and absolute Creator. **But that same reason and logic would compel any honest being, when viewing the turmoil, imperfections, and inequities of Urantia, to conclude that your world had been made by, and was being managed by, Creators who were subabsolute, preinfinite, and other than perfect.** [116:0.1-2]

The Grand Project of the Ages

Process theology, an American invention of another kind, represents a philosopher's version of Tom Joad's "big soul." It also agrees in broad outline with the *UB*'s evolutionary theology outlined above. But I noted in chapter 3 that process philosophy needs more clarification regarding one piece of the puzzle: how God can remain utterly transcendent while self-limiting his Deity manifestations in order to enable cosmic evolution.

As a Tom Joad might put it, the "big God" should remain infinite while making it possible for "little-gods-in-the-making." Or, as the Urantia Revelation expresses it, time and eternity remain in creative polarity because *infinity encompasses the capability of self-limitation.* "The Father is infinite and eternal, but to deny the possibility of his volitional self-limitation amounts to a denial of this very concept of his volitional absoluteness." [4:4:4]

As such, God as Primal Father is a self-emptying or *kenotic* God—as many contemporary theologians also teach.[124] As the *UB* explains, the Father delegates "every power and all authority that could be delegated" and bestows "all of himself and all of his attributes, everything he possibly could divest himself of, in every

---

[124] Among these are Philip Clayton (a Protestant) and John Haught (a Catholic).

way, in every age, in every place, and to every person, and in every universe." [10:1:2]

God is able bestow these gifts because of a self-imposed limitation on his infinitude. And significantly, this kenosis reflects "the outworking of the infinite love of the Universal Father." [32:4:10] Accordingly, God calls forth the possibility of an evolving universe of loving relationships. The Father-Mother creates a finite space in which other subabsolute beings can engage in independent action for the sake of self-divinization. And the Divine Person also provides these finite beings with the resources they need to move forward with safe passage. A biblical analogy may help here: out of love, Yahweh parts the Red Sea to allow Moses and the chosen people to safely pass to the promised land.[125]

In the first "step," the Father-Infinite bestows all that is possible to bestow—including absolute personhood—on his coequal divine partners. God also sources Paradise, the gravitational and energetic center of all things. Then, together with the Son, the Father creates (in eternity) the central universe, and the Infinite Spirit "eternalizes" along with these eternal worlds. After the creation of the perfect central universe, the imperfect realms of space and time appear— the seven superuniverses comprising approximately seven hundred thousand inhabited galaxies—along with their evolving creatures.

In a sense, the perfect central universe is the *thesis*, the perfecting space-time universe is the *antithesis*, and the soul-making and cosmic individuating activity of God's creatures is the *synthesis*.[126]

The outworking of infinite love also supplies energy so that the evolving realms can operate sustainably. In eternity the Father unveils the *Unqualified Absolute*, the stupendous reservoir of energy that vitalizes the unfolding realms of space, wherein "we live and

---

[125] This image is suggested by Stuart Kerr, author of the first full-length book about the Supreme Being entitled *God, Man, and Supreme–Origin and Destiny* (CreateSpace, 2016).

[126] This idea appears in the work of Steve McIntosh in *Evolution's Purpose: An Integral Interpretation of the Scientific Story of Our Origins* (Select Books, 2012) and is also found in the writings of William S. Sadler, Jr., one of the original Contact Commissioners of the Urantia Revelation. He is the author one of the very best secondary works on the *UB* available, *A Study of the Master Universe: A Development of Concepts in the Urantia Book* (Second Society Foundation, 1968).

move and have our being" [Acts 17:28]. This cosmic power supply is known to today's visionary scientists as the *quantum plenum*, a technical concept inherited from quantum physics that I discuss in Appendix D, "The Quantum Plenum and Space Potency." This nonliving energy that is inherently resident in space itself as *space potency*—along with the divine energy of life itself—"proceeds" from the Father-Infinite in a beginningless and endless stream to all universes.

God also lovingly delegates the oversight of the evolutionary domains to the evolving Deities of space-time known as the Supreme Creators. The so-called Creator Sons and Creative Daughters are the most important members of this corps.[127] Like all of the Supreme Creators, they are both divine *and* evolutional. They create and rule local universes with a love and mercy that reflects the Paradise Deities from whom they take origin. Operating as coequal male and female Deity complements, they carve out local universes of millions of inhabitable worlds and then create, out of the dust, the evolutionary biological lineages that produce the intelligent animals that we call humans—who then receive directly from the Father their unique personalities and God Fragments. (See Appendix B for more information about our local universe Creators, known to us as Mother Spirit and Christ Michael, who incarnated as Jesus of Nazareth.)

This beautiful quote encapsulates the overall work of the Supreme Creators:

Unqualified Paradise Deity is incomprehensible to the evolving creatures of time and space. . . . Therefore does Paradise Deity attenuate and otherwise qualify the extra-Paradise personalizations of divinity, thus bringing into existence the Supreme Creators and their associates, who ever carry the

---

[127] In the local universes the Creators evolve: "The [Creative Daughter] presence . . . evolves from a living power focus to the status of the divine personality of a Universe Mother Spirit; the Creator Son evolves from the nature of existential Paradise divinity to the experiential nature of supreme sovereignty. The local universes are the starting points of true evolution, the spawning grounds of bona fide imperfect personalities endowed with the freewill choice of becoming cocreators of themselves as they are to be." [116:4.8]

light of life farther and farther from its Paradise source until it finds its most distant and beautiful expression in the earth lives of the bestowal Sons on the evolutionary worlds. [116:2.3]

By attenuating or emptying himself in all of these ways, the Father sets the stage for the project of the ages: the grand dialectic between eternal God as *existential and infinite* and space-time Deity as *evolutional and finite*.

Here's a summary description of this cosmic dialectic:

God removes himself from all-pervading perfection and infinitude. A nonperfect "gap" appears that we call the finite realm, in which creatures can evolve. This realm provides a space, conditioned by time, in which imperfect creatures can swing back to God as perfecting beings. As philosopher McIntosh puts it, God's kenosis "leaves a vacuum which evolution rushes into, restoring organized information, value, and consciousness, increasingly by steps."[128] And as the *UB* says, "Emptiness does have its virtue, for it may become experientially filled." [117:2.8]

This dance of the perfect and the perfecting is like a joyous universal symphony in which one of the leitmotifs is descent and the other is ascent. God's divine power and love descend from Paradise and, in passionate response, evolving beings ascend back to their Creator, streaming in to the center of all things from their home worlds out in the far periphery of the evolving universes. And this magnificent journey requires "a love supreme" to make it all transpire. Allow me to quote at length:

> The enlightened worlds all recognize and worship the Universal Father, the eternal maker and infinite upholder of all creation. The will creatures of universe upon universe have embarked upon the long, long Paradise journey, the fascinating struggle of the eternal adventure of attaining God the Father. **The transcendent goal of the children of time is to find the eternal God, to comprehend the divine nature, to recognize the Universal Father.** God-knowing creatures

---

[128] Steve McIntosh, *Evolution's Purpose: An Integral Interpretation of the Scientific Story of Our Origins* (Select Books, 2012), p. 175.

have only one supreme ambition, just one consuming desire, and that is to become, as they are in their spheres, like him as he is in his Paradise perfection of personality and in his universal sphere of righteous supremacy. **From the Universal Father who inhabits eternity there has gone forth the supreme mandate, "Be you perfect, even as I am perfect." In love and mercy the messengers of Paradise have carried this divine exhortation down through the ages** and out through the universes, even to such lowly animal-origin creatures as the human races of Urantia. [UB: 1:0.3]

When described in this way, the universal dance seems almost unfathomable. It encompasses imperfect beings from trillions of inhabited planets, each striving to attain perfection by their own choice-experience. All of them become like "migrants headed to the north country of Paradise," but in this case the resources for their journey are plentiful. As the First Source and Center of all things, God can meet all the capital requirements of the project. He provides the endless reservoir of energy, the strategic plan, the project design, the support personnel, and the final goal—a place on Paradise that is reserved for the pilgrims hailing from thousands of galaxies.

In the outward phase of God's divine emanation (as it is revealed in the great dialectic), a self-limiting but self-distributing aspect of God descends into time and space in the form of what are sometimes called the *Descending Sons of God*. The creative work of these descending beings "incarnates" into evolving space-time reality as *almighty power*—a technical phrase (discussed later) that stands for the totality of the activity of the evolutionary realms. This outward phase of the dialectic is also known as *primordial God* in process theology.

During the *inwardly* moving phase of the dialectic (known as the *consequent God* in process theology), self-organization and evolutionary emergence is the great theme. Those ascenders who aspire to perfection "rock" back to the eternal center of all things. During their long, long journey to Paradise they actually do achieve perfection—that is, those who previously opted into Thought Adjuster fusion.[129]

It is fascinating to note that the Creator Sons (and all other Descending Sons who incarnate on planets) are able to achieve an analogous fusion of unlike elements. By virtue of incarnating, these Creators "acquire the natures and cosmic viewpoints of their actual local universe children." [116:4.9] They literally become the eternal *synthesis* of Creator and creature, containing the experiential essence of human nature in their divine being. For example, the soul and the human essence of our Jesus of Nazareth is a treasured possession that eternally resides in the bosom of Christ Michael, our local Creator Son.[130]

And now, let's factor in the role of the Supreme Being as we dive further into the divine dialectic.

I've often noted that the spiritual realities depicted in the *UB* are ultimately personal. Accordingly, the evolving universes are managed by the Supreme, a *divine person-in-the-making*. She could well be described as the orchestrator of the cosmic symphony, but she does so from behind the scenes; as we will see shortly, her divine personality is currently enshrouded.

The Supreme is, first of all, the universal *synthesis* of the incoming and outgoing activity of the great symphony, we are told in the *UB*. She portrays the sum total of the cocreative interaction of the creatures and the Supreme Creators, as explained in this statement:

---

[129] Here is a helpful summary in *UB* phraseology: "In the persons of the Supreme Creators the Gods have descended from Paradise to the domains of time and space, there to create and to evolve creatures with Paradise-attainment capacity who can ascend thereto in quest of the Father. **This universe procession of descending God-revealing Creators and ascending God-seeking creatures is revelatory of the Deity evolution of the Supreme, in whom both descenders and ascenders achieve mutuality of understanding,** the discovery of eternal and universal brotherhood. The Supreme Being thus becomes the finite synthesis of the experience of the perfect-Creator cause and the perfecting-creature response." [117:1.2]

[130] By engaging in and completing a series of such incarnating activities over eons of time, they achieve the undisputed sovereignty of the local universe of their creation. When our Creator Son completed his life on Earth as Jesus, that was his final bestowal in the likeness of one of his creatures. After his resurrection and ascension, he became the "Master Son" of our local universe. See 21.5.

The evolving divine nature of the Supreme is becoming a faithful portrayal of the matchless experience of all creatures and of all Creators in the grand universe. In the Supreme, creatorship and creaturehood are at one; they are forever united by that experience which was born of the vicissitudes attendant upon the solution of the manifold problems which beset all finite creation as it pursues the eternal path in quest of perfection and liberation from the fetters of incompleteness. [117:1:6]

The Supreme is an on-the-fly unifier of Creator and creature experience. At any one point, she is the up-to-the-moment *summa* or "embodiment" of evolution in all domains. The Supreme is, simply put, *the product of all experience*. She grows to completion in and through the efforts of evolving creatures and evolving Creators. She encompasses and totalizes the choice-experience of all space-time spheres as well as of all higher-dimensional worlds.

Think of her as the cosmic Mississippi River. She receives and registers within herself[131] the incoming stream of the experiences of incarnating avatars such as Jesus; the steady flow of the skillful efforts of divine administrators at all levels; the rivers of uncountable ministering activities of the angelic orders; and the rivulets of all the soul-makers hailing from the trillions of lowly planets.[132] All of this time-space activity contributes to the emerging experiential nature of the Supreme; nothing of lasting value is ever lost, including the souls and personalities of those who *don't* survive. These, too, contribute something of value.

But Supreme is even more than this. She is actually more akin to a living and personal organism whose "evolving soul" is actualizing within her.[133] In fact, the Supreme has direct analogues to our inner sacred triad, whose selfhood reality is evolutional; her divine selfhood is also in the making over time.

---

[131] The revelators state that they are not certain, but it is believed that these "registrations" of creature experience occur through the *persons* of the Supreme Creators. See 117:5, "The Oversoul of Creation."

[132] The aggregators of these "flowing waters" are the seven superuniverses, the great agglomerations of thousands of inhabited galaxies.

[133] In this connection see "The Living Organism of the Grand Universe" at 116:7.

We generally see ourselves as comprising body, mind, soul, spirit, and personality. In the same way, the Supreme has a composite identity. Roughly speaking, her components are technically known as the *Almighty Supreme* (her "body and soul," which is the entirety of the energies, personalities, and structures of space-time); *the Supreme Mind* (bestowed directly by the Infinite Spirit); and *God the Supreme* (the Supreme's so-called "spirit-personality" derived from the Eternal Trinity).

In other words, she is not just an evolutional "big soul." She has real personhood, mindedness, and self-awareness. In her guise as God the Supreme, she even has will, for we read that she is a "volitional and creative participant in [her] own deity actualization." [117:3.7]

But mark well this odd circumstance: *her personality is not contactable by the evolving universes.* It abides out of reach in the perfect domains of the central universe—and actually resides on a unique world therein.

Like all other personalities, God the Supreme (God as the Supreme *person*) is unchanging. Her personality functions as a unifier—much like ours does—but in her case it unifies and systematizes the activities of the body-mind-soul-spirit complex of the grand cosmos. But she will not be available as a person operating recognizably in the space-time realms until *all* of her constituent elements (i.e., the Almighty Supreme) achieve evolutionary completion. In that awesome moment, she will emerge for all of us to engage with—and will be designated by the formal title of "*the Supreme Being.*" Only then will she be contactable as a universal Person in her own right, possessing a fully integrated mind, body, soul, spirit, and personality.

Again, this is much like our own growth challenge. Just as we have to unify all the components of our selfhood in order to achieve adult maturity and much later undergo Thought Adjuster fusion, so does the Supreme have to "fuse" all of her parts into one integral whole.

You and I engage in soul-synthesis by striving to actualize higher meanings and values in our life experiences while embedded in the vehicle of our body-mind; and the Supreme goes through a roughly similar process, but on a gigantic collective scale. This is known as *power-personality synthesis*—an advanced concept in the *UB* that is a bit beyond the scope of our discussion. But in brief: The aggregate almighty power of the evolving universes (her body and soul), through the meditation of mind (her Supreme Mind), fuses "at the fulfillment of time" with God the Supreme, her spirit-personality. When this jubilee event of the ages occurs, an exalted Deity whose personhood is resident in the central universe literally unites, forever, with the entirety of the perfected space-time universe—that is, all of its perfected energies and all of its perfected beings, and that means all of *us*.

The upshot is that the Supreme Being has a *telos*. Her evolution will culminate when all of us, creatures and Supreme Creators alike, succeed in perfecting ourselves and loving one another with the love of the Father-Mother of all Creation. It is then that she moves from a noncontactable status to being universally contactable.

But must you or I be around for this greatest of all festivals? It turns out that making our unique contribution is highly desirable, but it is not necessary that we participate. If any one of us rejects the path of self-perfection, someone else will fill the experiential void we leave behind. This is a great tragedy for us, but not a lasting barrier to the Supreme.

> The great challenge that has been given to mortal man is this: Will you decide to personalize the experiencible value meanings of the cosmos into your own evolving selfhood? or by rejecting survival, will you allow these secrets of Supremacy to lie dormant, awaiting the action of another creature at some other time who will in *his* way attempt a creature contribution to the evolution of the finite God? But that will be his contribution to the Supreme, not yours. [117:4.12]

For a fanciful analogy to the culminating event of cosmic evolution, think of the Supreme as the impresario of a cosmic opera who modestly remains backstage. We cannot personally contact her or actually see her visage until the curtain falls at the end of the performance. When everyone in the great performance hall (including the audience, the singers, the chorus, the orchestra, and those back stage) achieves perfection at the end of the great opera (a very lengthy one indeed), she then saunters out for the lengthy applause and loud cheers. She takes a slow bow. Flowers are thrown. And thus begins the greatest party of all time, in which all things are shared universally.[134] This quote explains it in a more sober fashion, as only the *UB* can:

> Man's urge for Paradise perfection, his striving for God-attainment, creates a genuine divinity tension in the living cosmos which can only be resolved by the evolution of an immortal soul; this is what happens in the experience of a single mortal creature. But when all creatures and all Creators in the grand universe likewise strive for God-attainment and divine perfection, there is built up a profound cosmic tension which can only find resolution in the sublime synthesis of almighty power with the spirit person of the evolving God of all creatures, the Supreme Being. [116:7.6]

Genuine God-realization dates from our fusion with the Indwelling Spirit—our Father Fusion. Fusion is, with very rare exceptions, unattainable in the flesh; we achieve this status generally on the fifth or sixth mansion world of the ascendant career, we are told. A finaliter, by contrast, is *hundreds* of levels beyond the afterlife status of God Fusion, having progressed tens of millions of years up the line. Individuals who reach that level enjoy an inconceivably vast career in the higher worlds of the afterlife.

So, what exactly does it take to get there? Hindus, most Buddhists, and many New Agers may think of themselves as having inhabited scores of bodies in their rounds of reincarnation on Earth, before they finally get "off the wheel" to disappear into the void of Brahman. And Christians may believe in the transactions of the Last Day, when the elect are bodily resurrected from the grave and ascend directly to heaven to dwell in their body of glory with Christ in eternity. But a finaliter, we are told, has progressed

---

[134] "Since all creature experiencing registers in, and is a part of, the Supreme, when all creatures attain the final level of finite existence, and after total universe development makes possible their attainment of God the Supreme as an actual divinity presence, then, inherent in the fact of such contact, is contact with total experience." [117:5.14]

through *580 glorified embodiments* in the educational worlds of the higher dimensions. In other words, they have ascended through 580 spheres of light, being *re-keyed* (in *UB* terminology) with new bodies on each higher world. Additionally they have sojourned for ages in the central universe training worlds, *outside* of the evolving realms.

Their intellectual education might be compared to having received several thousand PhDs after being trained to perfection in all disciplines of study. But they have also advanced to an equivalent degree in socialization, having fraternized with ascenders from millions of planets in situations that would make the *Star Wars* bar scene look like a bland Starbucks in a white suburb of Chicago. They've been taught and ministered to and companioned by myriads of celestial beings of all orders, high and low. Plus, of course, finaliters have attained levels of spiritual realization utterly beyond our conception.

Here is how the *UB* attempts to depict their final embrace with the Universal Father on Paradise: "Some day, **doubt not, you shall stand in the divine and central presence and see him**, figuratively speaking, *face to face*." [5:1.9]

Having recognized the Father on Paradise, finaliters will not only have attained perfection but also completed their preparation for a new career in their *post-perfection* existence. In addition to their training in all subjects and practices imaginable and unimaginable, we are told that they have been given eons of education in administration—not for running a heavenly hotel or cosmic educational center but rather specialized training in *universe* administration.

And their final destiny? Out beyond the inhabited galaxies are the vast uninhabited realms—those billions of galaxies in outer space that, we are told, are not yet populated. And here the finaliters will pursue the adventure of the coming ages. They will embark on this voyage of future eternity only after the Supreme Being has personalized, in that moment when the last of the inhabited galaxies of the space-time realms become fully settled utopias of light and life. And even then there will be much, very much, more adventure to be had.

Special Supplement on the Urantia Revelation

SECTION 1

An Apologia

Many believers in *The Urantia Book* maintain that that the text is not the product of human authorship of any sort. As evidence, they point to its coherence, originality, and literary richness, as well as its evident mastery of an astonishing range of topics spread out across 2,097 pages comprising 196 Papers (chapters). Adherents claim that writing at this level of depth and brilliance is simply impossible of accomplishment by any one human author or by any conceivable group of writers—especially given that there is no evidence of monetary compensation and virtually no possibility of social recognition (since no human names are attached).

But it would only be natural for those outside this circle of followers to see this work as a channeled text like so many others, perhaps containing dictations from spirits but very likely contaminated by the perspective and prejudices of its human channel. No serious critic, however, has argued that the *UB* is simply a literary hoax pulled off by a few playful geniuses interested in the pleasure of fooling others.

New facts added to the public record in the past decade or so add complexity to the question of authorship. In the first section of this apologia I briefly cover recent copyright litigation and historical research, and in Section 3 I summarize new discoveries based on the fact that the revelators used human sources.

All of these factors, when considered together, render the issue of authorship a controversy that may never be settled. Nevertheless, I do believe that *The Urantia Book*, whatever the technique of its reception, stands in a class of its own among allegedly inspired works. The evidence I have come across in decades of my own research shows that, as a literary artifact, *The Urantia Book* is unique in the annals of scripture, channeling, and purported revelation—for at least the four reasons provided below.

The first consideration is the known facts about ownership and copyright. An oracular work that comes through an identifiable human person is considered to be that person's intellectual property, even if they claim that it was dictated to them or through them by discarnate beings. Channeled works are routinely assigned valid copyrights because of their observable association with a human conduit—a typical case being the *Conversations with God* series by Neale Donald Walsch. But *The Urantia Book* differs from the established norm because there is no legally admissible evidence of a human medium. In several lawsuits, no material evidence of human authorship (either as a work for hire or a composite work) was produced by the original publisher, the Urantia Foundation. Due to this and other factors, the copyright was declared invalid in 2003 and *The Urantia Book* entered the public domain.

Although the courts were unable to ascertain a human author for the *UB*, the work does have many peripheral human associations. The most important of these was the man now known as the "contact personality," who remains anonymous to this day—which is also highly atypical. Almost every other comparable case has involved a person whose identity was almost always publicly known, and these individuals were usually deeply involved in the revelatory process, along with witnesses and assistants who were present for the reception or presentation of the revelatory materials. An archetypal modern example is case of the psychic channel Edgar Cayce; a classic premodern example is that of Muhammad, the paragon of the prophetic revealer of a text who goes on to found a religion. But by all accounts, the contact person for the Urantia Revelation was not a psychic or a teacher or a prophet, and witnesses state that he was an ordinary businessman who was "unconcerned" with the transmission process that occurred over a period of over thirty years.[135]

A Course in Miracles (1976), a channeled tome in ways comparable to the Urantia Revelation, poses an interesting contrast. The "scribe" for *A Course in Miracles*, Helen Schucman, was originally granted a copyright with the designation of "Anonymous (Helen Schucman)." The *Course* lost its copyright in 2004 not because her authorship was disputed but because the text had

---

[135] The original contact person for the Urantia Papers is long ago deceased. The text states the following about him: "The Adjuster [i.e., Indwelling Spirit of God] of the human being through whom this communication is being made enjoys such a wide scope of activity chiefly because of this human's almost complete indifference to any outward manifestations of the Adjuster's inner presence; it is indeed fortunate that he remains consciously quite unconcerned about the entire procedure." [110:5.7]

been widely disseminated before its copyright registration. Schucman was not indifferent to the revelation that poured through her from the "Voice" (which she later identified as Jesus) over a period of seven years, and posthumous accounts make clear that she had a complicated personal relationship with the effort.

Most channeled works also have an informal set of associates who enable the reception, publication, and dissemination of the material. For example, Schucman, a professor of psychology at Columbia University at the time of her contact, was assisted by her colleague Bill Thetford, who typed and compiled the handwritten materials, after which a few other volunteers helped to get the book printed and distributed. Walsch had almost no support system other than his original publisher, Bob Friedman of Hampton Roads Publishing. But the human support for the Urantia Revelation was of a different and unparalleled scale. The reception of the Papers was fostered by a formalized group of six humans known as the Contact Commission, along with an invited group of several hundred participants known as the Forum. The interaction of these two groups with the celestial authors was kept secret until the Urantia text was completed almost twenty years later. This interactive process shaped the content of the Papers, but there is no compelling evidence that the Contact Commissioners or the Forumites had any hand in the actual writing. For further details on the story of the physical reception and editing of the Urantia material, please see Section 3, "The Origin Story of the Urantia Papers."

This process was also unique because there is no other case in which hundreds of people from all walks of life helped shape the drafting of a revelatory text. The Forum consisted of many professional men and women but also included farmers, housewives, secretaries, office workers, and common laborers. Today we know all of their names, and I have spoken with many of their descendants.

By contrast, channels of comparable texts in modern times were solo acts who had no resort to coauthors, editors, or readers to help shape early drafts. And in most cases, they were charismatic individuals who personally founded religious movements. Aside from the well-known case of Edgar Cayce, other examples include Helena Blavatsky (founder of Theosophy), Alice Bailey (founder of the Ageless Wisdom extension of Theosophy), Rudolph Steiner (founder of Anthroposophy), Ellen White (cofounder of Seventh-day Adventist Church), and Mary Baker Eddy (founder of the Christian Science movement and Church).

In almost each case, these high-profile personalities had their names attached to their revelatory works and their careers profited in some way by their work with purported higher beings. But none of those involved with the Urantia Papers gained celebrity or made money from the process, nor does anyone today. In fact, its early leaders did not found a movement. Even Joseph Smith gained great fame by promulgating the Book of Mormon, but he paid the price of persecution. The key person in the *Urantia Book*'s Contact Commission, Dr. William Sadler, died in 1969 without fame or fanfare and had spent a fortune in time and money on the process of publication and dissemination. Sadler and his associates saw themselves as educators and disseminators of a text, and almost all of them eschewed the idea of founding a religion, sect, or movement.

The second reason the Urantia text is unique is that almost all other channeled works are dictated by a single incorporeal being, such as Djwhal Khul in the case of Bailey, El Morya in the instance of Blavatsky, and Jesus in the case of Schucman. At most we may hear about the involvement of a small group of unseen beings, such as Mormon and Moroni in the case of Joseph Smith. The Urantia text, in contrast, is a composite work of a corps of numerous celestial beings, some of whom authorized or sponsored the project and others who served in the role as authors of individual Papers or groups of Papers. Twenty-three separate beings are attributed as authors, some by name, while others are designated by the order of being they belong to, such as Divine Counselor, Chief of Archangels, or Perfector of Wisdom. (Almost all are unique to the *UB*, and in each case they are briefly described within the text itself.) In addition, the work must have also been compiled and edited by a highly adept celestial editorial team with superb grasp of English, given that the Papers are widely considered to be well written and highly consistent in style and content. (For more on the authors of the text, see Section 2, "Key Celestial Authors of the *UB*.")

Thirdly, typical channeling involves mind-to-mind communications or inner dictation, but the preponderance of the public record reveals that the Urantia materials were not at any point transmitted through the mind of the contact person. Rather, they physically came into existence by a largely unknown means and with minimal human involvement, as explained in Section 4. Why such a methodology of transmission? Usually, channeled works are the result of what can be called autorevelation or personal revelation, which can be edifying for thousands of readers in a particular place and time. But a purported epochal revelation such as *The Urantia Book* should have no connection with the limited viewpoint of a human personality or founder, even one as great as an Apostle John or an Emanuel Swedenborg. According to the Contact Commissioners of the *UB*, their main reason for not revealing the identity of the contact person was that the revelators did not want any human being ever to be associated with the origin of *The Urantia Book*. The revelators wanted it to stand on its own as a singular work that would be suitable for all places and cultures in coming generations and also be widely translated.

The last of our four reasons for the uniqueness of *The Urantia Book* compared to other inspired works is the difficulty that one has in conceiving even the possibility of human authorship. The *UB* contains an internally consistent and integrative presentation of theology, science, cosmology, philosophy, psychology, anthropology, and history. No one has yet been able to explain how or why a 2,000-plus-page book with no known author is able to accomplish so many intellectual feats.

For example, as noted, the *UB* contains a massive biography of Jesus in Part IV. Even the man who is arguably the *UB's* chief critic—the famed debunker and science writer Martin Gardner—considers this narrative to be an especially "well-written, impressive work." He says, "Either it is accurate in its history, coming directly from higher beings in position to know, or it is a work of fertile imagination by someone who knew the New Testament by heart and who was also steeped in knowledge of the times when Jesus lived."[136] This backhanded compliment begs the question as to why an anonymous hoaxer would engage in a writing task of such audacious proportions. Parts I through III of the text are, in my view, even more herculean examples of high-quality writing and research.

Dr. Phil Calabrese, a mathematician and statistical expert who is a veteran student of the *UB*, asks us to imagine a group of scholars secretly cooperating in the endeavor of quietly putting together the highly detailed cosmology and science sections of the Urantia Papers. "Without the benefit of computers,

---

[136] Martin Gardner is the author of *Urantia: The Great Cult Mystery* (Prometheus Books, 1995). Gardner had written previous bestsellers, but *Library Journal* advised librarians *not* to purchase this book for their collections. According to a critique by Dr. Meredith Sprunger, "Gardner's book abounds with misinformation, erroneous assumptions, and fantastic speculations" and "classic logical fallacies," which Sprunger details in an article entitled "The Purpose of Revelation: A Response to Martin Gardner's *Urantia: The Great Cult Mystery.*" A prominent early leader of the Urantia movement, Sprunger had a PhD in psychology from Purdue, was a professor at major colleges, and was a lifelong Protestant pastor.

their research team would need to find the best human thinkers in astronomy, geology, paleontology, chemistry, physics, biology, botany, and all other fields. They would also need to selectively use their ideas and sometimes even their phrasing, but avoid all of their blunders." The effort as a whole would have to be the most audacious literary charade of all time. According to Calabrese, *The Urantia Book* predicted many scientific facts that were implausible at the date of its publication in 1955 but that have been subsequently verified as correct. Among these are: continental drift and plate tectonics,[137] the existence of hundreds of millions of galaxies, large-scale cosmic structures (walls of galaxies), huge red shifts, and the existence of neutrinos with mass. "Its track record of predictions is far better than that of any human scientists, while also successfully avoiding systematic errors, unlike our scientists. . . . On statistical grounds," he writes, "only superhumans could have written the science and cosmology of *The Urantia Book*.[138] But Calabrese's bold claims don't settle this complex issue. Many daunting questions about the *UB*'s science remain to be answered—especially its claims about genetics, subatomic particles, and its rejection of Big Bang cosmology. These fall beyond the scope of *Your Evolving Soul* but will be addressed in my future writings.

At the same time, it must be understood as well that the science of the Urantia Revelation is not to be considered inspired. It would be better to call its science and cosmology heuristic, even if some of it is prophetic. Rather, as earlier noted, it claims only *that its historic facts and religious truths will remain valid*—as stated in a section entitled "The Limitations of Revelation," excerpted here:

> **Mankind should understand that we who participate in the revelation of truth are very rigorously limited by the instructions of our superiors.** We are not at liberty to anticipate the scientific discoveries of a thousand years. **Revelators must act in accordance with the instructions which form a part of the revelation mandate.** We see no way of overcoming this difficulty, either now or at any future time. We full well know that, **while the historic facts and religious truths of this series of revelatory**

---

[137] The geology section of the *UB* describes a billion-year-old supercontinent that subsequently split apart, forming the continents that exist today. A professor of geology named Mark McMenamin writes, "This amazing passage, written in the 1930s, anticipates scientific results that did not actually appear in the scientific literature until many decades later." See *The Garden of Ediacara: Discovering the Earliest Complex Life* (Columbia University Press, 2000).

[138] See "The Coming Scientific Validation of the Urantia Book," by Philip Calabrese, PhD. http://urantia-book.org/archive/readers/coming_sci_val_abstr2.htm

presentations will stand on the records of the ages to come, within a few short years many of our statements regarding the physical sciences will stand in need of revision in consequence of additional scientific developments and new discoveries. [101:4.2]

In accord with this disclaimer, I have discussed in *Your Evolving Soul* many of the *UB*'s teachings about religion and spirituality. I compare this material to current thought on these subjects because I believe it remains highly relevant. But what about its purportedly prophetic historical facts? I will cover that subject in my next book, but we can briefly say here that, in particular, several discoveries in the last few decades have been supportive of the *UB*'s extensive account of our planet's prehistory. Among these are Gobekli Tepe, the archeological site in Turkey that is revolutionizing our understanding of pre-Sumerian history. But most important is the research funded in part by the History Channel a decade ago. This effort has established the credibility of a prediction exclusively made in the *UB* that a primeval civilization, heretofore unknown, once existed in the Eastern Mediterranean in the proximity of the island of Cyprus. Advanced ocean-bottom research nearly one mile down off the east coast of Cyprus reveals that now-sunken land once bridged Cyprus to present-day Syria, just as is stated in the Urantia text. On two different expeditions, evidence of a manmade structure was identified on this surface, a discovery hailed worldwide in major media. This sunken land, according to *The Urantia Book*, was the actual site of the Garden of Eden of biblical fame. (Please see further discussion of Eden in chapter 6.)

It happens that I was the editor and publisher of an illustrated book about this discovery entitled *Discovery of Atlantis: The Startling Case for the Island of Cyprus* (Origin Press, 2003) by Robert Sarmast. The author's pioneering efforts also produced the first underwater expedition, led by Commodore Robert Bates, USMM. The findings were favorably covered by the BBC, CNN, and mainstream newspapers around the world. Sarmast's book was updated following a second expedition funded by the History Channel and was broadcast as the lead program in its *Digging for the Truth* series in 2007. Sarmast's writings provide exclusive underwater maps and outline his original findings in ancient history, mythology, and natural history to make a case that a lost civilization lies underwater off the south coast of Cyprus, which Sarmast identified as Atlantis. (See: http://discoveryofatlantis.com/.)

The Eastern Mediterranean location is an original thesis in the tradition of Atlantis research, one that Sarmast argued matches more closely than current theories (such as Boliva, Antartica, and Thera) to the physical clues provided in Plato's *Critias* and *Timaeus*—the original sources for the story of Atlantis. (Distinguished British author Colin Wilson wrote the preface to the second edition of *Discovery of Atlantis,* in which he renounces his own thesis about the location of Atlantis that appeared in his bestselling 2001 book, *The Atlantis Blueprint.*) It happens that Sarmast, Bates, and all of their associates who have pursued this thesis are *Urantia Book* students who believe that the story of Atlantis actually refers to the Garden of Eden account in the *UB*. Finally, I should add that Commodore Bates has plans to mount a third expedition to the site using much-improved research technology.

Extensive reports on the Gobekli Tepe and Cyprus discoveries, plus articles on many other claims in the *UB* about science and history that have been corroborated, can especially be found at UBtheNEWS.com, edited by Halbert Katzen.

In closing, I cite this important statement by the *UB*'s authors, which offers five reasons why an epochal revelation can be of great value in clarifying human knowledge by:

1. The reduction of confusion by the authoritative elimination of error.
2. The co-ordination of known or about-to-be-known facts and observations.
3. The restoration of important bits of lost knowledge concerning epochal transactions in the distant past.
4. The supplying of information which will fill in vital missing gaps in otherwise earned knowledge.
5. Presenting cosmic data in such a manner as to illuminate the spiritual teachings contained in the accompanying revelation. [101:4.5]

After decades of study, I believe that the *UB* does meet these five criteria powerfully enough to be what it claims to be: an epochal revelation to all of humankind. In *Your Evolving Soul*, I have attempted to show how fruitful the Urantia text can be in clarifying our knowledge of self and soul, but these teachings on cosmic spirituality are just one part of the *UB*'s overall contribution. I believe that my work and that of many other colleagues working in this field is just the beginning of the harvest.

Key Celestial Authors of the *UB*

Unlike *A Course in Miracles* and other such channeled books, the Urantia Revelation is said to be the product of a large and diverse corps of celestial authors. In this brief section I mention a selection of the celestial beings who were either sponsors or coauthors of the Urantia Papers.

At the top of the angelology scale of the *UB* we meet beings of direct origin from the Paradise Trinity known as the *Ancients of Days*, who preside over our own galaxy supercluster, *Orvonton*. Recall that Orvonton is one of the seven great inhabited superuniverses—as explained in chapter 2 and elsewhere. The Ancients of Days (and others they authorized) organized a wide array of celestial beings to be authors of specific Papers in the Urantia text, we are told. These beings are called ancient because they are the very oldest in the evolving universes, and there are just twenty-one of them; every superuniverse has a governing trio of Ancients of Days who serve as administrators.

The Ancients of Days who oversee our own superuniverse directly sponsored Part I of the *UB*'s presentations to our planet, we are told. And among the very highest types of celestial authors of the text are the *Solitary Messengers*. One is the author of Papers 107–112, which describes the personality, the Indwelling Spirit, and the evolving soul—the inner trio that is the main focus of this book. An entire Paper is devoted to the work of these beings, who are of direct origin from the Infinite Spirit. They are described as the "personal corps" of the Third Person of the Trinity.

Roughly in the middle of the grand holarchy are celestial beings called *Melchizedeks*, who are known on high as the educators of the universes. They are the authors of many of the more philosophically advanced materials in the text, including Papers 100–103. These Papers offer the *UB*'s teaching on the psychology and philosophy of religion, providing essential background for the general discussions in *Your Evolving Soul*.

At the bottom of the angelology scale are the *midwayers*—known by that name because they exist in an invisible domain *midway* between humans and lower angels such as *seraphim*. Midwayers are able to connect directly with us physically because of their close energetic proximity to the material realms. Many miracles having to do with direct auditory communication, instantaneous physical healing, and changes in the location of physical objects are quietly carried out by our midwayers cousins. Because they can draw nearest to us, they were the invisible interlocutors of the human group in Chicago who first received the Urantia Papers between the years of 1924 and 1945. (See Section 4 for a sketch of the history of the revelatory process.) A special commission of midwayers who followed Jesus closely in his life were the authors of Part IV of the book, "The Life and Teachings of Jesus."

SECTION 3

Human Sources for the Urantia Revelation

I earlier broached the fact that the authors of *The Urantia Book* made use of human sources, doing so when such humanly derived content met their strict criteria.

As I understand it, their task was to present *revelatory content* pertaining to hundreds of topics. These are ideas and issues they were required to cover by virtue of their revelatory mandate. For example, it can easily be inferred that they were charged with restating Jesus's Sermon on the Mount for the upliftment and edification of modern ears, while also making sure that the new version of this teaching conformed to what Jesus really said and meant.

But how far they could go with unique revelation also had limits; wisdom demands that new truths being imparted to a planet not be too far ahead of the evolutionary trajectory of its peoples at the time of revelation. The following statement clarifies this important point:

> Revelation is evolutionary but always progressive. Down through the ages of a world's history, the revelations of religion are ever-expanding and successively more enlightening. It is the mission of revelation to sort and censor the successive religions of evolution. **But if revelation is to exalt and upstep the religions of evolution, then must such divine visitations portray teachings which are not too far removed from the thought and reactions of the age in which they are presented**. Thus must and does revelation always keep in touch with evolution. Always must the religion of revelation be limited by man's capacity of receptivity. [92:4.1]

The immediate intended audience for the *UB*, it seems to me, was educated English-speaking men and women who had been enculturated in the modernist mindset of the mid-twentieth century, especially in the milieu of liberal Christianity. The crucial task of the revelators, I believe, was to significantly upstep the worldview of this first generation of readers while remaining a potent disclosure for other progressive people around the world and in future generations.

To make this work, they engaged in what might be called "revelatory grafting." Their charter was to attach new limbs of truth to the existing stream of human thought; but to do so successfully, the writers had to insure that an "immune response" was not triggered in their readers that would cause them to reject the new material. At the same time, they needed to supplant certain mistaken ideas, and do so authoritatively. (For a typical example of such a correction, see "Erroneous Ideas of God" at 4:5.) And so, what might be called a rhetorical revelatory protocol was adopted: First, the celestial writers were obliged to seek out the finest examples available at that time of the previous *human* expressions of a particular idea needing clarification—for example, the existing concepts of the meaning of Jesus's death on the cross. Next, they were to carefully select suitable passages and phrasings from this humanly derived text and insert them in such a way as to create an infrastructure of meaning around which they could weave new superhuman concepts that they were permitted to reveal. Finally, they added facts and concepts about this topic that they were mandated to communicate but which were entirely absent from the annals of human thought.

Thus, for example, if the proper understanding of the crucifixion could not be found in the Bible, the writings of the Church Fathers, or in any extant theological works, then the *UB*'s authors could freely weave in purely revelatory material. The result in this case is the section called "The Meaning of the Death on the Cross" at the end of Paper 188, which breaks new ground in Christology. While this particular section departs widely from mainstream Christian thought, it should be noted that most of the humanly sourced material presented in Part IV, "The Life and Teachings of Jesus," is derived in part from the New Testament. But great deal of this narrative is also entirely revelatory, such as the story of the missing years of Jesus in Papers 124 through 135.

The extraordinary Part IV contains 77 Papers and spans 774 pages in the original edition. It is remarkable that its depiction of Jesus affirms cardinal points of Christian doctrine, including the Incarnation, the resurrection, the raising of Lazarus from the dead, and other miracles; but the *UB* also states that the virgin birth, the blood atonement, and the physical resurrection of the dead at the end of the age are myths. (Turn to chapter 6 for more on this subject.)

The revelators provide two explicit acknowledgments of their revelation methodology in the text. The first appears at the end of the Foreword, where the celestial author known as a Divine Counselor states that "more than one thousand human concepts . . . assembled from the God-knowing mortals of the past and the present" were utilized in the writing of Part I. He also states that this mandate was promulgated by "the superuniverse rulers." (For more on these beings, see Section 2. The Divine Counselor's disclaimer includes this important statement:

> In formulating the succeeding presentations . . . we are to be guided by the mandate of the superuniverse rulers which directs that we shall, in all our efforts to reveal truth and co-ordinate essential knowledge, **give preference to the highest existing human concepts pertaining to the subjects to be presented**. We may resort to pure revelation only when the concept of presentation has had no adequate previous expression by the human mind. [0:12.12].

At the opening of Part IV, the writer of the narrative indicates that the ideas of "more than two thousand human beings who have lived on earth from the days of Jesus down to the time of the inditing of these revelations" were used as sources. The passage below sheds additional light on the revelatory mandate and how it was applied to the forthcoming biography of Jesus:

> As far as possible I have derived my information from purely human sources. Only when such sources failed, have I resorted to those records which are superhuman. When ideas and concepts of Jesus' life and teachings have been acceptably expressed by a human mind, I invariably gave preference to such apparently human thought patterns. . . . **My revelatory commission forbade me to resort to extrahuman sources of either information or expression until such a time as I could testify that I had failed in my efforts to find the required conceptual expression in purely human sources.** [121:8.13]

Note that this celestial author, a so-called midwayer being, also states that a superhuman "revelatory commission" set the parameters of his work.

In the early decades after the publication of the Urantia Revelation in 1955, it was enough for most readers just to cope with the shock of revelation. Few were concerned about human sources in those days. But *UB* students eventually began to make exciting discoveries. For example, a book authored by Harry Emerson Fosdick, a prominent liberal theologian and minister of the 1920s and 1930s, was recognized as a source early on.

The rigorous search for what are now known as the source texts accelerated in the early nineties and was led by Matthew Block, an independent scholar who had been a graduate student in theology at the University of Chicago Divinity School. Since then, he and other researchers have discovered innumerable parallelisms—passages found in more than one hundred books that can be correlated with specific sections in *The Urantia Book*. Block now believes that he and his colleagues have identified the human sources used in portions of about 150 of the *UB*'s 196 papers. According to Block, "The source texts were all published in English and the source authors were, with few exceptions, Americans or Britons born in the 19th or 20th centuries."[139]

Block provides what he calls parallel charts that graphically illustrate the technique, displaying in the left column the source material that was used by the revelators and, in the right column, the correlated *UB* passage. In hundreds of cases, we can see that the revelators have inserted lines, sentences, and even whole passages from books by prominent thinkers of the day, and then have deftly interlaced the revelatory materials in and around this humanly derived skeleton of ideas. Sometimes the writers depart widely from an original source text after they "quote" it (almost always without attribution); other times they deviate moderately from it; but in some instances they rely on the human material substantively. It's comparable to a journalist who accurately quotes a source, if even just one phrase, after which they go on to refute, modify, or support the source's statement.

Block and others are far along in the effort to map out which parts of the *UB* were revealed for the first time and those that are in some portion humanly derived. This task is not as difficult as one might think, because the revelators make no attempt to disguise their human sources. It has now become obvious

---

[139] The most extensively used source, according to Block, is a four-volume textbook, *The Science of Society* (1927). The results of Matthew Block's heroic effort to find and decipher source texts can be viewed at this comprehensive website: http://www.urantiabooksources.com/. His only printed book to date is entitled *Source Authors of the Urantia Book* (Square Circles Publishing, 2002), written under the pseudonym of J. T. Manning.

to researchers that the revelators *want us* to discover the source texts they utilized. We are meant to return to these books with due appreciation to the outstanding historic value of these human writings, much like some of us still enjoy the "Great Books of the Western World" that were once taught at colleges around the country.

But even more important is this crucial point: revelation, like soul-making, is a cocreative cultural activity carried out by superhumans in close cooperation with mortals. It's a superior blend. Revelatory discourse is something like taking a superb wine that has been aged by the finest human vintner and combining these barrels with wine miraculously created by Jesus at a new wedding of Cana. The high achievements of human thought are rewarded by supplementation through a merciful downreach that provides new facts and truths. The result is a seamless integration of human observation with revelatory correction.

SECTION 4

The Origin Story of the Urantia Papers

The Urantia text came into being during a complex process that was initiated in 1911 (some say 1908) and completed in the early 1940s—most likely in the year 1942—but some believe the final editing of the *UB* concluded as late as 1945. The origin story has been shrouded in secrecy and mystery until the last two decades or so, when ongoing historical research into private archives, diaries, written testimonials, and oral histories, as well as evidence provided in the aforementioned federal copyright lawsuits, revealed a large amount of new information and lore about the process.

According to the records we have, there were no direct witnesses to the formal transmission process of the original materials comprising the Urantia Papers. No one ever saw the purported contact person or anyone else write down these source materials. (But there *are* witnesses to the informal and unofficial communications, which are also discussed below). According to all the accounts we have, the Papers first appeared in hand-written form but *not in the handwriting of any known person.* The best available handwriting-analysis experts were unable to trace the written materials to the alleged contact personality or any other person involved. Yet, for a period of a few decades, voluminous handwritten documents frequently appeared in direct association with the contact person or in close proximity to him, according to all accounts. These materials were various drafts of the Papers that physically appeared in succession over at almost two decades.

The contact personality (sometimes also known as "the sleeping subject") was described by one reliable source as "a hard-boiled businessman and a member of the Chicago Board of Trade and Stock Exchange." Over the entire time of contact, the celestials also engaged in informal verbal communications through him, we are told, in the manner conventionally known as channeling, usually by speaking through the vocal chords of the contact personality after he was rendered deeply unconscious by some mysterious force. At times there were also dictations to members of the Contact Commission that appeared as short written messages of practical import. (There were also cases of "direct voice" contact—actual audio communications from unseen beings that were heard, as it were, "in the air" during the frequent meetings of the Contact Commissioners.)

According to the testimony, the contact person was not personally or physically engaged with the process other than to allow his body to be used in informal oral communications having to do with logistics and practical concerns of the revelatory process. The promulgation of the written content did not occur in any known manner through the vehicle of his body or mind.[140] Preliminary informal "channeling" through the contact is known to have existed as far back as 1908, but the formal written Papers began to appear in succession on February 11, 1924 and continued to "manifest" for the next eighteen years. The physical papers were carefully typed up and proofread over these years.

All of these celestial transactions occurred in the city of Chicago. The main locus was the large home of a distinguished physician, psychiatrist, professor, author, and public speaker, Dr. William S. Sadler, and his wife Dr. Lena Sadler, also a well-known and respected physician and author. Their place

---

[140] The evidence seems to indicate that the informal communications between the celestial authors and the human contact group for the Urantia Revelation took place via a technique similar to that of Edgar Cayce and his interlocutors. According to the sources I have consulted, it transpired in a manner not unlike any number of other case of channeling, mediumship, or oracular activities before and since. These instances might be called classic channeling as contrasted with "epochal revelation" of the sort that is unique to the Urantia Revelation. The so-called Teaching Mission is a controversial case of contemporary channeling that has involved scores of contactees who are Urantia students, many of them veteran readers, and occurring decades after the publication of the *UB*. These "transmitter-receivers" (the term they use) have long claimed to channel three types of beings (1) some of the original celestial authors of the *UB*, (2) other beings introduced in the Urantia text, and (3) "ascended" humans speaking from the afterlife. This movement has continued up to the present, and in recent years has been extended its purview into another celestially inspired activity known as the *Magisterial Mission*, which purports to provide the teachings of the *Magisterial Son* who is soon to incarnate on Earth (or so it is claimed). The umbrella for both of all these newer contact missions is known as *The Correcting Time*. The massive series of thousands of transcribed lessons linked with these activities began in 1987. All of these teachings are highly referential to the Urantia Revelation, but these phenomena and the associated claims are outside the scope of the present study. This material is covered in my forthcoming book, *Romancing the Universe*.

in the near-north side of the city was also the meeting place of the Forum, the initial group of several hundred readers of the early drafts who Dr. Sadler trained as a surgeon and physician, and had also studied briefly in Vienna with Sigmund Freud. Because of his prolific writing and research and decades of clinical practice, he was known by some in his day as "the father of American psychiatry." He wrote a widely used psychiatry textbook and was author of several dozen other books, many of these directed to the popular reader. He and his wife were also pioneers in preventive medicine and in their earlier careers were Seventh Day Adventist ministers. Lena Sadler was especially known as a pediatrician and for her pioneering work in women's health, but died in 1939 before the completion of the reception of the Urantia Papers. Her husband lived on to see the book printed in 1955 and died at age 93 in 1969.

One scholar and trained historian, Sioux Oliva, PhD, has concluded that Bill Sadler himself was the contact personality for the revelation, but covered his tracks to remain anonymous. According to her controversial thesis, Sadler invented an origin story about an unknown contact person who never existed, doing so in order to protect the revelation from a direct link to any possible human association with the writing process. Sioux's enormous effort to uncover new facts about the Sadler family, the Contact Commissioners, and their associates in the Forum is exemplary, but her concluding speculations seem to overreach her own historical data. (See *Dr. Sadler and the Urantia Book: A History of a Spiritual Revelation in the 20th Century*). Martin Gardner, the famed skeptic and science writer, took the position that the contact personality must have been Wilfred Kellogg, a brother-in-law of Lena Sadler who was a member of the Contact Commission. Virtually all other researchers believe that neither of these two men were the contact, or "conduit," and that it must have been some other unknown person living very near the Sadler home. And this is the universal testimony of Sadler and the other direct witnesses.

According to these latter sources, each new Paper came into existence in the proximity of the contact personality, always in hand-written form. It would purportedly *appear*—either on a table in his bedroom or miraculously in a nearby safe or other locations. Some reliable oral accounts indicate that Papers were either "materialized" as hand-written text and then dematerialized once they were typed—or more likely, were very quickly hand-written by an unseen being while the contact person and his wife slept at night. According to Bill Sadler, Jr., one of the Contact Commissioners, "I think you would have seen a very exciting phenomenon, a pencil moving over paper with no visible means of propulsion. That's where the physical writing was consummated."[141]

Dr. Sadler explained in an account first published in 1929 that—despite all sorts of probes and tests—he and his associates could detect no discernible link to the contact personality's mentality, personal beliefs, worldview, or handwriting style. Eventually, all of those who were personally involved came to believe that the writing was actually carried out by unseen celestial beings and was not generated somehow through the human mind of the contact person. Sadler himself, with his hard-core scientific training during an era of logical positivism, remained a skeptic longer than all the others involved in the process. He even invited other scientists as well as debunkers and magicians, including even the likes of Harry Houdini, to investigate the phenomenon, in order see if these outsiders might come up with an explanation for the materialization of the Papers. He finally accepted the miraculous explanation in 1936, after all 196 Papers had come forth, many of them in multiple drafts, but with no trace of a human author.

Here is a brief overview of the revelatory process: Once a new Paper of the revelation appeared, it was carefully typed and checked, and then read aloud at the Forum meetings that were held every Sunday afternoon beginning in 1924. After the reading of a Paper, Forum members would immediately ask questions, which were written down and later sorted and classified. It is believed by some that these new questions were presented by the Contact Commissioners in closed meetings; it is also reported that the celestials simply monitored the human reactions to each new Paper in the Forum meetings. And then, like clockwork, a new draft would appear soon thereafter. This procedure continued until 119 Papers had been compiled in 1934. And then, to the great surprise of all, the last 77 Papers appeared *all at once*. This material became the 774-page Part IV of the text, the beloved "The Life and Teachings of Jesus." This was the capstone of the process and of the revelation. After its appearance, the Forum was invited for one more round of interaction. The entire corpus was presented once again to the Forum, new questions were asked and more reactions were monitored, and then the final drafts of the 196 Papers appeared, culminating

---

[141] The source of this quote is what I consider to be the best existing history, authored by Larry Mullins with the assistance of Dr. Meredith Sprunger: *A History of the Urantia Papers* (CreateSpace, 2010). See chapters 4 and 5 of this book for a detailed account of the revelatory process. Ernest Moyer is the author of a well-researched but controversial alternative history entitled *The Birth of a Divine Revelation: The Origin of the Urantia Papers* (Moyer Pub, 2000).

in 1942 or soon after. After many years of proofreading and typesetting, plus a delay requested by the celestials, the book was first printed in 1955, has been through innumerable re-printings, and has been translated into 17 languages.

SECTION 5

The Historicity of Revelation

We have been told that the Urantia Revelation "is intended for the coming age," but we also know that its human sources—though of very high quality—predate the middle of the twentieth century. In addition, we are aware that each of the 196 Papers was edited several times by the revelators in response to queries from the Forum in the period of 1924 to around 1942 (or a bit later) in Chicago, as mentioned earlier. The lore of those heady times indicates that several Papers were actually withdrawn because they were beyond the comprehension of the Forumites. And at least one very difficult Paper ("Diety and Reality," Paper 105) was incorporated into the text because of the persistent questions by Contact Commissioner Bill Sadler, Jr. I can testify that the resulting presentation is too advanced for most of us.[142]

It is an undisputed fact that the readers in the Forum presented hundreds of questions through the Contact Commission, although we don't know very much about the questions themselves. New drafts of each Paper that came forward over the nearly twenty years of the revelatory process addressed their most pertinent questions. Early histories indicate that the operating slogan for this unique cooperative effort between these humans and the celestial authors was "No questions?—no Papers!"

In this connection, it is an interesting fact that a legal theory once entertained by the Urantia Foundation was that because the Forumites

---

[142] Bill Sadler Jr. was the only child of William and Lena Sadler. He was an original member of the Contact Commission and the author of several important studies that are still in print. Fortunately, many of his lectures in the 1950s that explicate the most important and difficult concepts in the *UB* were recorded and are also available online. Many readers of the revelation consider these talks to be unsurpassed by any other commentary in their quality, depth, and humor. The Sadlers were a family of orators.

had shaped the *UB*'s content through their questions, a possible interpretation of copyright law might allow that legal human authorship be granted to this group.

It is undeniable that an interactive process conditioned the content of the Urantia Papers. Part of the mandate of the revelators was to directly respond to the intellectual trends of the early twentieth century—an evolutionary approach that is considered optimal for an effective planetary revelation. But there are other important implications as well. First, it is entirely wrongheaded to think of any revelation as inerrant. There are no infallible scriptures and never will be, as this statement makes clear:

> But no revelation short of the attainment of the Universal Father can ever be complete. All other celestial ministrations are no more than partial, transient, and practically adapted to local conditions in time and space. While such admissions as this may possibly detract from the immediate force and authority of all revelations, the time has arrived on Urantia when it is advisable to make such frank statements, even at the risk of weakening the future influence and authority of this, the most recent of the revelations of truth to the mortal races of Urantia. [94:2]

Purportedly revelatory texts can only be approximations of what we might think of as ultimate truth because they are conditioned by the needs and the mentality of its recipients in a particular time and place. Revelation is always at least partially an evolutionary product.

Secondly, the revelatory process is not unlike like the manner in which the individual soul evolves. I've explained that in the process of soul-making, the Indwelling Spirit of God reaches down to meet the highest thoughts and feelings of its human ward as these rise upward in the heart in an effort to grasp the living truth and make choices based on it. The resulting soul-substance is a beautiful cocreative blend, but it is never itself pure spirit.

Third, a revelatory mandate requires pure revelation as well. Crucial errors that are blocking the further evolution of consciousness do need to be corrected through a major download of grace. For example, decades of research have found no significant human sources for Papers 107 through 112, which are critical to the *UB*'s original description of the inner triad that I present in this book. When the revelators want to make sure to correct humankind on key issues, one can easily sense the authoritative tone; you will find this in many instances, including Paper 111, the *UB*'s principal discourse on the human soul.

And finally, the spiritual import of an inspired text requires exegesis over time. Revelatory scripture needs to be reinterpreted and adapted in the light of current evolutionary thought and the existing human predicament on the ground. Because human knowledge is progressing at an exponential rate and we are caught up in times of very rapid social change, I have little doubt that some of the interpretation I provide in *Your Evolving Souls* will itself go out of date. In that light, I invite you to enjoy my effort in the spirit of these times.

Urantia Cosmology and Current Astrophysics

W e know that the celestial authors of the *UB* skillfully wove human sources into their revelations, but their revelatory efforts with regard to cosmology and the physical sciences must have been an exceedingly complex editorial challenge. As I understanding their mandate, they were required to coordinate the very best human knowledge in these fields with a limited set of revelations about the physical universe, while at the same time not over-revealing in such a way as to stymie scientific curiosity and discovery. The result is that the text offers its disclosures about the physical universe in the phraseology of the scientific discoveries accepted at the time the *UB* was authored (in the 1920s and 1930s), yet it is also clear that these Papers go far beyond the cosmological paradigm of that generation of scientists. (The primary Papers concerning astrophysics and cosmology are 11, 12, 32, 41, and 42.) This approach, I believe, will inspire future scientific discovery but will also serve the overall evolution of human consciousness.

With regard to astrophysics, the *UB*'s revelatory descriptions appear to match and possibly transcend today's human knowledge of this field some eight decades later, but these statements also appear alongside now-outdated information from a bygone era in the history of science. According to veteran *UB* student and amateur astronomer John Causland, "The book's astronomy is phrased in the language in use at the time. . . . [Yet] with some amazement, I began to see that the Urantia cosmology actually told a story suggestive of a physical universe that only now we're beginning to comprehend." (See www. UBastronomy.com).

Causland suggests that the revelators must have timed their teachings to coincide with the work of astronomers such as Edwin Hubble, who was the first to discover the existence of galaxies outside the Milky Way. Causland speculates that before the *UB*'s celestial authors would have been permitted to reveal the size, structure, and age of our universe, our scientists would first have had to "earn" some rudimentary knowledge of the existence of far-flung galaxies and other large-scale formations outside of our own galaxy. This occurred with Hubble's first measurements, dating back to 1929, including his crucial discovery of the so-called red shift—a finding which proves that other galaxies and structures not only exist, but are rapidly receding away from one another.

Causland states that because the revelators had to utilize human sources around whose limited vision they could weave specific revelatory information, they also provided confusing or ambiguous indications about this extragalactic universe of universes. In following their mandate to not reveal too much, they seem to have unnecessarily muddied the waters with quantitative data that is now known to be quite far off. The celestial authors also incorporated and blended several contradictory models of the universe extant in the early twentieth century. Further, they used terms such as "nebula," "galaxy," and "universe" almost interchangeably, as scientists did at that time; today these words have far more distinct meanings. Due to such complicating factors, the Urantia Book's strictly physical cosmology is no longer reliable in a number of details.

For example, the Urantia text offers two apparently contradictory models of what constitutes a *superuniverse* (the most important large-scale unit of the inhabited evolutionary universe, which is discussed in chapter 2 and also in the Supplement in Section 2). Some passages in the *UB* depict our superuniverse, named *Orvonton*, as coextensive with the Milky Way galaxy, while other statements strongly (and accurately) imply that Orvonton is vastly greater in size.

Causland goes on to show that our superuniverse simply cannot be a single galaxy that contains a trillion inhabited planets, as some interpreters of the *UB* believe. (As a reminder, the *UB* states that there are seven superuniverses, each containing about one trillion inhabited worlds.) Instead, Orvonton is most properly a designation for a massive clump of thousands of galaxies now known to be the Virgo Supercluster. At his website, Causland lists other superclusters with names such as Perseus, Centaur, and Formax. These vast formations of thousands of galaxies seem to be equivalents of the Virgo Group and thus are candidates for entry into the catalogue of the seven great inhabited superuniverses.

It is my own speculation that the superclusters that have been clearly identified by astronomers may well be the ultimate constituents of the evolving inhabited universe known in the *UB* as the *grand universe*. Our own Milky Way galaxy (a *minor sector* in *UB* terminology), which contains a mere billion inhabited worlds, is but a small unit of Orvonton.

John Causland makes one more fascinating point: Some astrophysicists appear to have settled on the idea that the universe may contain a gravitational center, which may be akin to the central universe, the heart of which is Paradise (and which we are told is the cosmic source of all material gravity). Since the 1980s, astronomers have called this center the "Great Attractor" and describe it as an unbelievably massive gravitational vortex toward which the great superclusters are moving.

APPENDIX B

Mother Spirit and Christ Michael: Local Universe Representatives of the Trinity

According to the Urantia Revelation, *Christ Michael* is the Creator and Father of our local universe which, when fully evolved, will contain up to ten million inhabited planets. He is also known to us as the historical person Jesus Christ who incarnated here on *Urantia*—our planet Earth. In partnership with the *Mother Spirit*, who is his Deity equal, Michael ministers from on high to each of us, his children on Earth. The reality of a Deity partnership involving Christ is a new revelation to our world.

The divine affection of Michael and Mother for us is typified (1) in the fact that Michael incarnated in the likeness of one of us, (2) by ongoing revelations of the "divine word" such as the *UB*, and (3) by the ministrations to us of the vast angelic host created by Mother Spirit.

Somewhat similar to traditional Christianity, *The Urantia Book* offers a Trinitarian theology of Father, Son, and Spirit, but it updates these ancient concepts by providing unprecedented detail in the context of a modern scientific cosmology (see chapter 2). The Eternal Trinity manifests in our local evolving universe through Christ Michael and Mother Spirit, who are Deity partners in the mission of representing the Trinity in space-time. We are told that this divine pair perfectly depicts to our local universe the essence of the eternal Deities that they represent.

Michael is the direct and replete personalization of God the Father and the Eternal Son (the first and second Persons of the Trinity) to this local universe. As explained in the Urantia text in Paper 34:

The Creator Sons of the Paradise order of Michael are the makers and rulers of the local universes of time and space. These universe creators and sovereigns are of origin in the Father and Son but each is unique in nature and personality. Each is the "only begotten Son."

In addition, we are told in this Paper that the Infinite Spirit—the third Person of the Trinity—*personalized* as the *Mother Spirit* for our segment of the universe. We also learn of our "encircuitment" through the Mother Spirit's *Holy Spirit* and through Christ Michael's *Spirit of Truth*.

A Mother Spirit does not and cannot incarnate in the flesh in the likeness of one of her human children, but Christ Michael actually has this singular function as a phase of his mercy ministry to inhabited planets. In his incarnation experiences he always manifests the infinite love and divine power of the Eternal Son *in perfection*. However, he is not the Eternal Son of the Trinity asserted in Christian doctrine. In fact, he is of origin from the Father *and* the Eternal Son.

In the final analysis, we can say that the founders of the Christian Church were correct about the spiritual relationships of the Trinity but never envisioned the complex factual reality of Trinity manifestations in the space-and-time universes that would be revealed centuries later in the *UB*.

Some Core Contributions of Ken Wilber

I noted in chapter 7 that with the triumph of scientific materialism, modernity found it convenient to trivialize or ignore the metaphysical teachings of the wisdom traditions. In his writings, Ken Wilber calls this great repudiation of the past "the disaster of modernity." To his credit, Wilber attempts to navigate from there to a new framework that transcends both the modern and postmodern critiques of metaphysics but still enshrines their essential achievements. In addition, he reframes the traditional teachings of the world's cultures—selecting from them the ideas that he considers to have universal import—and incorporates them into his Integral Map along with the leading ideas of modernity and postmodernity that he finds worth preserving.

In Wilber's first take on this ambitious reconstruction project, he turned to what Aldous Huxley called *perennialism*, the notion of a grand hierarchy of universal levels of existence also known as *the Great Chain of Being*—perennial because it can be detected in almost all traditions worldwide. According to this vision, reality is composed of various nested levels or stages of existence, ranging upward from body to mind to soul to spirit. The Great Chain also referred to living beings, ranging from inanimate matter to plant and animal life, to humans, then to an angelic hierarchy, then extending up to God at the apex. But perhaps the better metaphor, says Wilber, is that of a "Great Nest." Each level in the Great Nest is qualitatively different from the previous one, yet each senior dimension transcends but always includes (or nests) its juniors. For example, at the smallest scale, atoms are part of molecules, which in turn comprise cells, which comprise tissues, all of which is transcended and included in organs of the body, then on to the entire person, and so on, progressing on up to nested levels of group consciousness and finally to global culture. One simplified version of nesting at a larger scale ranges from *physiosphere* to *biosphere* to *noosphere*, each sphere transcending and including the previous one.

Later in his work, Wilber built upon the traditional divinization teachings of the East and West in a similar way. For example, in *Transformations of Consciousness* (Shambhala, 1986), Wilber and his coauthors compare the theosis teachings of Eastern Orthodox Christianity with similar teachings about levels of consciousness in Islam and Eastern religions. In increasingly refined versions of this work ever since then, Wilber has extended the integral project into sophisticated new descriptions of human development and spirituality that I cover in chapters 7 and 9.

We noted in chapters 5 and 6 that with regard to human nature, many traditions present only two levels (the "body and soul" of substance dualism, which are not necessarily nested). We also saw that some monistic and nondual traditions made no hard distinctions at all between levels and substances. But we've also seen that more advanced esoteric systems in the past have distinguished soul from spirit.

Wilber's own early system followed Sri Aurobindo's and other sophisticated maps that designate up to a dozen levels or more in the spectrum of consciousness and self. In an effort to simplify, Wilber borrowed terminology from Vedanta and Buddhism, describing the progression of stages of consciousness as extending from gross to psychic to subtle to causal to nondual. These "sheaths" stand for increasingly rarefied levels in the spectrum of ontologically real energetic substances—or a gradation of frequencies, as some might say.

He depicts the ultimate disappearance of the self into a blissful nondual state as the highest achievement of the practitioner. I see this state as comparable to attaining the first level of circle-making (the highest level) as described in chapter 4. Along this line, in *Integral Psychology* (2001), he describes what might be thought of as Thought Adjuster communication: "Looking deep within the mind, in the very most interior part of the self, when the mind becomes very, very quiet, and one listens very carefully, in that infinite Silence, the soul begins to whisper, and its feather-soft voice takes one far beyond what the mind could ever imagine. . . . In its gentle whisperings, there are the faintest hints of infinite love."[143]

In a related passage, he adopts the traditional Platonic stance that the soul is a static substance: "There is a timeless nature about the soul that becomes perfectly obvious and unmistakable: one actually begins to 'taste' the immortality of the soul, to intuit that the soul is to some extent above time, above history, above life and death."[144]

Wilber's ideas in this "classic" period of his thought diverge from the Urantian understanding of the evolving soul. In the latter, progression depends on human choices and actions in the world. Wilber's view of reincarnation is especially revealing in this connection. At first, he sharply distinguishes the soul as understood by the wisdom traditions from the popular belief in reincarnation. In the classical view, the soul, cannot (according to Wilber) be a container of memories experienced in one's current or past lives. In the world's great traditions, he said, the soul had only two defining characteristics. First, it was regarded as "the repository of one's 'virtue' (or lack of it)—that is, of one's karma, good and bad." Second, the soul was a measure "of one's 'strength' of awareness, one's capacity to witness the phenomenal world without attachment or aversion."[145]

One can see the possible Buddhist bias in these characterizations. In particular, Wilber considered the memories of one's life to be strictly a phenomenon of mind, not soul. The upshot, in his view, is that any past life memory refers to some other phenomenon, not memories in the personal soul. Wilber has never been able to align himself with the idea that the worthy events of human experience are memorialized in and as the soul.

In his more recent thought, beginning with *Integral Spirituality* (2006), he dispenses with the idea of pre-given ontological soul or spirit, an approach adopted from postmodern theory that he calls *the post-metaphysical stance*.[146] Drawing insights from what postmodern philosophers call the *myth of the given*, Wilber now steers around the

---

[143] *Collected Works of Ken Wilber*, vol. 4 (Shambhala, 1999) p. 421.

[144] Ibid., p. 538.

[145] Ibid.

[146] See *Integral Spirituality: A Startling New Role for Religion in the Modern and Postmodern World* by Ken Wilber (Integral Books/Shambhala, 2006).

question of ontology as being almost meaningless in a multiperspectival universe. There are no absolutely real and preexisting entities such as souls or spirits or levels of consciousness such as psychic, subtle, and causal, he declares. When we enact a given "world-space," we generate perceptions of different phenomena that may arise in that zone and which appear to exist, but such perceptions are only possible or plausible because we inhabit and act from that particular "perspectival zone." Writes Wilber: "[There is] no pre-given world, but simply a series of worlds that come into being (or co-emerge, or are tetra-enacted) with different orders of consciousness."[147]

Wilber concludes his intricate argument in *Integral Spirituality* by calling for the "integralizing" of the world's religions, whereby they become transformational and inspirational "conveyor belts" of evolutionary progress. The intent of this great educational project would be to foster the growth of the world's peoples through the various quadrants, lines, states, and levels of consciousness development in ways that are compatible with the best concepts, models, and scriptures of their traditions. He further argues that a genuine "evolutionary enlightenment" of humankind becomes possible if planetary civilization finds a way to honor all perspectives, all religious traditions, and all levels of consciousness, through the method of transcending and including the best facts, knowledge, and insights from each. And Wilber has pursued this worthy endeavor of catalyzing the integralization of the world religions ever since, through his more recent books and through the Integral Institute and its associated website, www.IntegralLife.com.

---

[147] Ibid., p. 260.

The Quantum Plenum
and Space Potency

For several decades, scientists have theorized about a mysterious source of cosmic energy available at the subatomic level. It is known among physicists by the technical name *quantum vacuum* or *zero-point vacuum*. Perhaps a more apt phrase (now used by some visionary scientists) is the *quantum plenum* or *cosmic plenum*.

Once an avant garde theorem, the idea of the plenum is no longer widely disputed; scientists can find no other way to explain the dynamism of universal emergence without identifying a vast energy pool that supplies the manifest universe in each moment, and which might provide part of the explanation for dark matter and dark energy. To better explain it, systems philosopher Ervin Laszlo has borrowed the idea of the *akasha* from classic Hinduism, and argues persuasively that all things are birthed from this enormous "unified field" of all energies, things, and beings.

In *UB* terms, the plenum should be understood as technically referring to an impersonal aspect of Deity called the *Unqualified Absolute*. The great plenum, according to the *UB* (and many cosmologists), is contained *in space itself*. Einstein himself once wrote, "We have come to the conclusion that space is the primary thing and matter only secondary."

To illustrate the cosmic plenum, imagine this scenario: First, isolate a certain portion of space—say, a cubic centimeter—in a fantastically efficient freezer. Remove all the vibrating energies of matter-energy by freezing it down so that it cools to a temperature of absolute zero. What remains after we reach this theoretic zero point is known as the *zero point energy of space-time*. According to the influential quantum physicist

David Bohm, this frozen cube of space—whose "manifest" (i.e., visible) atoms and energy are now absolutely motionless—is nevertheless pregnant with vast quantities of invisible cosmic energy. Bohm and other physicists have argued that the total "unmanifest" cosmic energy in our cubic inch would be equivalent to a million Hiroshimas.[148] In other words, a stupendous primal energy reality underlies all phenomenal reality. Bohm and many others who have followed him believe that the manifest cosmos as a gigantic hologram that is projected from this unmanifest deeper ground.

This picture has recently become a common view. But if I have my history of science right, it turns out that the idea of the plenum was first systemically described in *The Urantia Book* in Paper 42, "Energy—Mind and Matter."

The *UB*'s authors call this energy *space potency*. "There is innate in matter and present in universal space a form of energy not known on Urantia. When this discovery is finally made, then will physicists feel that they have solved, almost at least, the mystery of matter." [42:1.3]

In the descriptions of the revelators, the store of energy in space is not absolute; it is unbelievably enormous but not infinite. Quantum physics describes the quantum hologram as an impersonal force without will or self-awareness, and the *UB* would agree, but its revelations uniquely explain that certain beings (as discussed in chapter 2) are able to manipulate this energy so as to bring into being nebulas that evolve into galaxies and planets. "*Space potency* . . . is the unquestioned free space presence of the Unqualified Absolute. [It] is responsive only to the personal grasp of the Universal Father, notwithstanding that it is seemingly modifiable by the presence of the Primary Master Force Organizers." [42:2.3–5]

---

[148] "The Unified Field—the zero-point vacuum of space-time—is infinite in its energy potential. . . . Quantum physics also theorizes that contained within every cubic centimeter (a mere small sugar cube in size) there is an approximate energy density/mass of 1094 grams (10 with 94 zeros following it). That's 39 orders-of-magnitude more mass/energy than the entire known Universe in every cubic centimeter!" (See http://cosmometry.net/infinite-energy-potential)

Acknowledgments

Writing a long book is a deeply personal and sometimes lonely process, but many good souls came forward to assist me in this effort.

The original inspiration for *Your Evolving Soul* came from Andrew Harvey, who told me almost twenty years ago that I was the right person to create this sort of introductory text. A personal meeting with Ken Wilber in 1999, during which we discussed *The Urantia Book* at length, led me to seek out the affinities of his work with the Urantia Revelation. Somewhat later, Barbara Marx Hubbard gave initial versions of the manuscript a strong vote of confidence, which buoyed me up in the early days of the writing. Others who offered inspiration and moral support along the way have included Phil Schanzle, Julie Perkins, Fred Harris, Donna D'Ingillo, Rob Davis, Dave and Meredith Tenney, Marty Risacher, Rob Crickett, Errol Strider, Elizabeth Kelley, Sheila Keene-Lund, Hal Katzen, Gard Jameson, Seana McGee, Richard Rosen, and Peter Laurence—but especially my housemate, Kenn Burrows, and my friend and coach, Holly Woods. In a more general way, without the *Urantia Book*-related education and fellowship that I have enjoyed for decades—all of which was made possible by the Urantia Fellowship and related movements and groups—I could never have found the confidence to publish my interpretations of the *UB*'s teachings on spirituality.

I had a different book in mind in 2014, but thanks to the visionary and inimitable Sean Esbjörn-Hargens and other open-minded folks at MetaIntegral, I was invited to give a paper on the Urantia Revelation at their international conference in 2015. That presentation was an unexpected success that inspired me to pursue a more philosophical approach to the subject matter and to engage more deeply in researching the connection between the *UB* and integral theory. Other integralists who have supported my efforts include Kurt Johnson, Dustin Diperna, Michael Zimmerman, and Steve McIntosh.

My own birth family has spent decades wondering about my interest in the Urantia Revelation, but in recent years they have supported this effort in numerous ways, including generously allowing me four months of retreat time at a family property. I am delighted today that each of my brothers, George, Nick, and Peter, are fans of *Your Evolving Soul*. My mother and her father were heartfelt believers in the Greek Orthodox tradition, and their example no doubt provided the predisposition that led me to *The Urantia Book* in the first place and to a lifelong interest in theology and spirituality.

On the editorial and production side, the greatest credit goes to my editor, who is known as the Writer's Midwife (she prefers to remain anonymous). I introduced her to the *UB* almost two decades ago, and she quickly became a fervent and brilliant student of the text. Now we have come full circle in that she has become my fervent and brilliant editor. No living person could have provided the quality and depth of editorial support she provided. Her standards of editorial excellence pulled me forward in the final weeks, providing a determination that reminds me of the horses that once carried Apollo across the sky, shedding light on all things. My hardworking graphics expert, Carla Green, brings it all together with equanimity—as she does for every Origin Press book—providing reliable and high quality production and design. And a special thanks also to the talented Mariah Parker, who designed the gorgeous front cover of this book. Thanks in addition to Michael Kerber, president of my distributor, Red Wheel Weiser, who has been patient with the many delays of this book while also giving wise input.

A number of friends read early versions of the manuscript and gave helpful feedback, including Dan Drasin, Sussi Rowland, Mike Painter, Jerry Lane, Jerry Gerber, Jacqueline Chan, Rich Scheck, and Alec Brindell. But the most helpful feedback of all came from an old friend, Matthew Rapaport, an expert student of the revelation and a disciplined philosopher.

More than a few people provided healing treatments and offered words of nurturance during the tough moments of this project, most notably Evan Reiff, Len Saputo, Donna D'Ingillo, Conde Freeman, Devatara Holman, and Satyvan McManus. And very special thanks in this connection goes to Katie Darling, who kept my body and breath connected to my soul and spirit during the months of intensive writing, all the while being a faithful, funny, and fascinating companion throughout the entire process.

Glossary of Terms

Adam and Eve

These unique beings serve as "divine reproducing couples" on evolutionary worlds with a purpose of ameliorating the shortcomings of human biological evolution as well as many other special duties. They comprise the order of "Material Sons and Daughters of God" (see entry) and typically reside on the system capitol (see "local system"). Our Adam-and-Eve pair materialized on Urantia nearly 38,000 years ago for the purpose of biologically uplifting the mortals of the realm. The progeny of Adam and Eve on Urantia were known as the "violet race." However, our planetary Adam and Eve had a very difficult mission compared to Adam-and-Eve appearances on other planets, because of the planetary quarantine on Urantia—a result of the Lucifer Rebellion—that isolated them from contact with the rest of the universe. Their story is recounted in the garbled record contained in the book of Genesis in the Bible and is updated for the modern age in Papers 73-76 in *The Urantia Book*.

adjudication; adjudication of Lucifer Rebellion

The case of *Gabriel vs. Lucifer* was launched early in the twentieth century before the courts of the Ancients of Days (see entry), concurrently with the reception of the Papers in Chicago that would later become *The Urantia Book*. Gabriel vs. An adjudication would mean that the quarantine of Urantia could be lifted so that all "off-world" communication circuits to the planet could be reinstated. The reasons for the rebellion and the story of its aftermath are discussed at length in *The Urantia Book* and especially in Papers 52 and 53.

adjutant mind-spirits; seven adjutant mind-spirits; adjutants of wisdom and worship

Adjutants represent the functioning of the "mind ministry" of the Infinite Spirit (see entry), and are of origin in the Mother Spirit of any local universe. Adjutant mind-spirits are not beings or entities, but operate more like connectivity circuits as they operate with the creature mind. The first five adjutants—the spirits of intuition, understanding, courage, knowledge, and counsel—minister to the lower levels of experiential minds (animals and humans), and the last two—the spirits of worship and wisdom—operate only in mortal minds with spiritual potential. Adjutant mind-spirits have been compared to the "seven chakra" system in Vedanta and other teachings about the human energy body. [See UB, Paper 36, sec. 5.]

Adjuster—see Thought Adjuster

Ancient of Days

In power, majesty, and scope of authority the Ancients of Days are the most versatile and mighty of any of the direct rulers of the time-space creations. They oversee the *administration* of superuniverses (i.e., galactic organizations that comprise approximately one trillion inhabited planets). In all of the vast universe they alone are invested with the high powers of final executive judgment concerning the eternal extinction of will creatures (e.g., the case of annihilation of Lucifer and Satan that concluded the Lucifer Rebellion). The Ancients of Days are the most perfect and the most divinely endowed rulers in all time-space existence.

architectural spheres

These worlds are purposely constructed for their intended uses. The local universe of Nebadon (see entry) contains over 600,000 of these spheres. While they may receive some light from nearby stars, these worlds are heated and lighted independently and therefore do not emit enough light to be seen by Urantia's telescopes. These worlds do not suffer from geologic instability or weather phenomena. They are made from morontia materials (see entry under "morontia"), which include one hundred additional elements that are not found on Urantia, and are very beautiful. Each of us will see our first architectural world when we awaken from the death experience, on mansion world number one. [See UB, Paper 15, sec. 7.]

Avonal Son
One of three "descending" orders of revealed beings or origin on Paradise in the central universe; also known as Magisterial Sons (see entry).

Billion worlds—see central universe

Christ Michael; Michael; Creator Son; Jesus Christ
Michael is our local universe father, creator, and sovereign, and is also know to us as Jesus Christ, who incarnated as Jesus of Nazareth on our planet. He is of the order of Michael—high beings with creator prerogatives who are also known as Creator Sons; they are directly of origin from God the Father and God the Son. In partnership with the Mother Spirits who are their equals (see "Mother Spirit"), Michaels create local universes and their myriad inhabitants, over which they rule with love and mercy. Their unending love for us is typified in the fact that they may incarnate in the likeness of their creatures on the worlds they have created.

central universe; Havona; billion worlds
Havona, the central universe, is not a time creation; it is an eternal existence. This never-beginning, never-ending universe consists of one billion spheres of sublime perfection. At the center of Havona is the stationary and absolutely stabilized Isle of Paradise (see "Paradise"). The mass of this central creation is far in excess of the total known mass of all seven sectors of the grand universe (the time-space creations).

Constellation; constellation level of authority
Constellations are comprised of one hundred local systems, and thus consist of up to one-hundred thousand inhabited worlds. The name of our Constellation's headquarters world is *Edentia*, and the beings know as the Most Highs (see entry) preside there. [See UB, Paper 43.]

cosmic mind
The cosmic mind encompasses all finite mind levels in the evolutionary universes.

Deity Absolute

The Deity Absolute is the summation of the absolute of all experiential and existential realities of all existent personal beings created by God. In essence, it refers to the "personalizable and divine values" that are manifest in universe reality as opposed to the function of the Unqualified Absolute, which pertains to that which is nonpersonal, "nondeified," and even randomly occurring.

Eternal Son

The Eternal Son is the great mercy minister to all creation. As the second person of the divine Trinity, he is known as the Original Son, and along with God the Father, he is the cocreator of other divine sons. He is the source of spirit, the administrator of all spirit, and the center of spirit in the universe and therefore all things spiritual are drawn to him; he is co-eternal and co-ordinate with the Father, and is a full equal to the Father. "The Eternal Son is the perfect and final expression of the 'first' personal and absolute concept of the Universal Father. Accordingly, whenever and however the Father personally and absolutely expresses himself, he does so through his Eternal Son, who ever has been, now is and ever will be, the living and divine Word. The Eternal Son is the spiritual personalization of the Father's universal and infinite concept of divine reality, unqualified spirit, and absolute personality. As the Father is the First Great Source and Center, so the Eternal Son is the Second Great Source and Center." [See UB: Papers 6 and 7.]

Fifth Epochal Revelation; epochal revelation

The purpose of revelation is to exalt and "up-step" the religions of evolution by periodic teachings that are tailored to the needs and capacity for receptivity of the mortals of a given world. Every inhabited evolutionary planet receives a series of epochal revelations throughout its history. *The Urantia Book* is one example of such a gift, and is the fifth such epochal revelation to be given to Urantia. The Fifth Epochal Revelation was designed to correct philosophical error, assess the evolutionary religions and sciences, and adjust planetary and human history to a factual account of events from the past.

fusion

The makeup of our being, our true self, is a combination of the personality, the soul, and the divine Father Fragment within. The goal of our personal spiritual evolution is the eternal fusion of these elements; in other words, these three aspects, when fused, are eternalized. For almost all of us on Earth today, fusion will only occur in our future heavenly life. Only a few documented cases of fusion exist while in a material body.

guardian angels; guardian seraphim

Although much of the existing teachings about guardian angels are based on myth, nevertheless they are real and play a crucial role in the spiritual destiny of mortals on all inhabited worlds. Their voluntary ministry is always to individual humans. These seraphim generally serve in pairs and are assisted by *cherubim* and *sanobim*. In the beginning of a mortal's life, one seraphim pair will oversee a group of one thousand mortals with assistance from a company of cherubim; but as humans ascend in spiritual attainment, the numbers served by a seraphic pair become fewer in number, until such time as we achieve the requisite spiritual status to have a pair of destiny guardians assigned to us exclusively. Angels do not invade human mind or interfere with the free will decisions of the mortals of their assignment, but they guide us into situations of learning and spiritual growth. At death, these "destiny guardians" become the custodial trustees of our life records, our identity specifications, and our soul, until we are repersonalized on the mansion worlds (see entry). They remain our companions for much of the time while we progress toward Paradise, simultaneously furthering their own advancement of seraphic education. [See UB, Paper 113.]

God the Father; God; Father; Paradise Father

God is love; as the universal Father, God is the first person of deity, the First Source and Center of all things and beings. According to the Urantia Revelation, the term "God" always denotes personality. God the Father is the infinite and eternal God of love, as well as Creator, Controller, and Upholder of the universe of all universes. The first person of deity—God the Father—loves us with an attitude analogous to that of a divine father; the love and mercy of God the Son, the second person of deity, can be considered akin to the love of a mother. God the Spirit is the third person of deity, also know as the Infinite Spirit.

Father Fragment—see Thought Adjuster

Havona—see central universe

Light and Life; Age of Light and Life

The goal of all inhabited planets, the final evolutionary attainment of any world of time and space, is known as the Age of Light and Life. When a world has reached this utopian state of evolutionary consummation, its achievements along the way will have included the attainment of one worldwide language, one blended race, one unified world religion, universal peace, and a very advanced state of prosperity and happiness.

local system

A local system consists of about one thousand inhabited or inhabitable worlds. Cold worlds or planets too near their suns, and other spheres not suitable for creature habitation, are not included in this group. One thousand local worlds adapted to support life are called a system, but in the younger systems only a comparatively small number of these worlds may be inhabited. Each inhabited planet is presided over by a Planetary Prince, and each local system has an architectural sphere as its headquarters and is ruled by a System Sovereign. Our local system, named *Satania*, is not yet complete. So far there are 619 inhabited planets in the system, and there will be one thousand when it is complete. Urantia was the 606th world to have life implanted on it within the system. The administrative head of Satania is a *Lanonandek Son* named *Lanaforge*. He has served since shortly after Lucifer was deposed and incarcerated for disloyalty to the universe government. [See UB, Papers 45 and 46.]

local universe; Nebadon

Our local universe, called *Nebadon*, was created by Christ Michael, and is ruled by Michael as Master Son and Sovereign, and by Nebadonia, our Mother Spirit or Divine Minister. The local universe administrative headquarters is *Salvington*, which is also the abode of Michael and Nebadonia. Nebadon is still in the process of formation and will eventually contain 10,000,000 inhabited planets. Nebadon is one of 700,000 local universes within the Grand Universe. [See UB, Papers 32 and 33.] In Urantia Book cosmology, Paradise is a stationary body at the center of the space-time universe (see "central universe" and "Paradise"), which is surrounded by a central universe of inherently perfect worlds, which is in turn encircled by seven discrete aggregations of galaxies (galaxy clusters) called *superuniverses*. Each superuniverse is comprised of 700,000 local universes. As stated, *The Urantia Book* indicates that a local universe is made up of approximately 10,000,000 inhabitable planets and is evolving toward perfection. Each local universe is ruled by one of the Creator Sons of God of the order of Michael.

Lucifer Rebellion

Lucifer was a high celestial being and brilliant administrator of a system of 607 inhabited planets, who with his first assistant *Satan* launched a rebellion against the local universe government of Christ Michael some 200,000 years ago. Lucifer's insurrection created pandemonium in the celestial hierarchy and on our planet—as well as in 36 other planets in our local system. Among other contentions, Lucifer claimed that the Universal Father does not really exist, and he attacked the right of Christ Micael to assume sovereignty of Nebadon in the name of the Father. The majority of celestial beings in the celestial hierarchy of our planet went over to the way of Lucifer, causing major distortions and aberrations ever since in the evolution and history of our planet. The planetwide era of conscious awakening known as the Correcting Time (of which the Teaching Mission is a part), was launched in the mid-1980s, we are told, after the final adjudication of the Lucifer rebellion in celestial courts.

Magisterial Mission

A visitation by a *Paradise Son* of the *Avonal* order occurs when a planet has reached an evolutionary limit of intellectual and ethical progress. These beings may also appear in judicial actions "at the end of an age" as so-called dispensation terminators. In this role they liberate sleeping survivors (those in repose after death) for resurrection in the mansion worlds of the afterlife. Each Avonal Son (also known as a Magisterial Son, see next entry) also has at least one incarnating bestowal mission, where he is born of woman, as was Jesus. On missions other than bestowals, they appear in visible form as adult males. Planets may have numerous Magisterial Missions.

Magisterial Sons

These beings are the joint creation of the Eternal Son and the Infinite Spirit, and there are about one billion in number in the grand universe, each one representing a new and divine ideal of loving service. They come into being as divine administrators, descending Sons who reveal themselves as servers, bestowers, judges, teachers, and truth revealers. They work closely with the Creator Sons, the Michaels, of each local universe. [UB, Paper 20, sec. 1-4.]

Most Highs; Most Highs of the constellation

Three so-called *Vorondadek Sons* rule over each constellation for a set period of years. These Most Highs are the invisible rulers of the polities or political organizations of humans on all planets as over-controllers of political evolution; they are occupied with groups, not individuals, and they foster the greatest good for the greatest number of people, without violating human free will. [See UB, Papers 43 and 134.] One hundred local systems (see entry) or about 100,000 inhabitable planets make up a constellation.

mansion worlds

In the afterlife, those mortals who survive the transition of death are repersonalized on these worlds; these seven heavenly planets are the first post-mortal residences for all survivors of life in the flesh. The mansion worlds are training worlds—the first two providing remedial training—whose purpose is to prepare us for the vast career ahead as we journey across the universe in our age-long ascent to God on Paradise. Some Teaching Mission lessons are based in part on the curriculum of the mansion worlds.

Michael—see Christ Michael

Michael Sons; order of Michael

This order of Paradise Son, some 700,000 in number in the universe, are created by the Universal Father and the Eternal Son. Each are known as the "only-begotten Son" because, even though they function alike in their domains, each has an individual personality that makes him unlike any other Michael Son. These Sons are the personification of the Paradise Father-Son, to and in their local universes. Each is destined to create a local universe of his own making, and with the

Mother Spirit, to create the living beings that will inhabit this physical creation. Each Michael must earn the right to govern his local universe creation as its sovereign, by completing seven bestowals, in which he incarnates as one of each order of beings that he himself created. In this way he becomes a wise, merciful and loving brother and Father to his sons and daughters. [See UB, Papers 21 and 33.]

Michael; Christ Michael

The creator of our local universe, Christ Michael, is Father and brother to all living beings of his creation, and is one and the same as Jesus Christ, who incarnated on Earth. He possesses and represents all the divine attributes and powers of the Eternal Son within the local universe of Nebadon, and has additional power and authority to fully represent the Universal Father to his creatures. To our local universe, Michael represents God; he is omnipotent, omniscient, and omnipresent. He is ably assisted by his consort, the Universe Mother Spirit, known as *Nebadonia*. His main concerns within his realm are creation, sustenance, and ministry. He does not participate in judicial affairs, as creators never sit in judgment on their creatures. [See UB, Paper 33.]

morontia

In the local universe, the morontia realm is the vast reality domain intervening between the material and spirit levels of existence. We are told that "the warp of morontia is spiritual; its woof is physical." While material planets have one hundred naturally occurring physical elements on the atomic chart (i.e., the periodic table of elements), the morontia realm has two hundred such elements. Morontia is a semi-material substance composed of varying mixtures of spirit and material energies; the more spiritual the mixture, the "lighter" the substance. (Morontia substance is normally invisible to the human eye.) The human soul is formed of this material as it grows during the mortal lifetime. With each step of progress through the morontia career in the afterlife, the ascender gradually becomes slightly less physical and slightly more spiritual, and each transition to a higher world necessitates a change of the body or life vehicle. [See UB, Paper 42, sec.10; Paper 48, sec 1.]

mota; mota of morontia

Mota is defined as that ability that allows additional intellectual insight into material and spiritual relationships. We cannot experience mota while in the flesh, but once we are removed to the mansion worlds, a new mind circuit provides the additional capacity to see the relationships of the spiritual universe with the material universe in greater dimension. The higher philosophical insights of humankind come close to emulating the function of mota, but fall short of actually performing as mota performs for ascenders. *The Urantia Book* explains it this way: "Mota is more than a superior philosophy; it is to philosophy as two eyes are to one; it has a stereoscopic effect on meanings and values. Material man sees the universe, as it were, with but one eye—flat. Mansion world students achieve cosmic perspective-—depth-—by superimposing the perceptions of the morontia life upon the perceptions of the physical life . . . Reason is the understanding technique of the sciences; faith is the insight technique of religion; mota is the technique of the morontia level. Mota is a supermaterial reality sensitivity which is beginning to compensate incomplete growth, having for its substance knowledge-reason and for its essence faith-insight . . . Metaphysics stands for man's well-meant but futile effort to compensate for the absence of the mota of morontia." [See UB: Paper 103, sec 6.]

Mother Spirit; Universe Mother Spirit

Just as Michael is our local universe Father, the Mother Spirit is our local universe Mother. As Christ Michael is a personalization of the first and second persons of the Trinity, the Creative Mother Spirit is a personalization of the third person of deity. She is Christ Michael's consort in the administration and in the ministry of love and mercy to the myriad of planets in Nebadon (see entry). Among the many powers and duties of Mother Spirits is the ability to give life; she supplies the essential factor of living plasm to all creatures high and low. She also loves and ministers to us through her vast retinue of angels and other ministering celestial beings.

Mystery Monitor—see Thought Adjuster

Nebadon

This is the name of the local universe in which our planet is located. Nebadon presently contains approximately 3,800,000 inhabited planets. It is a relatively young universe and sits on the outer edges of *Orvonton*, the superuniverse in which it is located. Nebadon is ruled by Christ Michael, also known as Jesus Christ, and his consort, the Mother Spirit, who are the creators of Nebadon.

Nebadonia—see Mother Spirit

Paradise
At the literal center of the cosmos, yet outside of space and time, is the only stationary body in all creation, and the Urantia revelation designates this reality as Paradise. God is personally present on Paradise, and from his infinite being flow the floodstreams of life, energy, and personality to all universe. Paradise is a stupendously large island located at the geographical center of infinity. All physical energy and all cosmic-force circuits, including all forms of gravity, have their origin at Paradise. It also has residential zones; all God-conscious mortal will someday attain and reside on Paradise.

personality
This refers to that part of a person by which we know them as unique, and designates those personal qualities that endure and which are recognizable regardless of changes in age, status, behavior or other external qualities. We are told that personality is a high and divine gift to each person from God the Father. It is that changeless metaphysical quality that confers upon them their unique identity in the cosmos, and could be called the "image of God" within us. Personality is absolutely unique and immutable; it does not in itself evolve, but its relationship with the indwelling spirit (Thought Adjuster) and the soul continually evolves. Functionally, personality also acts as the unifier and integrator of all aspects of an individual's relationship with his or her environment.

Planetary Prince
A Planetary Prince appears on a world when it has for the first time evolved primitive human beings of will status. Although a Planetary Prince is invisible to the humans, his staff is not. The staff sets up schools and teach a variety of skills, such as basic cultivation of the soil, home building, and spiritual culture. The classes are progressive in nature; the mortals are taught agriculture, food preservation, government,

sanitation, pottery, metal working and so on. The students are then sent out among their people to share the knowledge. The Prince and his staff normally stay on a world, teaching ever-higher concepts of wisdom, philosophy, brotherhood and religion, until a planet reaches the Age of Light and Life. Urantia's Prince *Caligastia* served admirably for 300,000 years before following his superior, Lucifer, into rebellion, about 200,000 years agao. Caligastia was then removed from his post. (See Lucifer Rebellion.)

quarantine; quarantined worlds

After a period of observation, worlds and systems that have partici-pated in open rebellion or disloyalty to the Creator Son are placed in isolation until the courts of the Ancients of Days (see entry) are able to rule on the matter. Urantia and 36 other inhabited worlds were placed in quarantine (all communications severed) when Lucifer and Caligastia went into rebellion against the universe government. The isolation continued for 200,000 years, until the adjudication took place in 1985. Our world is now being normalized and brought back into the communication circuits through the action of Michael's Correcting Time.

seraphim

The order of seraphim are the angels we have come to know in litera-ture and story. A large category of beings created by the local universe Mother Spirit, they serve in a myriad of ways throughout a local uni-verse. There are over five hundred million pairs of seraphim on our planet. [See UB, Papers 26, 30, 31, 37-40.]

soul

The indwelling spirit or Thought Adjuster is a perfect gift of God, but the soul is an experiential achievement. As we choose the divine will in our lives, the effect of this experience is that our soul grows in sub-stance and quality. We are told in *The Urantia Book* that the indwelling spirit is the *father* of our soul, just as the material mind—as a result of its moral choice—is the *mother* of the emerging soul. In the afterlife, it is the soul alone that survives death and becomes the container of our actual identity, through the agency of our personality.

Spirit of Truth

This is the unique spiritual endowment conferred on each person on this planet from our Creator Son, Christ Michael. This high and pure spiritual influence was first gifted universally to humankind on the day of Pentecost, just after Jesus' resurrection. The Spirit of Truth enhances each person's ability to recognize truth. Its effectiveness is limited by each person's free-will consecration of his or her will to doing the will of God, but its influence is universal. When actively sought, the Spirit of Truth purifies the human heart and leads the individual to formulate a life purpose based on the love of truth.

Supreme Being; God the Supreme

The Supreme Being is the evolving deity of time and space. He is not a direct creator, but he is a synthetic co-ordinator of all creature-Creator (or "cocreative") universe activities. The Supreme Being, now actualizing in the evolutionary universes, is the Deity correlator and synthesizer of time-space divinity, the ultimate summation of the value-laden import of all personal experience of all creatures on all worlds. The Supreme is the "world-soul" who is the repository of the universal akashic field always being created by evolving souls everywhere.

Thought Adjuster; indwelling spirit; Father Fragment; Mystery Monitor; Adjuster

This is the specialized Urantia Book term for "God-within"—the indwelling spark of God—and we are told that an actual fragment of God the Father that indwells every normal-minded and morally conscious human being. The TA is wholly subservient to our will, yet represents the actual will of God, resident in our own minds. Through the practice of stillness, meditative worship, and loving service to others, we can attune ourselves to the influence of this inner divinity, thereby discerning the will of God for us as individuals. Also known as the Father Fragment or Mystery Monitor, the Adjuster is God's gift to each of us in addition to our personality, and its influence arouses our hunger for perfection, our quest for the divine. In addition, our Thought Adjuster and our material mind, working together, actually create our soul (see "soul"). According to *The Urantia Book*, the great goal of our spiritual evolution is to actually fuse with the Adjuster—i.e., come into complete union and identification with the indwelling spirit of God, and by so doing achieve immortality.

Trinity; Paradise Trinity
This refers to the eternal deity union of the Universal Father, the Eternal Son, and the Infinite Spirit.

Urantia ("you-ran-sha")
Urantia is the name by which our planet is known in our local universe, according to the celestial authors of *The Urantia Book*. Urantia is said to be a disturbed planet by virtue of its participation in the Lucifer Rebellion, and yet is a blessed planet because it was the site of the incarnation bestowal of Michael, as Jesus of Nazareth.

Selected Bibliography

Combs, Allan. *Radiance of Being: Understanding the Grand Integral Vision.* Paragon House, 2002.

Chudhuri, Haridas. *Sri Aurobindo: Prophet of Life Divine.* Cultural Integration Fellowship, 1973.

Crickett, Rob. *The Father Fusion of Jesus: The Christian Gospel.* CreateSpace, 2016.

DiPerna, Dustin. *Streams of Wisdom: An Advanced Guide to Integral Spiritual Wisdom.* Integral Publishing House, 2014.

Eadie, Betty. *Embraced by the Light: The Most Profound and Complete Near-Death Experience Ever.* Bantam, 2002.

Elgin, Duane. *The Living Universe.* Berrett-Koehler, 2009.

Edmundson, Mark. *Self and Soul: A Defense of Ideals.* Scribners, 2000.

Goldsmith, Joel S. *Practicing the Presence: The Inspirational Guide to Regaining Meaning and a Sense of Purpose in Your Life.* HarperCollins, 1991.

Goetz, Steward and Charles Taliaferro. *A Brief History of the Soul.* Wiley-Blackwell, 2011.

Griffin, David Ray. *God, Power, and Evil: A Process Theodicy.* University Press of America, 1991.

Finlan, Stephen and Vladimir Kharlamov. *Theosis: Deification in Christian Theology, Volume One.* Wipf & Stock, 2006.

Fowler, James. *Stages of Faith: The Psychology of Human Development and the Quest for Meaning.* HarperCollins, 1981.

Gafni, Marc. *Your Unique Self: The Radical Path to Personal Enlightenment.* Integral Publishers, 2012.

Gardner, Martin. *Urantia: The Great Cult Mystery*. Prometheus Books, 1995.

Hodgson, Peter, ed. *Hegel's Lectures on the Philosophy of Religion: The Consummate Religion*. University of California Press, 1985.

Hick, John. *Evil and the God of Love*. Palgrave Macmillan, 2010.

Hill, Roy L., *Psychology and the Near-Death Experience: Searching for God*. White Crow Books, 2015.

Hillman, James. *The Soul's Code: In Search of Character and Calling*. Grand Central Publishing,1997.

Hoeller, Stephan A. *Gnosticism: New Light on the Ancient Tradition of Inner Knowing*. Quest Books: 2002.

Hubbard, Barbara Marx. *Conscious Evolution: Awakening the Power of Our Social Potential*. New World Library, 2015.

Hugenot, Alan Ross. *The New Science of Consciousness Survival*. Dog Ear Publishing, 2016.

Johnson, Kurt and David Ord. *The Coming Interspiritual Age*. Namaste Publishing, 2012.

Jung, C.G. *Two Essays on Analytical Psychology*. Princeton University Press, 1972.

Keene-Lund, Sheila. *Heaven Is Not the Last Stop: Exploring a New Revelation*. Document It Publishing, 2010.

Kelly, Joseph F. *The Ecumenical Councils of the Catholic Church: A History*. Liturgical Press, 2009.

Kelly, Sean. *Individuation and the Absolute: Hegel, Jung, and the Path to Wholeness*. Paulist Press, 1991.

Laszlo, Ervin. *Science and the Reenchantment of the Cosmos: The Rise of the Integral Vision of Reality*. Inner Traditions, 2006.

Leonard, George and Michael Murphy. *The Life We Are Given*. Tarcher/Penguin, 1995.

Lossky, Vladimir. *The Mystical Theology of the Eastern Church*. St. Vladimir Seminary Press, 1997.

——*The Image and Likeness of God*. St. Vladimir Seminary Press, 1974.

Makari, George. *Soul Machine: The Invention of the Modern Mind.* Norton, 2015.

Manning, J. T. *Source Authors of The Urantia Book.* Square Circles Publishing, 2002.

Markides, Kyriacos C. *The Mountain of Silence: The Search for Orthodox Spirituality.* Doubleday, 2001.

McIntosh, Steve. *The Presence of the Infinite: The Spiritual Experience of Beauty, Truth,*

and Goodness. Quest Books, 2015.

—— *Evolution's Purpose: An Integral Interpretation of the Scientific Story of Our Origins.* SelectBooks, 2012.

Medhus, Erik and Elisa Medhus, MD. *My Life after Death: A Memoir From Heaven.* Atria Books/Beyond Words, 2015.

Moltmann, Jurgen. *Theology of Hope.* Fortress Press, 1993.

Moore, Robert. *The Care of the Soul: A Guide For Cultivating Depth And Sacredness In Everyday Life.* HarperCollins, 1992.

Moyer, Ernest. *The Birth of a Divine Revelation: The Origin of the Urantia Papers* (Moyer Pub, 2000).

Mullins, Larry with Meredith Sprunger. *A History of the Urantia Papers.* CreateSpace, 2010.

Neal, Mary. *To Heaven and Back: A Doctor's Extraordinary Account of Her Death, Heaven, Angels, and Life Again.* WaterBrook, 2012.

Newton, Michael, *Journey of Souls: Case Studies of Life Between Lives.* Llewellyn, 1994.

Olson, James. *How Whole Brain Thinking Can Save the Future.* Origin Press, 2017.

Pagels, Eliane. *Beyond Belief: The Secret Gospel of Thomas.* Vintage, 2004.

Palamas, Gregory. *The Triads.* Paulist Press, 1983.

Parti, Rajiv. *Dying to Wake Up: A Doctor's Voyage into the Afterlife and the Wisdom He Brought Back.* Atria Books, 2016.

Russell, Jeffrey Burton. *A History of Heaven: The Singing Silence.* Princeton University Press, 1997.

Sadler, William S. *A Study of the Master Universe: A Development of Concepts in the Urantia Book*. Second Society Foundation, 1968.

Saint Augustine. *Confessions*. Hackett Publishing Company, 2006.

Schwartz, Gary. *The Afterlife Experiments: Breakthrough Scientific Evidence of Life After Death*. Atria Books, 2003.

Spira, Rupert. *The Transparency of Things: Contemplating the Nature of Experience*. Sahaja Publications, 2016.

Steiner, Rudolf. *Knowledge of the Higher Worlds and Its Attainment*. Anthroposophic Press, 1947.

Ware, Kallistos. *The Inner Kingdom: Volume 1 of the Collected Works*. St. Vladimir Seminary Press, 2000.

Wattles, Jeff. *Living in Truth, Beauty, and Goodness: Values and Virtues*. Wipf and Stock, 2016.

Whitmont, Edward C. *The Symbolic Press: Basic Concepts of Analytical Psychology*. Princeton University Press, 1969.

Wilber, Ken. *The Integral Vision*. Shambhala, 2007.

———*Integral Psychology: Consciousness, Spirit, Psychology, Therapy*. Shambhala, 2000.

———*Integral Spirituality: A Startling New Role for Religion in the Modern and Postmodern World*. Shambhala, 2007.

The Urantia Book: Indexed Version. Uversa Press: 2012.

The Urantia Book: Revealing the Mysteries of God, the Universe, World History, Jesus, and Ourselves. Urantia Foundation, 2008.

Index

When attached to a page number: n for footnotes and f for figures

D

daimon, 192
Dalai Lama, 168–169
Dante, 39–40, 110
De Anima (Aristotle), 103
death, to primitive peoples, 95
decision-making
    and action, 157–159
    on ascension, 45, 105–106, 222
    for ideal life, 72
    moral, 196
    and suffering, 228
    and Thought Adjuster, 60, 64
    and will, 212
deification, 120–125
Deities
    associates, 23, 24
    compassionate, 119
    creator, 36–37, 57, 232–235,
        232n
    evolutionary, 79, 83, 229
    God and, 231
    incomplete, 226–227
    Jahweh, 117
    master, 35
    Michael and Mother, 37–38,
        79n, 235, 235n, 273–274
    and personality, 177
    Persons of, 31, 33
    primal, 31–32, 34
    of space-time, 35
    subordinate, 117, 119
    Supreme Creators. *See* Supreme
        Being
    of the Trinity, 31, 72, 74
Demiurge, 117, 119, 227
depth, as self-expression
    dimension, 174
descent, of God, 230–234
destiny, 23, 38, 63–66, 72

dialectic, cosmic, 233–240
Dickens, Charles, 26
Dickinson, Emily, 4, 17
Diperna, Dustin, 206, 206n, 208
direction, as self-expression
    dimension, 174
*Discovery of Atlantis: The Startling
    Case for the Island of Cyprus*
    (Sarmast) 422, 249
Divine Comedy (Dante), 39
Divine Heart, 60
divine indweller. *See also* Spirit,
    Indweller
    arrival of, 196–199
    feeling, 199–204
    as God's love in humans,
        189–191
    and imperfect beings, 199
    naming, 191–196
    theisms on, 192
Divine Monitor, 198
Divine Mother. *See* Spirit, Infinite
Divine Parents, 26. *See also*
    parental, God as
divine will, 78–79
divinization. *See* deification
Djwhal Khul, 244–246
dreams, 17, 77n
dualism, substance, 99–102, 103,
    128–129
dualism of body, 99
dukkha, 168
*Dying to Wake Up: A Doctor's
    Voyage into the Afterlife and
    the Wisdom He Brought Back*
    (Parti), 15

job (vocation), 69, 72, 217–218
John, Secret Book of, 114
Judaism
  on afterlife, 96
  on fallen state, of world, 115
  on image of God, 97
  and Jesus, 29, 56–57, 117
judgment, 105
Judgment Day, 104, 239
Jung, Carl, 17, 68, 71, 77n, 168,
  174, 191, 221

K

Kant, Immanuel, 134, 159n
karma, 96, 127, 127n
Katzen, Halbert, 250
Keats, John, 6–7
Keene-Lund, Sheila, xxvii
Kellogg, Wilfred, 261
kenosis, 230, 233
Kezer, Robert, 208, 209
Kharlamov, Vladimir, 123
kindness, 13–14. *See also* service to
  others
King, Martin Luther, 212
knowledge (gnosis), 119
kosmocentric, 149, 149n

L

lamp, inner, 199–202, 203
Laszlo, Ervin, 279
lessons, in afterlife, 159, 166, 220,
  240, 251–252
Lessons from the Light (Ring), 10
life, purpose of, 217–219
Life after Life (Moody), 7
Life Carriers, 24–26
life impressions, 127
life passing before your eyes. *See*
  life reviews

life reviews. *See also* near-death
  experiences (NDE)
  accounts of, 12, 14–15
  of author, 3–4
  by celestial beings, 12–13
  by celestial guides, 17, 22
  Dickinson on, 4
  epiphanies in, 15
  of the misguided, 61
  as multiperspectival, 15, 63, 143
  and near-death experiences
    (NDE), exclusivity to, 16
  negative feelings toward, 11
  and souls, 5, 16–17
  storage of, universally. *See*
    records of life
life-story-as-a-whole, 4–5, 10
  47-48. *See also* life reviews
light, inner, 199–200, 203–204
limitations, of God, 230–231
lines of human development. *See*
  human development, lines
  of
Living in Truth, Beauty, and
  Goodness (Wattles), 77
Long, Jeffrey, 9
love
  applied, 33–34
  celestial guides, showing, 12–14
  in circles, 80, 82
  from consciousness, higher
    states of, 203
  as energy, 231–232
  God as, 27, 30, 33, 58
  of Indwelling Spirit, 215
  of others, because of faith,
    26–27, 53, 63, 77
  as personality characteristic,
    183–184
  of Thought Adjuster, 198–199